The Awakening

The Essene Legacy
BOOK TWO

Channeled by Al Miner and Lama Sing

Cover art and book design by Susan Miner

Second Edition 2016

ISBN -13   978-0-9791262-8-4

1. Spirit writings 2. Psychics 3. Trance Channels 4. Essenes
4. Expectant Ones 5. Jesus Christ 6. The Awakening
I. Miner, Al II. Title

Library of Congress Control Number: 2010910413
Printed in the United States of America

For books and products, or to write Al Miner,
visit our website: **www.lamasing.net**

to the Guardians who gave their all

CONTENTS

Dear Reader,

It has proven a challenging, if joyous task to attempt mediating between the realms that Lama Sing inhabits and our own third dimensional one. In each instance we have made every effort to be utterly true to the sense of what Lama Sing is offering to us while honoring the vast expanse between us and their recounting of scenes that took place over 2,000 years ago in another tongue and culture. To be sure, Lama Sing was not only translating inter-dimensionally, but also, for our benefit, was relating events as they transpired in real time in a language (ancient Aramaic, for the most part) which often has no words that gracefully lend themselves to twenty-first century American English.

And so, we have tried to carefully discern when it was important to remain totally true to the exact wording (for example, to bring you more completely into the moment in time-space that is being depicted) and when to allow the thoughtful substitution of contemporary idiomatic English, in order that your being carried along by the narrative flow remains largely uninterrupted by your pausing to puzzle or even stumble over the text itself. So, although much of the archaic language and syntax has been preserved, some has been respectfully altered. Finally, the use of Maidens and Sisters refers to those twelve who were chosen as living embodiments of virtues to surround the Master, to mirror for Him that which He already is; the use of maidens and sisters designates those who prepared the way for His coming, sometimes generations before the Birth, as well as those who served Him according to their souls' intent.

The Editors

Chapter One

Of One Purpose

hose who have made the preparations, near and far, have made the way passable at last. The children and others engaged in the sacred works may now return to the area of the Three Holy Mountains.

During the past months as these preparations were unfolding, many of the children's parents established themselves in the outlying cities, communities, and outlands. Now, excitement and questions abound among the children as they bundle up their belongings, preparing for the journey ahead. Some are exceptionally excited, for they know that the months of being separated from their parents or other family members will soon end. They have been told there will be a gathering to reunite them with these loved ones.

Elob is speaking with Anna, Judy, Ruth, and many of the other sisters, as well as with several of the guardians, those ever ready to preserve their people, the children who hold the Promise, and the Word. "I shall find the means to visit now and then." He smiles warmly, clasping Judy's and Anna's hands in his own. "I have learned so much from you and your people."

"And we, of course, from you," Judy replies.

Elob resumes, "I must continue to oversee our works and to insure that the intent of the Promise is carried off into far distant lands and hearts. Some will hear Him, others will actually see Him in His journeys in later days. It is our guidance and our honor to serve with you to fulfill the prophecy and the Word of God.

"Our people who will be journeying and residing with you will keep me informed, for we have learned to see through each others' hearts, minds, and eyes." He squeezes their hands. "So I will oft look upon you, and perhaps you will feel my touch just as clearly as you feel this now."

He releases their hands and turns to Ruth. "Thou art truly blessed, good woman. The gifts of your spirit and the power of your faith will remain here among our people as that to be sought after."

She bows her head, taking his outstretched hand in both of hers. After a brief moment, she looks up. "Sweet Elob, ever shall I hold you in the temple of mine own heart, where God dwells. For I know you. You are His messenger and His servant. I will be honored to oft review the memory of you." Surprisingly, she leans forward.

Knowing it is her intent to offer him what is perhaps one of the highest and most intimate of blessings, Elob, too, leans forward, and gently places his forehead against hers.

"You are my brother ... ever," she whispers.

"And thou art my sister, ever and beyond."

They step back to gaze for a moment into one another's eyes, and a song of prayer begins from the group just beyond. All bow their heads. When the prayer is complete, they lift them to bid one another a final farewell.

"Will you see us off in the morning?" Judy asks.

Elob shakes his head. "No, this is my good-bye to you. But remember, it is only our bodies that will part. Our spirits will always be one. I prefer this time," looking up into the early evening sky, "to make what I call a final affirmation of oneness to those from whom I will separate. I have learned that at this time of day the power and purity are profound. There will be much for you to attend to, many children's questions to answer." He smiles broadly. "Go now, with my blessing and God's. We will be with you, not only by means of our emissaries, but in our ceremonies and other works as well. Therefore, if you have a need, call." Speaking no more, he gestures the Essene gesture of love, then turns and strides up the familiar pathway, rounds several large outcroppings and disappears.

"Oh-h ..." Anna murmurs, her hands covering her heart, "it is as though part of me has been removed."

Judy places an arm about her. "I know. But, as he said, he will always be with us. The children will sing songs of him in generations to come."

"Look what he has given us," Anna continues. "He and his people saved us. And they freed our brethren. They called us forth from darkness and gave all they had to give."

Ruth places a hand upon each of their shoulders. "Come now, what manner of teachers are we if we cannot remember that which we teach? Elob is the spirit of God manifest in a beautiful being, a true son of God. Surely, no matter where we are, we will feel his love, his oneness with us, and his support of the Promise. Come. Gather yourselves up and strengthen your spirits. Remember the purpose, remember the work." She turns her sisters and leads them down towards where the children are encamped.

"The adepts have provided many beasts of burden, much to the delight of the children," one of the guardians observes.

"They have thought of everything," replies another. "For all practical purposes, we will look like any other trading caravan. They have even provided the goods with which to barter, if need be. These are truly our brothers and sisters."

The children are struggling to get to sleep, as the sisters busily move about, helping this one or that.

A sweet voice comes from up on a plateau, and then another over to the side, then another. The adepts have come in their own manner, in their own custom, to bid the group farewell and perhaps to help the children, as they know very well the excitement that abounds here. Their music is sweet, haunting, and the words, though unknown, incredibly beautiful. It is as though a mystical essence of swirling orbs of light is being carried by the gentle breeze, reaching out, touching and embracing each child.

As the sisters continue to move about, they beam, shaking their heads, for upon each child's face is a heavenly smile.

It is yet early dawn, minimal light, but they are moving.

Members of the guardians, the warrior priests, have gone to the forefront with several others to the right and left flank.

On they all move, the children chattering, joking and laughing.

Anna turns to look at some of them and then glances at Ruth. "This is certainly different from our other journey to this place."

"Praise God," Ruth replies. "Look at them! How they have grown. How they have brightened. It is true. The Promise is awakening. You can see it and feel it."

So they journey and the days pass, but the children's excitement is undiminished by the physical exertion, for they are strong and vibrant. Their many outings into the arid wastelands have strengthened them remarkably, and the nourishment and the teachings have given them a resilience perhaps twice that of other children their age. Beyond all this, the brilliance of their spirits shines so strongly that one can presume quite clearly that this is the force which empowers them, that whether or not their bodies are taxed to their fullest extent, this inner light renews them. And they know it.

The excitement is barely containable. It is mid-morn, and the children can see their beloved Sea once again.

"May we go to it?" squeals Zephorah. Glancing about, she sees a guardian making the sign that all is well.

Anna laughs, "Go ahead, children. You have certainly earned it."

The scene is delightful, heart-warming. Like a swarm of beautiful little butterflies rushing toward a single destination, the children run splashing into the water. Soon the entire caravan has reached the water's edge.

The children are having such fun that they fail to note a solitary figure perched upon a large boulder, his stout staff glistening in the now mid-day sun.

"Well! It appears your memories are not very long," the figure shouts. "No, short indeed! You cannot even remember an old friend. I guess I will sing a song to cheer myself up."

Screams and shouts abound, for there is beloved Jacob, who has now begun to dance and twirl about slowly, wiggling his hands vigorously. As though he were some great creature with an insatiable itch, he moves this way and that, pretending he doesn't see them as they struggle to clamber up the boulder to embrace him.

"Wait a minute!" He feigns surprise as he turns and looks upon them. "I know you!" The children fall silent, their faces glowing. "You are ... No, that is not it." The children begin to giggle. "I think you must be ... Ledotia! No, not Ledotia. She is up there, up the mount. Well, my goodness! I believe you are Mary."

Mary blushes and giggles. "And I believe you are Jacob."

"You are right. Your memory is longer than I thought." And in the blink of an eye, he slides down the face of the boulder with remarkable ease, using his staff adroitly to balance and guide himself. "Oh, that was quite joyful." He looks up, rubbing his backside as he does.

The children, of course, overwhelm him, and in but a

moment, a swirling mass of them and Jacob are all rolling about on the ground, as he kisses faces and calls them each by name.

Then, down the mount many other children rush, laughing, yelling, calling out, running to embrace the others.

Off to the side, Joseph asks Anna and Ruth, "How was your journey?"

"Oh, Joseph! My heart is gladdened to see you again. And, of course, you," Ruth calls out to Jacob. She chuckles as Jacob, now leaning on his stout staff, simply nods in return.

"Zechariah, you look well. Have you been accepted into your village yet?" questions Anna.

"Oh yes. The Word of God is like a magical key." He smiles brightly. "All is well."

They turn to greet the many others, exchanging embraces, news, and such, and the day passes in this way.

The entourage has moved up into the embrace of their blessed residence in the Holy Mountains. The children have fallen fast asleep, for their day has been filled with rejoicing, and their dreams beckon them, as here and there, quiet songs are sung to small groups. Many of the young maidens, covered only lightly, some with heads touching, are lying out in the open under the stars. Friends, brothers and sisters, relatives, the elders, and all of the tribe are walking about, bending to stroke the forehead of each of these sweet sleeping gems.

"How are Elob and the brothers and sisters?" asks Joseph with quiet excitement.

"They are quite well. Elob said to speak his greeting unto you, and say that he sends the strength of his faith and love to all of you, and to the Promise."

"Goodness!" Joseph remarks. "The children are all so bright and vibrant. It is obvious they have gained much. It is also obvious that the light is growing within them. Are the

Maidens chosen?"

"For the most part," Judy responds, glancing at her sisters, smiling. "But they are all such beautiful children that even with our complete focus, we are having difficulty discerning which ones shall fill the sacred symbol and the tenet."

"It will come," he replies. "I am certain it will come."

"Well," Jacob chimes in, "if one needs only a dozen, having twenty or more is quite nice, I should think."

All smile at this and glance about to acknowledge members of the other tribes who have gathered here, some of whom had gone into hiding as the adepts of the School of the Prophets had warned them to through the guardians.

Judy sighs deeply, looking about the encampment. Small campfires are everywhere. Turning to look at Zechariah she asks, "Are we safe? I mean, are the pursuers ..."

Zechariah smiles and nods. "Those who had sworn vengeance against us are now battling some great foes to the northeast. God is wondrous. Now the question is one of ... How shall I say this? We no longer need to be cautious of those who would seek to vanquish us, but now our focus should be on the further unification of our peoples. On the morrow, several elders will arrive from other tribes. Their path, their belief ... Well, their seers have a different vision than ours."

The sisters gasp as their hands go quickly to their chests.

"Do not be too concerned. They are needed, and we should like to bring them into the spirit, into the understanding, of what we believe to be truth."

Jacob is rocking slightly, leaning on his staff as he does. "I will speak to them."

Zechariah and Joseph laugh as Zechariah follows with, "Well, certainly, if you speak to them, Jacob, that will make all the difference."

"That is meant lovingly, of course." Joseph laughs again. "Actually, I do not know anyone who could turn you down when you are determined to do something."

"Well," Jacob, replies, "I will only be the messenger. God will do the work." A moment of silence follows, and then he throws his head back in a mighty laugh.

The conversation brings them to the end of the day. It is past twilight, and the visiting groups have arrived. Tradition calls for the evening prayer, though much of the usual formality and tradition is dispensed with as they gather for ceremony. Out of honor, they ask Mathias and Thaddeus, the two emissaries from the main distant tribes, to lead the prayer. The foods are blessed, and when the nourishment, the prayer, and the passing of the cup have been completed, the groups gather at the council fire. It is a very impressive sight, for these are all people of great light.

"We have heard of your works," Mathias begins, "and we have been following in a similar manner with the groups of children who are under our care."

"Are they well?" asks Anna.

"They are. And as is the plan, we shall bring them here in groups in the very near future, according to that which is agreed upon."

"That will be wonderful. I so long to see them again."

Mathias smiles. "Do you believe that the children are truly those forces that will awaken the One who comes?"

Silence.

Judy rises to be recognized and is called forward.

"We honor you, Judy. Your reputation goes before you. We have heard of you and the two seers." Mathias glances around to see them seated towards the rear, their faces serene.

Judy kneels and thanks Mathias and Thaddeus. "We do believe this. We hold in our hearts that from the children, there must be chosen twelve. That from those twelve, the Hand of God will come to rest upon one, and that upon that Maiden, the Word of God shall descend and He will come."

"These are departures from our teachings." Mathias responds gently, for he can see the sincerity with which this revered teacher called Judy speaks. "How are we to reconcile this with our custom?"

"Is our custom so different from yours," questions Joseph, "that we cannot come together in support of one another in order to make the way passable for Him who comes?"

"There are questions about much of what you believe, dear Joseph," continues Mathias. "For instance, there is a question in our hearts and minds as to whether or not all of this, if we are to accept it, is to be represented in a feminine body."

Joseph, greatly moved and struggling to find words to express what he feels, is surprised and delighted to hear a firm, clear voice speak.

"What gives birth to any form of life that is not of the feminine?" the voice questions.

Mathias leans to look. "Who art thou speaking?"

Zelotcse steps forward into the light of the fire. Anna, Judy, and Ruth glance at one another with a smile.

"I am called Zelotese. I have other names, but the name is of no great consequence. I am knowledgeable of one of your great teachers."

"Name that one," Thaddeus presses.

"He is called Elijah." A murmur goes through the group. "And his Healing Spring is just a short way over there."

The visiting group murmur among themselves, for this is a well kept secret.

"I am come from a school not unlike this very mountain upon which Elijah claimed his oneness with God. We are of the one purpose that reaches back to the heritage of your own people and beyond. For we know of the sons of God."

Again the visitors' elders murmur among themselves. *Who is this man to speak in such a way?*

"When so very long ago the Light entered the Earth to show those who had become entrapped in it the illusion thereof, your elders were with Him. And I, as well."

"You were with Him in this time? And you know this?"

"It is so, Mathias. You may question me about it as you wish, and I will answer. For now, however, let us speak to the question in the hearts and minds of your people. Enos is aging, this we all know. Who will follow him? Who will lead?"

All glance around at one another.

"It must be a heart and spirit open to see truth in spite of that held in their own mind and heart. Is there such a one in this gathering?" He glances about with remarkable authority.

There is silence as his eyes move about the group in such a way that all feel as though they have been touched by this one called Zelotese. "Is it within you, Mathias, to set aside that which seems to be separate and to claim that which is alike? Have you the courage of spirit to be all you truly are? I call you forth, in the Name of God."

Remarks and exclamations are all about, for rarely has anyone ever spoken to an elder in such a tone.

Mathias is stiffening visibly, an apparent inner struggle going on, for he is true to that which he believes. He has led his people to this point, and those of Thaddeus as well, for Thaddeus has always looked to him for guidance.

"If it troubles you that the twelve are feminine in body, then ask your seers to look beyond. But tell them not aforehand what I speak to you here. Let them see it independently of me and tell it to you. My spirit tells me it will be the same."

Another murmur moves throughout the group, for of what spirit does this man speak?

"There is but one God, and He bears that Name as thou knowest Him. Therefore, am I one with Him."

Now voices are sounding loudly back and forth, and arms are waving about.

Judy, Anna, and Ruth are seated in silence, looking at Zelotese, as are Zechariah and Joseph. Jacob is only rocking, smiling, looking down into the flames. Curiously, Zelotese turns to look down at him and in that moment, Jacob's eyes come up to meet his. They smile and Jacob nods.

Zelotese looks up, his face strong. "If you are to believe in your purpose as the Expectant Ones, then it begins here and now. There can be no more division. There can not be separateness, but only oneness. If you cannot cleave unto the ideal, the purpose, and unto building and making the Way passable for Him to enter, then how shall you call yourselves? For I could not call you Essene if that were so."

Strong comments and shouts break out, but Zelotese speaks loudly over the din. "Hear me out, then speak as you would. Yes, my spirit and the Spirit of God are one. And my brothers and sisters are one with me now, even though a distance away. I know they are here and they know it. They look upon you, as do I … through my eyes and my heart. I tell you this to demonstrate to you the power of oneness, the claiming of an ideal that has no division, that cannot be deflected towards illusion this way or that, but is so filled with faith and hope that the way is strong and purposeful, ever.

"He is to be born of one of these," gesturing broadly to where the children are resting. "This we have seen and this we know. And He will be nurtured and taught, not that He will need to be given information. Rather, He will be taught how to manifest it here in this realm of finiteness. The very qualities which are of Him, He will see reflected back to Him, nurturing Him, supporting Him. Just as a babe would suckle unto his mother's breast, so will each of the Maidens of their spirit, nourish and reflect back to Him all that He shall bring from within Himself that is of God. Is there one among your elders who believes that they could do as these Maidens shall? If so, let him stand now before all."

Looking around, he singles out one of the stern, wrinkled faces. It is he who spoke so vociferously when Zelotese called out, *God's Spirit and mine are one.* "You, sir. You read the stars, do you not?"

The man's eyebrows arch. "It is so. I can see in the stars that which can guide us."

"And you have injured yourself on your left side. It was a fall as you were climbing onto a high place. Let me see … That was one season ago."

The man looks quickly this way and that. "So you can see. Many of us can see!"

"Well, let me ask you … Are you willing to do that which these Maidens shall do?"

His face softens as he glances down and then up. "This, a man cannot do. That is a woman's place."

"So be it then. Why do you question, Mathias, if one of these, your own seers and elders, speaks it?"

"How is there to be balance for Him if He is surrounded only by the feminine?" Mathias counters.

"You are missing the spirit of what I give to you. He is His own balance. We do not give to Him that of which He has need. We shall give to Him that He shall know whereof He comes. I tell you this … As soon as the words fall from His mouth and He hears Himself speak them, He will know.

"And He will call upon you, sir," turning to look at the astrologer again, "and you will look upon Him and know that what I speak to you now is only truth, and He shall carry it forward upon His journey through times of joyful service, and other times as great pain and sorrow. And He shall ask of you certain things. If you wish to know them, I will speak to you apart from all the others, that you may know my words are true. When He comes into the fullness of His being, before He leaves, He will speak the very words I will give unto you."

"How is it you know this?" the astrologer questions.

"He gives these to me now, that I might speak them to you … and to all of you, dear friends. Know the Way. Know that it is purposeful. Set aside that which could divide or separate. And I ask you humbly, claim that which unites you. If you can meet this challenge, Mathias, then I foretell that you will become the leader of your people. If you cannot, your name will fall away and another will step forward." Zelotese smiles broadly for the first time. "But I know it shall be you because I can see in your heart, above all else, the wish to serve God. Embrace this path, I pray thee. It is *the* path.

"I thank you all for letting us speak … I, and my brothers and sisters who are with me." He gestures his own salutation of honor to all, turns, and strides away.

Absolute silence.

"Quite a man," remarks Mathias softly.

"He is that," Joseph responds gently. "He is a prophet. He is a healer. He is a seer. He can read the stars. He knows the plants that heal. And I could go on."

"How is it he knows all this?" questions the astrologer.

"He is an adept from the School of the Prophets. He is all that he has said to you, but much more. He has journeyed for several years to be here with us because he heard the Call. He knows the Promise. He is one with it. He is my brother."

To hear Joseph make such a comment is awe-inspiring to all of these people.

Judy rises again, and is recognized. "I and the seers have together oft looked to the future with a dear friend, Elob, who is as a master of the School of the Prophets …"

"Elob, you say?" Incredulous, Mathias interrupts and turns to look at Thaddeus.

"Yes, that is his name."

It is Thaddeus who now speaks. "In working with our dreams and visions …" He gestures to his scribe. "Bring it to me." The scribe searches through rolls of parchment, selects one, and brings it. "See, here? It is recorded. Mathias had a vision. It awakened him and called to him. In it was a man called Elob!"

"You see?" prompts Judy. "And it was Elob who sent

Zelotese here."

Mathias bows his head and his hands come up. He places them together in front of his face and bobs. "Praise God! Praise God! So be it. We are one with you."

"But may I finish?"

"Yes. But I tell you, Judy, our peoples are with you. We will support you. We will support the Promise."

"That is wonderful." She glances about. "But I feel I must tell you this, and I have been chosen to speak it. There will come a time, when He is quite young, that He will go forth. Zelotese and others like him will guide Him to their own lands. He will see the reflections of truth through the eyes of those peoples and their teachers. And He will share the Promise with them, that they can, in turn, gift it to their people, that others who follow may also manifest the truth of God unto those who follow them. And in this manner will the teachings, the truth that He brings, be offered to all people."

Again there is silence.

"How long shall He be with us? Have you seen this?"

"Yes, Mathias ... perhaps a dozen years or so, not many. Then, we all agree, it will be purposeful for Him to journey. We have already begun the preparations. Many of our peoples have gone forth, aided by the adepts from the School, given the means and guided by them to foreign lands."

"Will that be our only time with Him?"

"Have not your seers seen and revealed this?"

Mathias glances down and then up again. "I pray you understand that their focus has been elsewhere because we believed separate from this path. But now I am certain if they open themselves, they can see it as well. Will you help?"

Judy, honored, nods and bows. "I, and, perhaps, even Zelotese." Again, a murmur goes through the group. "His mastery of such things is wondrous. I had believed that the elders gave me great gifts and that the Spirit of God rested His hand upon my heart and opened it. But, I tell you ...

Zelotese is one with God. I have seen him often when only the purpose of service seemed to keep him here. He is filled with the love and compassion of God, equally balanced with the truth and honor of God. He is like a rod of righteousness, as we see him." She glances about and receives affirmation from all of her brothers and sisters. "Yes, we will. But I wish to tell you, if I may, several more particulars."

"Please," Mathias continues softly. "We are with you. We wish to know all that will help, all that we can know to empower ourselves and to contribute to you and the Work."

Judy sighs, pleased at this. "It is as Zelotese said."

Mathias smiles and nods. "Do continue."

"He will return from the tribes that have come from afar." There are joyful responses and murmurs. "When He does so, after a time He will begin His true work. Thereupon, He will call forth twelve to walk with Him, and many more to do His work. These things I have seen, and I might direct your attention to some of the ancient writings and prophecies that go back to the Shining One in the ancient lands, where the Forces of Light and Dark first met.

"So, you see, in His work, He will bear the gifts from the twelve Holy Maidens. Each one that He calls forth has already had the seed of her gift sown within her, either by us, or, as we have seen, by the Hand of God. Thus, I offer this in humbleness as an understanding to you and to all your people: That which begins, begins according to the order of nature nurtured by the feminine spirit, guided, taught, strengthened, and encouraged by it. Not apart from the masculine spirit, for all about, look and see (and we call upon you and your people to join with us) ... Always there will be those at the ready to provide any such balance, any such honor, wisdom, truth, or enlightenment as flows from the masculine aspect of God in the form of you and your brothers.

"But for now, we must give our work at hand considerable attention, and so it is important that twelve are chosen, each of whom also choosing of her own volition. This process has been carefully, lovingly nurtured, as we have encouraged you to do with the group of candidates you have in your own midst. For should there be the return of that which would seek to vanquish us and should the unforeseeable happen, we must be prepared, no matter what, to fulfill the prophecy: that all twelve Tenets of Truth, the Holy of Holies, be represented to and evoked from Him.

"It is the Son of God who comes bearing the example and the teaching which will awaken others to know themselves as sons and daughters of God. He will give us the example, the gifts, the truths which we know can set all people free who are willing to hear, to see, and to claim. The adepts have looked beyond that which we can see. I can share their visions with you at another time, for they are most profound.

"For now, let me state that what we see of such importance, and rightfully so, is only the beginning. After His passing, many times of testing and challenging will follow so that each soul on Earth during His walk here with us now or in the future as they hear His message or Word will have the opportunity to choose it. And as the Wheel of Life revolves for them and their spirits journey ever upward upon it, He whom we now await, the adepts have told us, will come yet again."

Vigorous discussion erupts among all of the peoples.

In a clear but gentle voice, Judy concludes, "It is a wonderful time, my brothers and sisters. I dedicate my life unto our Lord, who comes. I beg of thee … Wilt thou not join us," gesturing towards her people, "in service unto Him?"

Chapter Two

Gems in the Crown

It is a brilliant spring morning. Even the most arid of lands is bursting forth in a bounty of color so brilliant that they seem to vibrate.

The maidens are delighting in wandering about, gathering a variety of flowers, careful to leave some behind for those who will follow. As they gather the flowers in their great baskets, they twirl about and sing.

Rebekah calls out, "I am so excited! The celebration will be tonight. We have waited so long."

"And we get to dance!" Zephorah twirls again.

As always, off to the side are the elder sisters, including Anna, Judy, Theresa, Ruth, and many others.

"It should be a wondrous evening, think you not, Judy?"

"I should say it to be so. But time will bear it out."

"Do I detect a doubt?" Anna asks Ruth.

"Oh, it is probably just a bit of anticipation."

"Ah, yes. We understand." Judy smiles, gazing off at one young maiden's bouncing head and then another's. "We are so near to the choice. And I know, as do you," glancing at both Ruth and Anna, "that some decisions will be made this very evening!"

"Well, it is likely to be so," Ruth begins softly, then brightens, her voice lifting. "But look at them! If we, ourselves, were to choose, perhaps we would do so based on some personal regard or favoritism. Who knows? Who can say what truly lies within one's heart and emotion?"

"You are no doubt correct." Judy sighs deeply. "Were it left to me, I would choose all of them."

They all laugh.

"Do you not ever wonder," she begins again after a long pause, "whether or not God truly … well, you know, and I mean this lovingly, needs our rituals and symbols, and the value we place upon such things?" She quickly looks down, almost as though slightly embarrassed at what she has stated, for she is considered one of the highest in terms of the great teachers. For her to question such things might well raise the eyebrows of some of the elders.

She continues, "I have always felt, as our young sisters out there," gesturing to the little maidens, "that it is good to question. It is good to ask. Because through the process, one discovers truth and, likely as not, strengthens both faith and memory of all that which is proven and valuable." Glancing up from the side, Judy studies Anna, whose face is smiling and bright. "Do you think that my question is indicative of a need of some rejuvenation of my faith?"

Though Judy's words could perhaps sound challenging, the warmth of her smile reveals the true nature of a heart seeking to gain insight from her beloved friend.

"Whose faith does not need a little bolstering now and then?" Anna smiles brightly.

"I would affirm that," Ruth adds.

"Are the children gathering the flowers for tea or for preparation of potions?" asks Isadore, having just arrived on the scene.

Almost in unison, the three each sisters respond. "No, not for either. These flowers are simply for the beauty of them. They are for this evening's ceremony.

"Ah, yes." Isadore observes. "The coming forth of the season. And perhaps much more, is it not so?"

"Perhaps so." Judy smiles and looks at Anna and Ruth, who nod and return her smile.

"Well, you three must feel … How do the children call it? Butterfly tummies."

Laughter rolls from her three beloved sisters, and Judy replies, "We do have our share of that, and I especially. In fact, we were just speaking of this."

"Well, tell you what … I have been doing a bit of gathering myself. See what I have here?" The sisters look down into Isadore's bag and see a wonderful array of beautiful petals and some stems and leaves. "I should like to prepare us all a wonderful tea. May I?"

The three sisters oo-o and ah-h and Anna smiles. "You had best make a large pot. Once those young ones smell your tea, they will all be over here."

"So I surmised." She gestures to several of the other sisters. Some bring bags of water, one has a large pot, and another brings various utensils. It seems only moments until the water is warm enough for the tea and herbs to be stirred into the pot.

Nearby, Ruth lifts her face into the steam. "I do not know if I will ever smell anything quite as aromatic and as stimulating as your teas."

Obviously pleased, Isadore smiles and rocks back and forth, her eyes closing as she does. "Thank You, Lord God, for Your many gifts, Your many blessings, and for these sweet sisters with whom to share this tea." Then she raises her hands and claps them very loudly three times.

This is all the children need. Laughing, they rush up to collect a small bowl and be served their tea.

The sisters gather a short distance away, busily speculating about the evening's ceremony.

"Do you think," asks Isadore, sipping her tea, "the School of the Prophets will send anyone? Surely they know."

"Oh, they know, all right." Judy replies. "Zelotese has so

confirmed. We have been told that they will be in special ceremony this evening, though they have not said much about why, other than simply pointing out that it is a sacred time." She glances around at the shadows, lengthening as the sun dips towards the horizon, and sighs. "How wondrous that God has provided such a means to acknowledge our growth, the building of our spiritual light."

"How so?" asks Ruth, noting Judy's gaze.

"The movement through each day, and the announcement of the forthcoming night ... How could anyone orchestrate such majesty, save God?"

"It is curious," Ruth agrees, "that so much of life seems independent of God, yet as we have been taught to see, feel, and know, it is so very evident that all is one."

Brushing an insect from her forehead, Isadore remarks with an impish little smile, "Even such creatures as those."

They all laugh heartily, gaining the attention of the children nearby, several of whom gravitate towards their elder sisters. Noting them, the sisters gesture them over, as always snuggling them and embracing them on their laps.

"Did you enjoy your tea?"

"Yes, it was excellent, Isadore. Thank you." Little Mary rubs her tummy. "It is magical when you gather the herbs and petals, and then prepare it for us. Even though you have taught us well, my tea never tastes quite like yours."

The elder sisters laugh, and Isadore replies, "Well, perhaps it will in time, and perhaps will even surpass mine, for you will add your personal sweetness to it."

Glancing down and wiggling her toes, Little Mary looks back up. "I knew it! That is what you do. You add your sweetness to it."

All the sisters laugh again.

"It is the power of one's intention that makes a thing either sweet or sour," offers Ruth. "Think you not this so?"

"Oh, yes," Little Mary replies. "But some people's intentions are stronger than others. I think mine is not grown yet."

Again there is laughter.

"What say you, Rachel?" Isadore asks.

"Well, I can make pretty good bread, but when it comes to making the tea, I either put too much of this in and not enough of that, or too much of everything. And it tastes ... Well, you have to put a lot of honey in it in order to get it down! And you know what?"

"No. What?" Anna smiles, delighted.

"It makes me perspire when I make it."

In the laughter which follows, Rachel laughs, too, for not only is it humorous, it is true.

"Perhaps you are adding too many of these." Isadore shows her the leaves of a certain herb."

"Well, I think only what you told me ... two or three to the bowl measure."

"That sounds right. Then, how about these?" Isadore holds up a handful of yellow petals.

"Oh, I love those. They remind me of sunshine. I probably put an extra measure of those in."

"There it is, then. If too many of these are added, they can cause the body to repel drosses. But that is a good thing."

"Well, not at the evening meal!"

And everyone laughs again.

"Sometimes it drips right off here." She points to her nose, adding, "and I have to ... Well, I have to check to see who is looking so I can wipe it away."

There follows a moment of silence, then laughter bursts out once again.

"You do, though," offers Anna, "make lovely bread."

"I think so, too," Rachel concurs rather proudly. "I like to put the little seeds in there. They give it such an uplifting flavor, do you not think it so?"

"Yes, I do. And I think yours is one of my favorite breads of all."

"Really? Better than Isadore's?"

Anna glances lovingly at Isadore, then back to Rachel. "Forgive me, Isadore … but yes, Rachel. Yours has an aromatic flavor. When I close my eyes, I can move into a meditation and see the beauty of the desert. I can see the long wadis and valleys of the embracing mountainside. I can hear the water trickling from hidden springs down below. I can hear the wind and the creatures of the air calling out, looking for friends and family."

"My! I thought it was good bread, but I did not know it was *that* good."

Everyone laughs yet again.

"Well, children, be about your works and gather up your flowers. Time is growing short. Look over here at the shadow from the mount."

They glance and quickly jump to their feet.

"I have almost enough." Little Mary shows them her collection. "What I gather now, I will bring to you, my sisters."

"I, too," echoes Rachel, and off they go.

A silence descends as the sisters have a second bowl of the wonderful tea.

Judy is looking into the reflection on the surface of her bowl of tea. "They are two. I know it." She sips slowly and glances up.

Ruth's eyes glaze as she focuses upon a distant spot. Everyone present knows that she is seeing. She blinks several times and turns to look at Judy. Her face is aglow, her eyes round and shining. "I believe it to be so, as well. I can see them mounting the temple steps."

The sisters whisper at this, in wonder and awe.

"Have you seen the others, as well?" Judy asks.

Ruth's eyes become glazed again. "I have seen some."

"Could you share with us?"

Again there is silence. Finally Ruth blinks again and looks over at Anna, whose eyes have become serious, though her face is warm, cheerful, loving. "What do you see, Anna?"

"I see two Marys," she responds, her eyes focused upon the mountain before them, wherein the School was originally established. "And I see several of the others. I see beyond that to when He comes, and I see Him and His friends laughing and playing, all under the watchful eyes of these Maidens, whom we now tend. Our time will come to reap the harvest of Spirit's bounty, to gather up the power of Spirit's light and hold it in a reservoir of light for those lovely Maidens who will be chosen.

"It is interesting to me … As I look far beyond," Anna continues, her eyes narrowing, "I seem to recognize some of them in the years ahead. But I hear our Lord calling to them, and I know not these names." Her eyes now blink and flutter and become themselves again, as she turns and glances around at Judy, Ruth, Isadore, and the other sisters, who, if they were pressed any closer, might fall over into the teapot.

Judy adds, "It is curious … those of our brethren who have gone forth into the outer worlds … I have gone off to see them, and I think I have seen them well. Those who are being helped, aided, by some of our brethren I know are having their hearts turned to focus upon the coming of the Promise. Then, when I journey back from such distant places, I see some of them coming forward."

"Do you know them, Judy?" Isadore, leans forward in great interest.

"Some I know."

"Can you name any?" Recognizing her own eagerness, Isadore smiles and settles back.

"Yes. I see Nicodemus."

There are oh-h's and ah-h's, for he is well thought of, even at this age. It is believed that he is likely to have a voice in the future among those of authority.

"He does keep his distance, though," observes Isadore.

"By design, I believe," Judy continues. "And what a

sweet man. Filled with the spirit. He will surely come."

Deep sighs sound all about.

"I, too, have seen and heard," Ruth adds, "and I, too, have heard names I do not understand. So I asked. One of the ancient ones came and said unto me, *He will call them by that which He knows them, and whether they are of that name in the present is of no matter to Him. For He will know that name by which our Lord God calls them.*"

There are great sighs and all make various sacred signs and symbols, bow their heads, and rock.

A great circle of generous campfires rings the outer periphery of the gathering, the greatest of them burning in the absolute center. Here and there come those to occasionally tend to one of the smaller fires and then take a position seated between two of them, so there is a continuous circle of fire and Essenes, all around the gathered council. This circle is very large, so under other circumstances it would be feared that such a great light might concern some outsiders who, noting it, might come to investigate. But the guardians are in place, as are those on the outer periphery, so it is known that all is well.

The elders are gathered in their position at the high point of this gently sloping ground. To either side are the elder sisters, the seers, the prophets, the healers, some from the School, some of the adepts who have journeyed here, the remaining guardians, and the elders of various tribes.

In the center are several groups of children, their faces shining, their garments flowing beautifully, reflecting the light. Streams of their hair are intertwined with rivulets of woven flowers. Each maiden sparkles in the iridescent light reflected by the petals of the blossoms ringing her face and cascading down over her upper torso. Some have woven necklaces of flowers, and have great bundles of them and are moving around the outer circle, offering a blessing and placing flower wreaths around the necks of those tending the outer flame, much to their delight.

Three claps sound, and the children scurry to resume their proper positions.

"While blessed beyond measure," Judy speaks in a clear voice, "as we celebrate the awakening of the Earth from its slumber, so do we celebrate the awakening of spring in our midst. For here we have the flower of our youth, adorned appropriately by the gifts of God from the lands that embrace us. I should like to thank our elders for their beautiful prayers, and those who have spoken so wisely and eloquently to open these ceremonies." She turns and bows, offering the Essene maidens' gesture of love to all those to whom she refers.

She then turns, hands upraised, eyes sweeping across all present as she repeatedly intones, "The grace of God be upon you. The grace of God be upon you."

When all have been blessed, she brings her hands down and places them over her face.

All fall silent, for everyone knows that Judy, High Priestess, now summons the ancients.

Slowly, she brings her hands down and spreads her arms wide. The only sound is that of the flames consuming the fuel upon these fires of sacred intent. She begins to rock to and fro, at first only her head, then exaggeratedly, and then her body swaying and her hands come in and out, in and out.

Finally, she stops, bringing her hands to rest upon the center of her being. "They are here," she murmurs.

"Do you have guidance for us, our beloved brothers and sisters who have gone before?" With slight, almost imperceptible motions of her head and upper torso, she speaks: "We are yet, as ever, with you. We come to you to celebrate, as those who shall hold the light for our Lord are awakening. God's Spirit and grace are with you all, as are we."

A flutter of greeting and praise comes from almost everyone present, for they know that the voice speaking through

Judy is, indeed, one of the ancient ones.

"May we call them?" Judy questions. "Is it time?"

Again, the almost imperceptible motion of her head and shoulders is followed by, "Some are called because they are awakened. Some have walked with their spirit for a number of Earth years. These can be called."

Again, silence.

Judy's voice rings out, "Wilt thou name them?"

The movement of her head and shoulders is followed by, "They will name themselves. Call them into dance and you will see, and we will return and confirm it for you. Call them to dance."

There is silence until Judy's eyes open. "We thank you. Praise God for the gift of you." Her hands come straight up, and then, clap, clap, clap.

The children jump to their feet, rush to positions, and outstretch their arms until only their fingertips are touching.

There is silence once again as all wait.

Then comes the thum-thum-thum of a sacred drummer from beyond a rise, seemingly within the holy mountain itself; then, from the side, floats a sweet sound somewhat like a flute; and over there, another sound, metallic, cymbal-like.

The maidens begin to turn to face one another and gesture the symbol of love. They turn again to each other and repeat this. They raise their hands, and the clapping begins. Perfectly aligned with the sacred drumming, they move, first one foot this way and the other that way, and 'round and about they move forward, and again, and again. Soon, they are twirling, many little swirling circles of color and light comprising a great circular spiral of light as the circle revolves, in the center of which is the sacred fire.

Suddenly, the drumming stops, along with the flute, the metallic sounds, and the others, and the children stand perfectly still in the absolute silence.

One steps forward towards the flame, bends and bows,

and we hear her tiny, but exquisitely clear voice ring out. "I am Zephorah. I come to You, Lord God, offering myself as a vessel of Your light, so as You would choose me." She steps back a pace, and we hear the drum. She spins and turns, then moves back to the circle.

To the side, another steps forward, and the drumming stops. "I give you the gift of my life's love, Lord God. I am Mary, your Daughter. I ask of You the glory of service, and I give of myself without limitation to that which Thou knowest to be aright." She steps back, and the drum begins and she spins about. As she does, many can see the light grow around her. Heads bob, some lean to whisper to one another such comments as, *Surely she is one of them.*

Another comes forward. "I, Theresa, have a life offered in service to You, Lord God. So as Thou would have me, I am Thine." Again, the drum and her little dance, and again, several whisper, *Here, too, the light here is evident.*

So it goes, so many, until the ceremony is complete. There is great rejoicing and many prayers.

Finally, when the children have been taken to their time of rest and prepared for slumber, the adults gather.

"Zelotese! How wonderful to have you with us again."

"I am honored to have been chosen to be here, Joseph." The brilliance of Zelotese' eyes is unmistakable. No question that this one is beyond any Earthly limitation. As one gazes at him, the image could come to mind of his brothers and sisters who are several days' journey away, yet, whose faces seem to come and go over that of Zelotese himself.

"And Elob ..." questions Jacob, "he is well, I trust?"

"Mightily so." Zelotese smiles broadly. "Unquestionably the hand of God rests upon him often. For there are days, and all of us have noted this, when he seems more youthful and vibrant than any in our entire group."

Jacob, rocking slightly, also smiles. "And what might those days be, if they could be discerned?"

"You are wise, Jacob. Of course, they are those days when the visions are clear, and often."

"Could you share some of the more recent good ones?" Jacob laughs silently.

"Of course. That is in part my purpose for being here. You are in the process of choosing the crown, are you not?"

"The crown?" questions Joseph.

"Yes, the circle of light that will surround Him. Each of the Maidens, we think of as a beautiful gem in the crown of light which will be His when He enters."

The silence is broken only by some of those on the periphery of the elders and seers who are commenting and smiling. For the prophecy says a king shall come, and Zelotese' reference to a crown pleases them greatly.

"Which of these do you see, if you can name them?"

"Some can be named, Joseph. Some cannot. For their names are not known yet."

"How so?" Joseph probes further.

"They will be given by Him. And they will be twice blessed because of it, in a manner of speaking. For how could any not be considered greatly blessed merely to seat themselves upon the symbolic twelve points of power."

Again, the seers, elders, and prophets of the Essenes, and several of those from the School of the Prophets, smile and nod, speaking quietly to one another.

"It is not so much a question at this point," Zelotese continues, now somewhat authoritatively, "who is who and what is what. It is, rather, a question of what remains before us to be done. Time grows short. Soon, very soon, shortly after the Twelve are chosen, She will become known."

"Do you mean that … Well," looking about, Joseph asks, "that this will happen close together?"

"As we see it, it will be very close together. Then, there will be perhaps two years only to prepare, and She will be told to make ready. She will be apart from us, and from these holy lands."

"How could this be?"

Zelotese looks at Joseph long and carefully. "You will come to know how so, and you will know clearly."

The gaze of Zelotese weighs upon Joseph in a way that stirs him.

"What sayest thou?" Zelotese' gaze is fixed upon Joseph. "And what of thee, Zechariah? Does thy spirit move at such words, as well?"

"Whenever in temple, I offer myself for whatsoever our Lord would have of me. I pray that I am a worthy vessel."

Only then do Zelotese' eyes shift to Zechariah. "Perhaps it can be said, Zechariah, that your role in this will be greater, and uniquely so, than many might surmise."

"Good brother," Zechariah questions, "can you reveal this unique role?"

Zelotese is smiling now, his eyes somewhat glazed, as though he is looking through Zechariah. "I can see only this much, my brother … that you shall have an important work at hand when He comes. And that the preparation will in many ways come to focus upon you for a time, and heavily so."

"Then I shall work all the harder. I shall do all I know to do, that I might meet my works and responsibilities, and serve them to my spirit's all."

Zelotese, eyes still glassy, nods and smiles gently. "I can tell you that you will do to a measure and a half."

A ripple of discussion goes throughout the group.

"Did they like our dance, Judy?"

"Yes, Zephorah. They loved it. And all of you children looked so beautiful."

"Did I speak clearly enough that all could hear?"

"Very clearly, Mary. Your voice was as the call of a beautiful bird in the twilight sky."

"Oh, that is good." She smiles and looks down, folding

her entwined fingers back and forth as she does.

"Did they like the flower necklaces we made for them?"

"Yes, Hannah. Some said they intend to dry them and keep them forever as a memory of your love's intent."

Hannah, too, smiles looking down, and straightens the garment over her knees.

"Was there a … Did a light come upon any of us?"

"Yes, Andra, there were lights," Anna responds softly.

"There were lights around all of you," Ruth adds.

"No, I mean *the* light."

The elder sisters look at one another. Finally Anna answers. "We are ever dependent upon truth and honor. These are pillars upon which the light of God rests for our people, and we ever strive, as you maidens know so well, to balance and match these with love and compassion. So it is in the spirit of our sacred honor and truth that I answer your question, and I gift it to you from the center of my being where the grace of God exists as love and compassion."

"Well, did I have the light around me?" questions Andra, her voice shaking

Quick glances from all of the elder sisters, and Judy nods that she will respond. "You had the light around you, Andra. It is believed that you are one of them."

Andra's hands sweep up to cover her face, and she begins to sob softly.

Two of the elder sisters move swiftly to console her.

"Why do you weep, child?" questions Judy.

"If I am one … and I thank You, Lord God … if I am, then there are only eleven more. Is it not so?"

"Yes."

"Then I weep for those who shall not be chosen. For we are many more than this number."

"Oh no, child. Know you not that the light of God will shine upon all of you? Know you not that the prophecy states there are those who will come to tend Him, to guide Him, to nurture, to protect Him, and that they shall be called the Holy Maidens Twelve? But that there shall be more at His side, ready at His hand and heart's direction to do His work who will be the Remainder? So then, equal is the joy to be celebrated here. For as you have chosen are you chosen. None will be left behind. None shall want for the opportunity to serve and walk with Him.

"Hear my voice clearly, sweet children. The light of your childhood is coming into its fruition. Like a plant waiting to blossom, so are you. When you bloom, the Call will come. And from your midst, one will be chosen. Think you for a moment. Here are we," smiling, looking around at the elder sisters, the teachers, and caregivers. "What shall our role be?"

The children gaze at those whom they have come to love so deeply, those who have nurtured them every day of their lives that they can recall. Save but small fragments of time, ever have these elder sisters been with them, some silently preparing meals, some mending garments, others weaving, some tending the soil and gathering up the harvest, all these things and more. And here, too, are the great teachers, who, the children suddenly realize, will step back as the light descends upon the Twelve and then, later, upon all the others.

Andra, her face luminous, looks from one to the other of the elder sisters, jumps to her feet, and rushes across to fling herself upon Judy, who receives her warmly, rocking her. "Forgive me, my sister." She sobs lightly, her face buried in Judy's neck.

"There is naught to forgive, my sweet Andra." She holds Andra's shoulders, looking closely into her eyes. "Remember the teachings. I am one with you. Your joys of service, your opportunities to bear gifts, are mine as well, and doubly so because I have been with you all these years. So my heart," she places a hand upon her own chest, "and your heart," doing the same to Andra's, "are one with Him," holding her palm up towards God. "It is important for you to go beyond your first reaction. For I say to you in the truth of God: All will be called. Not one shall be left behind, unless they choose it to be so."

Judy, Anna, Ruth, and many of the others, look about at the children and at one another in absolute silence.

"So, now, let us prepare for our nourishment."

The children excitedly move into position.

"Oh Lord God, we come unto Thee again this eveningtide. Nourish our spirits that we might grow stronger, brighter. Guide Thou us unto that Thou would have us know, and show unto us those works that Thou would have us do. But, as ever, do we pray, Lord God, that Thou lift up our spirits into Thy embrace, and as our bodies rest and rebuild, so, too, we ask, bring our spirits to rest at Thy bosom and nourish us. Build us up that on the morrow we shall be the greater light."

No power is greater than the power you are willing to claim.

No light can ever be any brighter than that light you find in the sanctuary within your own being and which you bring forth.

No wisdom is sharper, keener than that which you have garnered through the journeys of your spirit, the experiences of your current lifetime brought to the altar of truth and honor within, and carefully weighed and measured, that your path becomes guided by this wisdom, and your service, thereafter great.

No song can be sung sweeter than the song of your own heart when it is filled with the joy and resonance of love. For love is the song of God spoken in the Word of God, which goes forth emanating from you in your being, in your word, your action, your deed. For love is the light of God, and it penetrates and transcends all illusion that such be revealed for its own nature and intent.

Chapter Three

Song of God

It is a beautiful and refreshing day in early spring. Among the many wadis or small valleys up and down the area called the Three Holy Mountains, we find a circle of the young maidens in the midst of an incredibly beautiful array of blossoming wildflowers and herbs of many different varieties, colors, and fragrances. Seated in a rather close circle, they are busy weaving, tying ends of flower stems together, fastening them into different garlands of bright fragrant color, chattering lightly amongst themselves.

Groups of the elder sisters, guides, teachers, and mentors are off to the periphery here and there. And in the distance, barely perceptible, several guardians are on higher ground.

The breeze moves up-slope from the sea below, carrying with it another collage of fascinating scents and fragrances. The entire atmosphere is filled with the charm and expectancy of a new season waiting to be called forth by the children of God.

Young Theresa is leaning over to look at Hannah's work. "I love the way you weave those long-stemmed violet flowers into your garland."

"Thank you, Theresa. And I am delighted by how you have placed those contrasting colors side by side." Reaching over, Hannah points. "Look how this white one and its yellow center contrasts that blue one, and over here, how the colors seem to merge together to make a unique band. What is your intention with this design?"

"I think of it as the different levels of our being, our consciousness. See here?"

Now the other children have stopped and are listening intently, respectfully. Several of the elder sisters have moved closer, noting that this is relevant to the work.

"Well," continues Theresa, "here is where we are as children. See? I blended many colors to indicate the different opportunities that are always present for us, as we have been shown and taught. Along here is where I made my choice for this path I have followed, and then where I explored this experience and that emotion. And here is where I began to awaken. See the daisies, how all the bright petals come together to surround the face of God in its center? It makes me happy to look upon these simple flowers. That is why I like to contrast them with the others." She points to the blues, violets, and an array of wonderful colors.

"And notice how I brought the teachings from our beloved sisters into the different stages of my awareness." She turns the garland over. "See? Here is my mind embraced by my heart, which these red flowers symbolize for me. Over here is the wisdom of my spirit ... still awakening, I might add." She receives confirming rivulets of laughter from her sisters. "And here is the blue, the Spirit of God and the light of our ancestors." Turning it over again carefully, she adds, "And here is my path ... the songs of my heart. See the yellow ones embracing the daisies, the wishes for my lifetime? Here, I have brought the lavenders and purples in, and here, the daisies are surrounded by the lovely greenery, which I think of as the Spirit of God giving life to my dreams and to my hopes." Having reached the end of her garland, "That is all I have for now because that is all the life I have for now."

Everyone laughs and applauds her, supporting her, and Theresa nods to them, smiling.

Anna has moved up behind Mary. "Sweet Mary, tell us

of your garland and its meaning."

The impact of its pure simplicity, comprised mostly of white flowers, some with subtle ruby-throats, is striking. Mary has chosen large, shiny, vine-like green leaves, and has woven the white flowers into the midst of them. For the most part, except here and there, her garland is singular in the colors of whites and greens.

Carefully turning it over in her hands and adjusting it lovingly across her lap, she looks up and smiles her almost shy smile, looks down, and begins to speak. "I have found it purposeful to place several blue flowers ... see, here, at the beginning of my garland? Rather like you, Theresa." Mary looks across at her and smiles. "I like to think of these as where I have come from ... the life before life." She glances up to look at Anna, now bending over her, and receives a nod.

"So, here, I move into life, itself. I've chosen the white flowers to indicate that this is a new opportunity. Here, I have begun to weave in the leaves of beauty and brilliance. See how they reflect the light? I like to think of these as opportunities being brought to me and the white flowers mingle with," turning her garland over, "and look to, the opportunities. And they test it within. Here, I have placed a group of mostly white, with very little other color in the midst of them, because I think of these as times in our youth that are the purest of all. We haven't had opportunity in this life to gain many beliefs, or needs, so the purity of our spirit still shines through.

"I have brought in a few blue flowers to indicate the opening of consciousness ... the awareness of God's guidance in dream, in vision, and all about." She gestures to the beautiful brightly colored slope on which they are now seated. "And here," looking back down at the garland, "I have mostly white again, for it was a period of time that I was mostly listening. Now I bring the greens in again for more opportunities, more teachings. Here is where we journeyed to our benefactors, the great teachers and prophets and seers of the School of Elijah. And here, I placed Elob. For I so love him," looking down for a moment, "because he brought us together in the Spirit of the One God, and he saved some of our ..." glancing around, blinking away a tear, "some of our sisters from great peril. So I honor him each day, and also in this garland.

"Here to the side, I have placed the symbol of our beautiful teachers, our elder sisters. And here ... This symbolizes Joseph, and Jacob, and Nicodemus, and all the others who are of such beauty, and whose beauty grows with each day. Now again, I have woven in mostly the white flowers." She holds it up and turns it towards all of her sisters. "But see here? God guided me to these soft ruby-throated ones. Aren't they lovely? I like to think of that as the heart and spirit coming together in oneness.

Once more, she turns the garland over. "Here is my dream and the fountain of light that comes when I tell God of my love for Him. And here is the future. I have placed a ring of beautiful blue flowers around the garland, for I know some day there will be such a spiritual Light that will come and be with us, whom we will nurture and protect and who will become, as we have been told ... a great Light unto all of the Earth. And this is where I have ended." She looks down.

A moment of silence follows, and then supportive comments and applause ring out from Mary's sisters.

Anna and Judy wander about the circle, bending and touching, as the children have gone back to their handiwork. Here we find Ruth bending to speak, her face very close to Andra's. "What is it you have created, Andra?"

"Well," she begins slowly, "I don't think it is as meaningful as some of the others, except maybe to me."

"Is that not important enough? If it has good meaning to you as a daughter of God, will it not, thereafter, be likely to have good meaning to others?"

Andra turns her face up brightly, looking into Ruth's. "How is that again, my sweet sister? Will you tell me, once more, that my heart will remember it forever?"

Settling herself next to Andra, stroking her hair gently, Ruth leans her back against one of the other little sisters, who responds by rubbing against her lovingly. Ruth then leans forward to gaze into Andra's eyes. "Think of it as a great harvest within you ... a storehouse of gifts, of potentials, of the blessings of God that are within you, and everyone."

Andra blinks and nods.

"When you take that which is good for you into yourself, Andra, and you can look upon it within and without and know it to be good, it becomes the pathway through which all that is within you can flow out."

"But is it not ... well, selfish of me to choose what I find joy in, rather than the example I see in the great teachers, the holy ones, the prophets? Should I not be as they?"

Ruth smiles and nods, carefully choosing her words. "You can be as they and yet be the uniqueness that you are, Andra. They reflect the potential that is you. That they do this in certain ways proves they know this truth that you and I are now discussing. They have chosen that which is the very best and highest for them, and which brings them the greatest joy, the greatest sense of purposeful life, each and every day. You do not see the holy ones seated, weaving baskets, do you?

"Oh, no. They most certainly do not weave baskets," and she smiles.

"Do you see them prepare the evening meals?"

"No, but they do bless it." Her face brightens.

"That they do. Do you see them afield, gathering herbs or roots, or harvesting the grains for our breads and biscuits?"

"Well, I see them out there, but they are not gathering. They are doing something else."

"Do you know what it is they do?" Ruth asks softly.

By now, many of the other children are straining to hear

the quiet conversation.

"I think they are being holy."

"Out in the fields?"

"Yes, I think they are being holy and their holiness makes the grains fat."

The children giggle at this, and Andra turns to look this way and that, smiling that she has brought laughter.

"Perhaps it is so, that their holiness does make the grain ... Perhaps we could call it full, abundant."

"Well, okay. But I like to say fat."

The children giggle again, trying to look down and appear busy.

"So," Ruth continues, "what do you think is within them, or about them, that their mere presence in the fields ... not sowing, not harvesting, but what in their presence alone makes the grains, as you say, fat?"

"Well, the light of God shines through them. They are so holy that there is light wherever they go, and I suppose that holy light is felt by the grains and makes them joyful."

"Then, let me come back to the original question. Do you think they have chosen to fulfill themselves according to what brings them joy, or not?"

"Well, I do not know, really. It seems that they are all pretty much the same. You know, just, real holy. I cannot see a great deal of difference in their holiness. But some of them are ... well, a bit more fun than the others."

The children all giggle again.

After glancing around, smiling at the children, Ruth comes back to Andra. "And those who are fun ... What would you say is the source of their fun?"

"Oh, that is easy! They know the laughter of God. Some of the others are very serious. That is their job. I suppose they have to be serious because they have to deal with serious things. And the others who have a little more laughter ... Maybe that is what their work is. Maybe God has said to them, *You do the serious work, and you do the laughter.*"

The children are very silent.

"Is that truly how you see it, Andra?"

"Well," shrugging her shoulders, "it does look like that."

"Do you think perhaps they have chosen because it brings them joy?"

"Well, I would choose the laughter before the serious works, I think. But I see the light grow so bright around some of those who do the serious works, and they do smile. They are obviously smiling at God, only I cannot see God. But they do, and they smile at Him. So, the ones who bring us laughter from time to time ... Do you think they hear God laugh?"

The elder sisters are all chuckling as Ruth answers, "I am sure they hear God's laughter."

"Why do I not hear God's laughter? I love laughter." Andra laughs to evidence this.

"And a mighty laugh you have, Andra. Everyone loves it. I am sure that in the future it will be a source of joy and brightness for others. But we are as travelers who have not made a choice upon which path to travel because we keep moving away from the true question here."

"Oh, yes, I have a habit of doing that. I love to see what is over here," pointing in one direction, "and over there," pointing in another. "I guess you know me pretty well."

"I do," Ruth replies, smiling. "And I also know you are very bright, and you know the answer."

Andra sighs deeply. "Yes. It is that I have a right to choose that which brings me joy, and as I do so, it opens me to let the joy of God in me come out and be a part of all that I am, all that I say, all that I do. Even in this garland." She holds it up proudly. "But sometimes my joy feels different than others'. And I think, *Uh-oh, Andra. You should have followed the joy teachings of the elders. You should not have created your own joy. You should have followed their example.* What can you tell me about that, Ruth?" She looks up into Ruth's face.

Glancing around the group a bit more seriously now, Ruth notes that one is studying them carefully. "What say you, Abigale, to your sister's question?"

"Well, I think that when we create something, when we have a thought inside our hearts, that is God speaking to us. I have heard God speak many times in a curious voice. You know? Distant, but near. I hear Him say, *Abigale, do this thing.* Or *Sing that song, it will bring joy. Just do it.* So I do, and it is true, just like the voice of God says … It brings a blessing to someone, sometimes to someone I had not noticed needed a blessing. So I trust the voice of God. You should trust it, too, Andra."

"Well, I do. Look at my garland. I did not copy anyone. I did it the way I felt."

"But what about *within* you?" Abigale questions gently. "Sometimes I see you very serious, like one of the holy ones. Other times, it brings me such joy to hear your beautiful laugh. Which of those is really you, Andra?"

The elder sisters are very attentive, noting carefully the uniqueness of each of the children coming forth here.

"You are right, of course. I do try to emulate the holy ones who have the serious works because I know that in doing them, there must be many blessings that will be given to others. And maybe they will see as we see. Maybe they will know as we know."

"Well, could they not get that from your laughter? I know I do." Abigale glances around, receiving nods, smiles, and gestures from all of the other sisters.

"Tell me what to do, sweet Ruth. Which should I do? That which my mind sees and knows to be good or that which comes from within and often has no reference outside me?"

Judy has come to seat herself by Ruth, who looks at her and smiles. "I think our sister, Judy, can tell you, Andra."

"Can you not tell me, Ruth?"

"Yes. I can."

"Then why are you going to have Judy tell me?"

"Would you prefer that I tell you?"

"Yes, I would." Andra turns to Judy. "Not because I do not love you, my sister, but only that Ruth feels like my own heart feels. You know my heart, do you not, Ruth?"

Smiling and nodding, Ruth glances at Judy, whose face is aglow with the recognition of the bond between these two.

Judy reassures Andra. "Ruth knows the same truths as I. "I know that your love is a pathway of understanding between you, and I know it is the same between you and me. But each of us must listen to the call, the guidance. You are doing that, and how righteous of you to state your wish. We all honor it. Ruth, please, if it brings you joy, serve our sister."

"It always brings me joy," Ruth begins. "The pathway to your heart is the pathway of truth, Andra ... all of you, sweet sisters. If you listen to the truth of your heart's song, the voice of God speaking to and through you, no matter what your journey may be, no matter what work shall come before you, that inner song of God's guidance will always keep you aright and true to that which is your ideal.

"So, yes." She turns, gazing down lovingly at Andra. "We would all encourage you to listen to your heart, to take from the serious holy ones that which you know to be good. But do not cover the beauty of that within you with what you see outwardly, no matter how good, how righteous, how purposeful you see it. It must, in order to be right for you, increase the song in your heart! In other words, test it to see, *Does it bring gladness to my heart?* That is the message, that is the purpose, for one's life."

There is absolute silence.

"There are times when I see a need," Kelleth adds, "and I think to myself, *Kelleth, ask the voice in your heart: Is it righteous for me as a Daughter of God to answer this call?*"

"And what does the voice say to you?" Anna questions,

having now moved closer to her.

"The voice says, *Do what seems right. Do what feels good to you.* Well, some works that come to me do not feel very good at all. In fact, they can be tiring and sometimes they are a little dirty." The children giggle, for Kelleth is known by all to dislike being soiled in any way, continually brushing her garment, cleansing and rearranging her hair. "And, you know … If we are Daughters of God, should we not outwardly be like God? And I think God is very clean."

The children break out in sumptuous laughter.

Kelleth smiles expansively, having brought such humor to her sisters. "Well? Is not God clean?"

Anna replies, "I should think the cleanest of all. But to get your hands or your garments a bit soiled in doing a work does not mean you are not clean and godly."

"Well, I do not look very clean with mud on my face and hands. And sometimes when we gather the roots for the stews and such, it is very muddy work." She sighs heavily.

"But do you not hold the thought of what you are doing before you?"

"Oh yes. I hold that before me, and I think to myself like, *Kelleth, these are good roots you are going to gather. God put them in the earth for you and for your people. They will bring great nourishment and make strong minds, hearts, and bodies.* Is that good to say?"

Anna smiles an affirmation.

"Then I think, *Kelleth, whatever soils your body cannot soil your heart or spirit unless you let it do that.*" She glances up at several of the other sisters and two of the disciples from the School who have come to live here to help in the maidens' awakening. "And so I think to myself, *Well, what is the problem here, Kelleth? Why is it that you just do not like being soiled?* And so, I think about all the things you have taught us … not to judge by the outer. Look within. And I think, *Well, it is hard to look within with a pair of hands,*" holding hers up, *"that are covered with stains or mud or soil. The first thing I see is all of that dirt."*

The children giggle again.

"But then, I gather up my thoughts like you taught us," pointing to Judy. "I created a basket in my mind, and I put my thoughts in there. Is that good?"

Judy smiles and nods.

"So, I take the basket with my mind-self and set it in a very special place ... a place to be nice to my thoughts. Then my mind-self walks along the pathway to find the cleanliness of God and to hear the song of God, so I can get over a dislike for being dirty."

Here and there the children giggle yet again.

"What do you think it is about the outer appearance that troubles you, Kelleth?" continues Anna.

"I remember one of the prophets said, *When you see a thing, if it gives you a feeling of goodness ... If you look upon a thing, and you see its light and you see its sweetness, then go a step further. And if it is the same, go even further.* So I say to my mind-self, *Look not at the dirt. Look to see if there is sweetness and goodness underneath it.* And a part of me says, *Well, why do some people not bathe? Why do they not cleanse themselves so that they can be seen easier, better?* "

"Maybe they do not know to do so," Anna suggests.

"Well, it seems like in the outer world, there are a lot of them that do not know that." Her voice trails off, her face sort of whimsically twisted as she remembers journeys through some of the outer world villages.

"That is very true," Eloise chimes in. "I, too, have seen that. A lot of people do not do their services. You know, they don't cleanse themselves inwardly or outwardly. You can tell when you are coming toward one from a distance, because ... Well, the fragrance is unique."

The children giggle and roll about.

Eloise looks back and forth to see if the elder sisters are

going to approve. They merely shake their heads, smiling, so she smiles and continues. "I tell myself, maybe I should give them some of our teachings. Maybe I should tell them that it is easier to find God in a clean body than in a soiled one. And that it is easier to smell the flowers that God brings to us," holding up her garland, "if one can get past their own smell."

This time the children howl with laughter.

"Is that wrong of me?"

"No, it is not wrong of you," Judy responds, "for it is truthful. But you know, of course, if you were to tell them such things, you could offend them."

"Oh, well, I know that. I know from the holy ones, that you speak gently of a destination. Not where they are at in the moment, but where you think they might find greater joy in being. You tell them of the result, the place to journey to, and they will want to go to it."

"How else might you share that with them?" asks Ruth.

"I could share that with them by example. That is why I agree with Kelleth. I think that being clean and bright lets them see your light and your gifts better. Is that not so?" Her chin juts out.

"Yes, that would be so. But it is not the only thing that would be an example or a teaching, is it?" Anna questions.

"No, but it is the first thing they see and smell."

Everyone laughs again.

Hannah joins in, "I think we could sing to them. Do you not think so, Mary?"

Mary smiles and nods.

"I think that if we sing to them, they will hear the sweetness. And if we speak words in our song, we can tell a story that they will carry in their heart, surrounded by the sweetness of the song. Is that not so?" She looks up to see Jacob standing off to the side. "Jacob, is that not so?"

"Always," Jacob responds softly. "You know me ... A joyful song is good for all the parts of one's being." He settles back in the shade of a boulder outcropping, placing his staff across his lap.

The children are fidgeting now, for their natural reaction at Jacob's appearance is to rush and pounce upon him with hugs and words of love. But they continue their weaving.

"What does a song do anyway, Jacob? And why do you love it so?" Hannah asks brightly.

"A song? Correct me if I am wrong, sweet sisters ..."

Ruth laughs aloud. "That is not likely, Jacob."

He smiles at her. "In order for me to sing a song," straightening himself to sit very upright, "I must reach down into here." He places his hand upon the mid-section of his body. "I must ask the life-force of God to give me the power to express something into the Earth."

"Why do you have to ask?" Hannah questions. "Can you not just do it? I am not asking to speak to you right now, and my voice is coming from right here, or somewhere in here." She looks about and rubs her body, again causing giggles. "So why do you ask, Jacob? Tell us. We want to know."

"I ask because I want the voice of God to be a part of all that I am and do. And especially, I want to ask the God within me to bring forth that which will bring me the most joy. See Andra? Abigale?" acknowledging their earlier comments. "If I bring joy to myself, and I call upon the voice of God to come forth surrounded in my joy, then what shall be the nature of the song which comes from me, if not joy?

"Then, I ask in my heart, *Have you any words to put with this joyful song?* My heart turns to my mind-self and spirit-self and says, *Give me the words to put into the gift of this love flowing into the Earth. Give me the creation of your wisdom, your teaching.* And my heart hears my spirit-self answer, *I will create one for you.* Then my mind-self says, *I have one that is already created, which is filled with goodness and teachings of strength. Why create another?* And my spirit-self replies, *I am always here to create in God's name.*

When my mind-self hears that, it says, *Oh, well … That is a good thing to do. You create it, and I will remember it. And if it is ever needed again, I can give it to you.*

"So my mind-self and spirit-self find happiness and joy in working together, and my heart-self gives it unto God within and the joy from the wellspring within. That is what I mean. All of me, all that is who I am … my past, my present, and what I can be … works together to bring forth song. So, when you hear my song, you are hearing and feeling all of this."

"Oh-h, Jacob! That is why your songs are always so much fun and so sweet. When I hear you sing," Hannah rocks to and fro, rolling her eyes up to the sky, "I think, *God sings through Jacob.*" Then she begins to clap her hands, and all the sisters follow and praise Jacob.

"Jacob, please give us a song. Will you?" Zephorah's eyes are large and round, and so filled with love, evidenced in their sparkle, that Jacob rises, comes over, and reaches a hand out to her. She looks down shyly, and then reaches her hand up.

Jacob takes her back to where he was previously seated. He pulls her up on one knee, cradled against him, one of his arms about her, and rests his chin upon her head. "I will if you will."

"Me? Sing with you? Alone?"

"Yes, why not?"

"Oh-h. I have those fluttery things in my tummy now."

Jacob begins to laugh, as do the children. "Well, here … Put your hand over the fluttery things. And I shall place my hand upon yours."

Zephorah closes her eyes, placing her hand upon her solar plexus, and Jacob's, dwarfing hers, comes to rest against it. "Oh, Jacob. That makes the lights and colors come into me, and the fluttery things all find a place to rest, and they glow. It makes me feel good. Thank you."

"What do you suppose it is that you are feeling?"

"I feel your goodness, Jacob." Zephorah's eyes pop open and she looks up at him. Momentarily she closes them again. "I want to keep feeling that." She smiles.

The children have stopped what they were doing and are sitting, gazing enchanted, for each one here knows the love and warmth of Jacob's touch, and loves him beyond measure.

"I send you, sweet Zephorah, the spirit of God that lives within me. My hand is God's hand. As I place it upon yours, it is the hand of God's love and compassion that you feel."

"Is that what God's love and compassion feels like?" Her eyes close again, as she leans forward into Jacob's hand.

"Yes, at least for you. It may have other qualities for some of your sisters and others. But for you, Zephorah, the hand of God comes to you with beautiful color and sound, does it not?"

"Oh yes. And I so love it." She opens her eyes and looks across the group. "Do you feel it, too, Mary?"

Mary smiles and nods, "Yes, I do."

"Hannah, can you feel it?"

Smiling, Hannah rocks a little this way and that. "I do feel it. It is as if your hand were upon my own tummy, Jacob. How about you, Abigale? Is this feeling also within you?"

"Yes, but to me it is like a wind, a warm gentle wind, like the one that comes up from the Great Sea. It is like a bird soaring. It is like the call of the wild creatures as they seek one another's companionship. Zephorah, how do you hear it?"

Zephorah rocks to and fro, her hands on her knees, and then side to side. "When I move this way, forward and back, I feel it as that which is flowing through me called life. It goes in and out, like my breathing, and it feels good and cleansing. When I go this way and that, first this side and then the other, it flows through my heart. It brings me love and I feel the love of God. All together, it feels like," reaching down to touch the petals of the flowers in her lap, "the softness of this flower petal. And it feels like the essence of some good foods."

The children giggle.

"No, I mean they make you feel good and content."

"And full, too," Theresa jokes.

"Yes, full, too. But, it renews me. That is what it feels like to me." She smiles and continues to rock. "Jacob, tell us … How do you call this forth?"

"Well, I call it forth in answer to your request, Abigale."

"Did I ask you to?" she asks with some confusion.

"You did not ask with your words. But you asked me by telling me that you had something that was unsettling. Remember the fluttery things?"

"Oh, yes! Can we do that, too? When we see someone who has, you know, something like the fluttery things, and it is unbalancing them, can we just bring the song of God forth and give it to them?"

"You can give it to them if they ask in a manner of their being."

"How can you know someone is asking in the manner of his or her being?"

"By what you perceive, Abigale, by what you feel, by what you know. I know that you are open and willing and that you are seeking. And I know that you love me, and our love is a bridge upon which all things can pass to and fro."

"Oh-h! I like that, Jacob. So, when we see others, if we feel love from them, or if we feel that they are sincere but maybe just don't know that we have the song of God in us to give to them, can we give it anyway?"

"Yes, you can."

"And we would not be …" Editha questions, "well, you know, doing a wrong thing?"

"Would you intend to be doing a wrong thing?"

"Oh, no. Of course we would not do that!" She looks

around at the others, who shake their heads, *no*. "But I mean, like the holy ones teach us about the Laws ... Would we not be doing a wrong thing? Maybe they need this."

"You are only offering a gift. They must choose to receive it," Jacob responds.

"Oh yes. I remember that teaching. But sometimes I am not very sure. Sometimes I ask myself, *Should I heal this little creature with the song of God within me, or not? After all, it can't even speak to me that I can understand.*"

The children have grown very serious, for they all know of such situations.

"Tell us how to know this, Jacob," she asks sincerely.

"By going to the place of knowing, within ... the same place from which the song of God comes. Knowing is evaluating what is against what can be."

"What is, is that that creature has a problem," Editha responds. "What is, is that if someone does not do something, it could perish."

Oh-h's and *aw-w's* come forth from the children.

"If the creature cannot speak to you, but if it is upon your path, go to your place of knowing and ask this: *Is it God who has placed this creature upon my path that I can give the Song of Life from God to it?* The knowing place will answer you."

"Sometimes it does, very clearly. But when I need a little help, what shall I do?" Editha is quite serious in her question.

"You test it against that which is righteous," Jacob answers. "If you are upon a pathway in life and it is brought before you as an opportunity to be a blessing unto that thing, then know in your heart that because your paths have crossed, it is a work of God. Offer it, and if it is received, then that work is done and you continue on. But if you see that your offering has not been seen or heard, then continue on, as well, thanking God for your opportunity to leave a gift behind. For what you have done is given a gift which that one, whether it is a creature or a person, can choose to receive when they are ready."

Theresa comes to sit in front of Jacob. "Well, when I give the Song of Life to a creature that has a problem ... you know, is injured or something ... the creature gets better, right?" She turns to look at all her sisters, who nod their heads. "But, when I give a gift to a person, they don't always get better, at least not while I am around."

"You have a very loving heart, little Theresa, like your namesake." Jacob looks up at the elder Theresa, seated to the side. "But a loving heart is not always willingly received. Some people do not see love the same way we do. Some people see love as something being used to manipulate them, or something weak, or something ... well, you know. So the best you can do is give it. Then it is up to them."

"Why do the little creatures receive our Song of Life," questions Hannah, "and people do not?"

"Why do you think?" Jacob asks.

Leaning back, Hannah rubs the side of her face with the palm of her hand. "Well, I know that we have been taught that people are working on things as parts of their soul's pathway ... things they brought from the past, or things that they agreed to do in this life ... and I guess it distracts them."

Jacob smiles and nods. "Sometimes it distracts them a lot." He leans back and laughs. This makes Andra laugh, and her laughter plus Jacob's brings laughter from all. "Enough for now." He places Zephorah back in the group. "Now it is time for Jacob to bring the creation of God's love and light into the Earth." He raises his hands up and twists them about, and that is all the children need.

They jump up and form a big circle, link their arms together, and begin to sway this way and that.

'Round and 'round Jacob goes, twirling, dancing, singing the song of praise to the One God, and singing the blessings of God to these children, who represent the Promise.

"I am leaving on the morrow," Jacob confides later that evening to Joseph and many of the elders and seers. "I am going to seek out a good … might I call it, connection with the courts, and such."

"We have Nicodemus with the adepts," counters Joseph. "Is that not sufficient?"

"No, not for now. I think we are in need of allies."

"I would have to question the wisdom of that. Quite a number know you, Jacob … know you well, and know your nature and your people. Think you not this to be risky?"

"I have measured this upon the scales, the table in my heart. And I have spoken to several of the seers and elders about it. It seems that I must answer this inner call. I know not why, but I trust the guidance."

Joseph and Jacob's eyes lock. Joseph can see clearly that this is so, and he honors Jacob. His face breaks out in a smile as he asks Jacob gently, "What about a traveling companion, my brother?"

Jacob's eyebrows arch. "Truly? You would leave here and journey with me?"

"I would in this very moment, if you will have me."

"Wonderful!" Jacob claps his hands together. "Just wonderful! We shall have such a great journey. We can visit the temples. We can visit some of our brothers and sisters. And you can help me, Joseph. I know you have a keen eye and great faith. We shall leave before the sun's light, before the children can have time to lament," and Jacob laughs.

"We have heard from several of the others," Jason comments, "by way of messengers, caravans traveling this way."

"What say they?" Joseph questions.

"All is well, and they are on a safe journey. They have made many good contacts, particularly our brethren who are journeying to the east. The Way is being made passable."

"Praise God! And the others … Have you heard from all of them?"

"Not from those to the north," Jason replies, "but then, the sea is great and unpredictable on that route."

"Well, when you do, please communicate that to us. You know where Jacob and I will be."

"We shall make several of the guardians aware of your journey and your presence. They will watch over you, this I promise."

Nathanael, the guardian accompanying Jason, suggests, "Might we offer an affirmation unto Him, who comes? Might we close our evening discussion with such a prayer?"

"Will you lead us?" asks Jacob.

"I shall. O Lord God, as Thou seest us here gathered in the intention of Thy work, help us to know that which is to be known. Guide Thou us upon those paths which are to be traveled. Open our hearts and minds to hear and see that which is to be heard and seen. But, most of all, Lord God, let us ever know and feel the presence of Your love, that we can place this before us in all that we are and do. As we come now to join You in our slumber, and on the morrow as we journey forth in Your Name, we send Your love before us as our intent, and it fills us with joyful expectancy."

Chapter Four

Such a Shining

several seasons have passed, and the Maidens and all the other children have gained much, especially those who are to be among the Chosen. They have been brought to a point of inner recognition that in addition to all the other tenets in the pallet of truth, each has a certain unique awareness that is to be a nurturing embrace for Him who comes.

This has been a wondrous day of rejoicing and celebration. Not only have the high holy days for this year arrived, but according to the great sages, they signal the beginning of a time of unique empowerment.

Benjamin himself has proclaimed that a great wave of light is about to enter the Earth. This has been validated and supported by many other seers and prophets among the host of Expectant Ones gathered here in the area of the Three Holy Mountains.

After the glorifying festivities at the sacred Healing Spring and the merriment with the children, much of the celebration has centered around the arrival of Elob and great numbers of adepts from the School of the Prophets.

In short, those who have gathered here are coming from near and far to celebrate with the children and all the tribes of the Expectant Ones

As they descend the temple steps, passing a small group of people, Joseph speaks to Zechariah with some urgency. "We must make haste, for we cannot travel tomorrow. We must move quickly."

Just then, a man stretches out his arm. He is huddled on one of the steps with his mate and two small children, one of whom he has clutched to his chest.

Zechariah stops. "What is it, good sir?"

Tears stream down the man's cheeks. "My son ... He is gravely ill and we have no coin, no means to provide. And we are exhausted."

"Why do you speak to us of this?"

"It is," he bows his head and strikes his chest, "God."

"You are here because of God?" Zechariah questions, glancing over at Joseph.

"Yes. We had felt that all was lost, with no way open to us or our sweet son, whom we named Adam in memory of the blessings of God."

Again Zechariah glances at Joseph, who simply returns his gaze. "Could you explain, good sir?" Zechariah kneels before the man and his child. His mate holds the other child, who also appears to be somewhat ill. The woman rocks and bobs, mumbling soft prayers.

"You see, sir, it was in a dream. God said to me, *Arise. Go, gather your family and take Adam to the temple. There you will find a man of light, and he will make it possible for Adam to be healed.*" The man, tears still streaming, raises his palm, arm outstretched. "You are certainly a holy one. We saw you, and you, good sir, come from the inner sanctuary of the temple. Are you he, of whom God has spoken?"

"Why would you think this?" Zechariah is now on both knees before the small family, reaching his hand out to uncover Adam's tiny face.

"Your head garment, sir. It is as in my vision ... the design, the pattern on it. I feel certain you are he."

"Did God say anything else to you?"

"Yes. He said that you would take Adam, and perhaps all of us, to a healing place. Tell me, sir … Tell me this is a true vision from God."

Zechariah, his hand upon the child's forehead, glances quickly at Joseph.

Nodding, Joseph understands that the child is with fever.

Zechariah turns his attention to the girl. Though it is apparent that she too is with fever, it is also clear that hers is not as intense as Adam's. "A moment, sir."

Zechariah stands, and he and Joseph move up several steps back toward the temple. "It is a work in God's Name, is it not, Joseph?"

"It certainly would appear so. But, remember … we must make haste. Can we tend to this and yet reach our destination in time so as to not break the tenet?"

"We can if we hurry. I shall acquire beasts for them to travel upon."

"Use care, Zechariah. Use good care."

"It is well. I shall meet you at the city gate, and I shall have two beasts for them to be carried upon. Are you ready?"

"I am," responds Joseph.

"Lead them to the west gate, and I will meet you there."

At the gate shortly thereafter, Zechariah waves to Joseph, who is indeed, leading two burros upon which they mount the man and one child and the woman with the other. Joseph has also acquired some food and skins of water. As the sun sets, the group begins their journey, moving quickly.

Elob and many of the adepts are gathered around the morning cookfire. Gathered with them are some of the seers and prophets and many elders of the various Essene tribes.

"You have seen the new energy?" Elob asks Benjamin.

"Yes. Not only I, Elob, but many here."

"How have you perceived it?" he questions further.

"First, in vision and dream successively, then in meditation and in ceremony. Most recently, as a wave of undulating light accompanied by beautiful sounds, seemingly coming from everywhere simultaneously."

Elob glances to his left and right at the goodly number of his adepts and colleagues. Many smile and nod, others simply look up, their eyes closed, evidentially giving thanks. He turns back to look at Benjamin. "We, too, have seen these signs. The wonder of the remaining holy celebrations just ahead and the longing in our hearts to see all the beautiful children again and how they have grown and learned and the joy of being with you, dear brother Benjamin, and all of your colleagues, would certainly be more than sufficient cause for us to joyfully journey here. But we tell you in the honor and truth of our pledge that our primary purpose for this visit is a result of what we have seen."

"Can you elaborate on that?" asks Benjamin, aware now that Elob and the others apparently know more.

"Yes, I can share with you what we have perceived ..." Elob is stopped in mid-sentence, for the sound of a single tone, a horn, comes from down in the valley. Its tone is pure, haunting, continuous. Then, silence.

Everyone everywhere, those preparing the morning meals, the elder maidens, the many, many sisters and brothers, stop as though frozen in mid-action.

Then, it comes again, powerful, pure, singular in its essence, hauntingly beautiful, and, again, followed by silence.

No one moves.

A third time the horn sounds. This time, everyone begins to move about quickly, for they recognize it to be a call from one of the guardians that there is a need, an urgent one.

Benjamin does not move, neither does Elob nor do the adepts. Rather, they bow their heads, and Elob begins. "O Lord God, we thank You for whatsoever opportunity has come before us. We know that it is Your hand that has guided unto us this coming work. We go unto it and that call in Your Name, Lord God, asking that whatsoever awaits us, You help us to see the way. Help us to be worthy to answer this call. Amen." Then he pronounces firmly, "So let it be written."

All of the adepts strike their chests with clenched fists, holding them there, and then slowly relaxing the fingers, palms facing downward, swing their hand out, as though pledging their heart unto the Spirit of God.

Zechariah and Joseph have helped the man and his family to the ground near the sea and have prepared a rudimentary encampment and a fire. One of the guardians, Jason, stands off to the left. Two others are up the hill just a bit, watching in the direction from whence the entourage came, to be certain that no one has followed.

Zechariah looks up at the great warrior priest. "His fever is worsening!"

"They will come soon. Be certain of this, for I know they have heard our call. Here. Take the herbs and let us make teas and potions for the fever." Justin bends and begins to stroke Adam's brow. Then he turns to the mother. "How is this one called?"

"We call her Theresa."

"Oh, so beautiful." He goes to the water's edge with garments of woven cloth, soaks them in the cool waters of the sea, and brings them up to the parents.

The mother and father remove the coverings from the children's heads and begin to stroke their brows and heads with the moistened cloth.

Moaning, eyes yet closed, Theresa manages to take a few sips of the tea that has been prepared for them. But Adam will not. Even as they attempt to stream some of it into him, he appears too weak to swallow.

In answer to the guardians' call, Josie and several other elder sisters are among the first to arrive from the School of the Prophets. Some of the adepts are with them.

Josie moves around to the side. Examining both children, she looks up and speaks to the adept who is called Naomi. "It is the fever!" She glances around at her other sisters.

They gasp and kneel, but remain a distance away, for it is known that the fever is very dangerous.

"We must call for help from the healers," instructs Naomi. "I can begin now, but I cannot do this alone."

One of the elder sisters rises swiftly to her feet. "I will go and call them. What am I to say?"

Tell them we are in need of the trinity of light."

Blinking and nodding, the sister moves swiftly up the slope and around the boulders and outcroppings. Before she gets very far, she is met by the group coming down. "Oh! I was coming to get you. Your teacher, your worker, Naomi," speaking to Elob, "asked that some of the adepts come to form a light of trinity or a ..."

Elob puts a hand on her shoulder and nods. "Rest easy. We know whereof you speak."

Benjamin is being aided down the slope as well, and soon all are gathered.

Looking up, Josie informs them, "It is the fever."

As the others before them, they all glance from one to the other. Two of the adepts move to position themselves so that, with Naomi, they form the triangular symbol. They ask that a blanket be placed on the ground, and that the children be placed upon it.

The father clings to his son, Adam, but Zechariah reassures him. "Please. Remember, your faith brought you this far. Can it not carry you a bit further?"

Looking down, the man kisses Adam's forehead. Again his tears fall upon the tiny babe's face. "But, good sir, if he is to depart now, I wish to hold him during his last moments that my spirit can insure his journey."

Zechariah glances around at all of the others, as more are

arriving. "How do you know of this thing?"

"We have had teachers come through our small village in the hills where we tend our flocks. They have given us these words and these understandings. And we have seen the peacefulness of many of our peoples who have gone beyond when they have lived the life and believed the belief that these teachers gave to us."

"And how are these teachers called?" questions Zechariah carefully.

"They are called Expectant Ones."

All glance quickly.

"Expectant Ones?" Zechariah probes.

"Yes. They tell of One who will come who will be our king … a light to the world they say. We know not of these things, but we know that they have given us many, many gifts. They have taught us healing ways and ways of finding many foods where we thought the earth was barren."

Smiling, Zechariah turns to look up into the faces of Anna and Judy, acknowledging their arrival, and then continues. "Sir, trust me. Give me your son. Let me place him and your daughter on this cloth, which is actually a special robe. It lies upon the earth which contains the Spirit of God, for all life comes from within the earth, does it not?"

The man's eyes search Zechariah's face. Finding only love and understanding in the eyes, which are so gentle, so loving, so understanding, he looks down one more time, bends to kiss Adam on the forehead again, and lifts him up.

Zechariah carefully takes the babe and places him next to his sister on the sacred robe arranged on the ground. The little girl occasionally opens her eyes and looks around.

Naomi is to the right. Her two brothers are positioned triangularly equidistant, one above and the other across from her. She extends her hands out toward them, palms directed straight at them, and they reciprocate, their arms extended, palms upright.

They begin to chant and pray, but their language is not known here, for it is an ancient one. Then Naomi begins to sway this way and that.

The elder maidens and sisters have gathered in good number now, positioning themselves to form a sacred circle around the three adepts and the two children. They have linked themselves in their traditional way and are swaying in a circular motion, silent, eyes closed, faces upturned to God.

The chant becomes louder.

Benjamin looks over at Elob who turns, his eyes gentle, but his resolve as obvious as the strength of a forest tree, unwavering no matter which way the winds blow. He nods at Elob's evident resolve, and then kneeling upon the ground, places his hands upon his knees, bows his head, and moves into silent prayer.

All continues in this manner for a time, until the three adepts stop simultaneously.

Then, utter silence.

Off in the distance, there can be heard the single sound of a great winged creature calling out.

Naomi turns abruptly to look up at Elob, who nods that he has heard it. She closes her eyes, but her body is stiffened, waiting, waiting.

Again the great bird calls out.

Naomi and many of the sisters bring their hands up to their chest, for they know that if there is no answer, only one child will survive.

Silence.

Again, the creature off to the west calls out a high, alluring tone, and … silence.

Naomi glances up at Elob once again.

Very subtly, his eyes fixed unwaveringly upon her, he shakes his head, signaling her to not change a thing!

Once again, she returns to her intense position, closes her eyes, and bows her head.

Suddenly, to the east comes a call, and the creature to the west answers more vibrantly, as though excited, again and yet again. The soft call from the east comes once more.

Naomi begins to weep. Some of the sisters know, for they have studied with the adepts and in particular with her, and they begin to weep, as well.

The others lean over. "What is it?"

"It is the spirit. It has heard our prayer and our call, and it has answered."

"The birds mean this? Is this what you say?" a sister asks.

"Yes, it is so. You will see. Believe now, without doubt, for we must strengthen our faith."

Again, the sisters become as one in a circle of light that symbolizes the logos of God, the complete, unbreakable cycle that is eternity. They rock one way very slowly to indicate the movement of life into the pathway of discovery. Then they rock the other way, symbolizing the movement back into spirit and the merging of the newly gained wisdom and understanding into the composite of their true being. And again, back into finiteness and experience.

It is Judy who begins the chant of the maidens, one very different from those of the adepts. It is a sweet singsong-like prayer, wordless, with only tones.

The sister across from her answers it, and then the one to the right, and then the one to the left. Now the cardinal points are awakened. Each of the other points responds until all twelve of these elder sisters in their sacred circle have brought forth the mandala of sound, the prayer of our Lord God.

Benjamin raises his head. His eyes open and he looks at the boy. "He is yet with us. You have done well. The power of your spirits in the Name of God has literally given life where death awaited. Now, I have seen the following ... Those of you, my brothers and sisters from the great School of our ancestor, tell me if my words ring true: We must bathe these babes in cool waters for a goodly time, then prepare an earthen bath for them where the drosses can be drawn out. You, sisters, prepare your herbal teas and this will break the fever. This I have seen."

"Which earths?" questions Judy.

"The red ones by the sacred trees."

"Yes, I have seen this, too," Judy responds, motioning to two of the elder maidens, who immediately gather up baskets to fetch the earth.

Elob glances about at his colleagues and then turns back to Benjamin. "We hear your words and see your vision to be true. We encourage you to go forth."

The children are bathed and cleansed, then given warm teas and broths. A warm earthen bath is prepared for each, and each is given the herbal aromatic treatments that the adepts know so well.

Now the color is moving back into Adam's face and he begins to take some of the broths and teas.

As Adam and his sister, Theresa, are being watched over by the elder maidens, the children who are the candidates have gathered near at hand.

"There is no more need for concern," Ruth assures them. "The fever is gone, now the body only needs to be restored. These two are safe."

One by one, holding a hand of an elder sister, the candidates come to kneel before the two little children. Each offers a gift, not a physical one (though some bring flowers or fragrant herbs), but the gift of her prayer, for each has her own way of praying, her own words, and her own ritual. It is considered a great gift, a great honor, to be given this by any one of these young maidens. But to receive from all of them, for there are nearly fifty gathered, is considered a rare honor.

"And what have you brought for these sweet babes?" Judy asks one of the maidens.

"My love of God."

"How would you do this?" Anna asks quietly.

"I would do as I have seen in visions, and as you and the others have encouraged us to believe, that as I do, it is as the hand of God that doeth the work, not only mine."

"Well then, be about your works and bear your gift to them." Ruth motions gently.

It is Mary who moves to kneel so she is between the two babes who are resting comfortably on thick piles of hand-woven, sacred cloth. She raises her hands so that the palms are upright. "I love You, Lord God," she begins, "and, there-fore, I love all that is, for Thou art the Creator of all. Let my hands now be Your hands. These creations of Your intention have fallen amiss. But now, they grow stronger. I pray, Lord God, that my hands bear to them the gift of my love for You." She bends and places her palms upon the children's brows and bows her head.

There is silence.

Suddenly, Anna gasps. Judy glances quickly at her and then back at Mary, and lifts a hand to her face. A tear forms in her eye. Before them all a light is growing from within this young maiden ... a golden light!

Adam coughs. Then his eyes pop open. Mary's hands still rest upon the foreheads of the tiny children. Theresa's eyes, too, open, and she looks about, struggling to see. As she peers up into the sweet face of Mary, she begins to smile.

Soon Adam begins to make sounds, his first in days.

Recognizing that voice, his father, and now his mother close behind, come running, fall upon their knees, and pros-trate themselves.

"Thank You, Lord God," the father begins, "thank You. Blessed be Your Name. It is true what the Expectant Ones said! It is true! Surely a king of righteousness comes. Surely you are His peoples." He looks up from his prone position and places his face down on the dirt, humbling himself before what he believes is the presence of the Spirit of God.

Mary's hands remain a moment or two longer, her smile so sweet. Now they move, so that each cups a child's cheek.

Theresa raises a hand to place it on Mary's, smiling. Adam just gazes at her, perhaps enchanted.

Mary glances up into the eyes of Judy and Anna, who simply nod and smile. Then she rises and walks away, softly repeating a prayer of thanks unto God.

She is quickly met by her sisters who all strive to embrace her, who all wish to be at her side. "It is not I," Mary replies softly to the many compliments from her sisters, "but we. For each of you gave your gifts. As when one would build a great temple, one rock, one stone will not do, but many together placed upon each other become strong and permanent. We are like those rocks, all of us. Soon, we *shall* build a temple. I know this now, for I felt the Spirit of God answer. And I know that my love of God was given back to me in order that I might give it as gifts to them." She turns to gesture at the two children being cradled by their parents.

"It is truly remarkable," Elob observes later, back at the encampment. "These young maidens have truly become as jewels in the crown of God. You have done well, my friends." He nods to the elders.

"With your help and that of your brothers and sisters," responds Benjamin. "It is righteous and joyful for us to have served with you, of course."

"How many days to the ceremony?" questions Elob.

"Seven," Benjamin replies.

Elob turns to Ruth. "All are well?"

"They are. And brightly so."

"And they know their Truth?" looking at Josie, Judy, and Anna, and so many of the others.

It is Anna who answers. "Actually, they have *become* their Truth, and when it is appropriate, they will know that there is One Truth of which they are twelve facets."

Elob smiles. "I should like to be present that day!"

Judy, too, smiles, tilting her head to the side. "Who wouldn't! Seven days ... What would you have us do, dear Benjamin? We are here to serve you and the Promise."

"Perhaps you could have your brothers and sisters move among the maidens. No differently than you have these past years so often, but to discern if there is any last need. If there is, you could tell us, for we know your sight is clear, all of you, and we wish to have fulfilled our work and our part of the awakening without reservation or limitation."

"Well then, it sounds to me ..." comes a voice from the edges of the darkness, "that it is time for celebration." Striding into the campfire's light, Jacob appears.

All rise and move quickly to embrace him.

He laughs heartily. "Well, I should not have thought to receive a welcome like this except from the children. Are they well?" he asks as he embraces one after another, puts a cheek to the side of each brother's or sister's face, touches a cheek, caresses a head.

"They are more than well, sweet Jacob," Anna replies. "They are brilliant. They shine."

"Well, they have always shined."

"You know what I mean, Jacob." She laughs. "Their spirits are shining through."

"Oh, wonderful. I suppose I shall not sleep this eve, awaiting the first opportunity to see such a shining." He throws his head back and laughs.

Judy raises a finger to her mouth, indicating to Jacob to quiet down a bit. "You will wake the children and that will be it! They will all be up here, looking for their beloved Jacob."

"Oh, sorry," he replies in a mocked, hushed voice. "But does that preclude the opportunity for a little song and dance? And, by the way, have you any good food left?"

They all laugh and quickly dispatch others to gather up a

great bowl of wonderful broth filled with sumptuous roots and herbs harvested from the surrounding lands.

Jacob sips a bowl of steaming tea and recounts his experiences, listening as well to those of Zechariah and of Joseph, and those who have established sanctuaries and gained credibility and acceptance in their communities, as much as anyone can in these times.

Glancing over at Benjamin, Jacob asks softly, "And the visions?"

"They are good," Benjamin responds, smiling. "The Light comes. We have all seen it. And we all know its truth."

"When?" questions Jacob.

"Seven days."

Each garment is carefully prepared. Every thread is examined and matched in size to the one next to, above, and below it. Each gown is carefully pulled and stretched so that it will drape itself humbly, yet regally, around the Maiden whose body it will embrace. Each gown is woven with the colors and patterns of sacred teachings. Each is washed three times in the sacred water. And each is anointed and blessed by the high priests and elders of all the Essene tribes present.

All of the gowns are then placed in the center of the elder maidens' sacred circle, who, together, call upon the eternal Spirit of God to become one with these garments and those who shall wear them.

The adepts, too, led by Elob, then perform sacred rites, blessing the garments and empowering them with the energies of their sacred teachings and their ancient ways.

Carefully, tenderly folded, the gowns are handed, four each, to Judy, to Anna, and to Ruth. These three are bordered to the right, left, and behind by the other elder sisters who are softly singing hymns of praise unto God and calling out for His Spirit to surround all of His children and to awaken them that they might know … He comes.

Let there not be that chamber within your life into which you place your faith, but rather let life itself be the chamber of your faith.

This will make for gladness. This will make for the manifestation of all that can be for a Child of God.

Chapter Four – Such a Shining

Chapter Five

$\mathfrak{She\ Is\ Chosen}$

In the predawn, the cookfires cheerfully warm all that is still embraced by the darkness. Though this is the holy season and so many have gathered, outwardly this day would seem little different from any other.

All of the Expectant Ones are following their traditions: the preparing and blessing of the food, the sending forth of the light of their spirits unto the needs of others, the calling upon those who are a part of this group who dwell no longer in physical body, and the honoring above all else of the oneness of all things. Having completed their celebrations of the morning all have returned to their various tasks to prepare for the coming events.

For the maidens, however, there has been considerable attention paid to their purification ceremonies. As they welcomed this very special, very holy day and asked of it its blessing and direction, there has been an air of electric excitement. Yet, they have been inordinately quiet, each searching within, asking, questioning, offering, though with a spirit of wonder and joy.

Now, into their midst come those whom they so love. At the lead is Anna, followed by Judy, then Ruth. Each carries garments of considerable beauty, so simple, yet so revered. For the hands that have prepared them have done so with the full intention that they be equal to the blessing that is known to be within the ones who will wear these garments.

Turning now to stand parallel to the group of young maidens, Anna begins. "Sweet sisters, we have here the garments that will be worn by those twelve of you who shall ascend the steps to the altar.

"Each of you bears a light that is exquisite beyond description and each of you knows the importance of that which you bear. Whether you are one whose foot shall trod upon the holy steps, or one who shall in times ahead walk with Him, all are equal. All are without limit in terms of inner and outer beauty. And now, we will give these beautiful garments to those of you who are chosen for this work."

Anna nods.

A number of the other sisters come forward. Each takes a garment and holds it in her hands until Anna, Judy, and Ruth stand, their arms now empty of their precious cargo.

The three sisters turn and face one another in a triangular pattern. Anna extends her hands to the center, then Ruth, then Judy. With their hands touching one another's, they bow their heads, and the twelve sisters with them, each now holding a beautiful garment, also bow their heads.

"We feel the sweetness of Your Spirit, Lord God," Judy prays aloud, "and we hallow it. We have known and been blessed by the beauty of these Thy young daughters, every one. As we grant to each the sacred garment for her journey to the altar of Thy Name, we ask as we symbolically do so, that Thou wouldst give unto her Thy tenets of honor and truth and eternal compassion and love. Strengthen her with the pillar of righteousness, that each shall know ever that she is Your Daughter. We call upon all of our brethren who have gone before us to join with Thee, Lord God, asking them to celebrate with us the anointing of that one who shall be the Maiden of Holiness. And we ask Thee to embrace Her sisters, those who walk with Her and those who shall encircle the ceremony. Let them all be blessed beyond measure, and let their hearts and spirits ever be one in gladness and joy. We call upon Him who shall come, lovingly, reverently: We await You, dear Brother. And we thank Thee, Lord God, for all that we are."

Several moments of silence follow. Then, Anna, Judy, and Ruth look up, glance at one another and note that each other's face is, in this moment, expressionless.

It is first Anna whose face warms, then Ruth's, then Judy's. "This is the day," Anna states quietly. They grasp one another's hands, tears glistening in their eyes. Swiftly, gently, they embrace one another, all three simultaneously.

All the young maidens and the others applaud, for these three, perhaps singularly, have walked upon the path of utter dedication, and it is clearly known that their spirits are within each of the maidens, candidate or nay.

Anna nods to Judy, who turns and walks to the first sister, takes the garment, turns, holds it up in silent prayer, walks directly to a young maiden, and outstretches her hands. The maiden bows and lovingly, tenderly, accepts the garment.

This sacred little ritual is repeated again and again, as these three, Anna, Judy, and Ruth, come to each of the sisters to collect the garment that she had carried to this morning's celebration, and then hand it to a maiden.

As each one receives her garment, she appears to be enveloped in light.

Judy notes this, as does Ruth and Anna who turn, smiling, knowing without question that these are indeed those who are chosen, for the light surrounds them now.

All of the other young maidens come rushing, rejoicing, celebrating. It is indeed an overwhelming sight, for not one feels any remorse, only joy. For truly all have been chosen, and this is widely understood and believed: Some become the instruments, but all are a part of that which makes it possible. All are looked upon with utmost honor. For in each who weaves the cloth, prepares the food, tills the soil, stands as guardian, offers vision or prayer, finds the herbs for teas or the roots that heal, whether seer or prophet, maker of pots or builder of huts … the equality of spirit is revered.

So the joy flows freely. All hold and claim the joyous thought: *He is coming! We shall be at the ready to cradle and nurture that which He will bring with Him that it can come forth freely, joyfully, and be received as in the embrace of a loving parent.*

Now, though activity seems to intensify, paradoxically, there is stillness. Many move about replicating activities they have performed so many times that they need not think about or involve themselves with them outwardly in any way. As one carrying fuel for a fire passes by another carrying skins of water, their eyes meet, and there is a curious moment, an empty space of wonder, and then the smile of rejoicing and on they go on about their duties.

Over to the side a large circle of many elders and holy ones from the different tribes has gathered to discuss various works. Off in another area is a group, interspersed in which are many of the adepts and Elob himself who is seated near Joseph, along with many others. In still another group we find Jacob at the center, speaking quietly, drawing diagrams in the soil at his feet, showing the various places where their kinsmen dwell in the outlands, and on and on. All are engaged in some aspect of preparation or discussion.

"I have some great butterflies in here again," Kelleth confides, rubbing her tummy.

Anna laughs softly. "Does anyone else?"

All twelve immediately raise their hands, and smile and giggle gently to one another.

"What do you think will happen?" Kelleth asks of Judy. "What have you seen?"

"Oh, I have seen many beautiful things, but do you not think it is good to wait and allow God to manifest in accordance with that which is appropriate? Or should I, a humble daughter of God, go in front of Him?"

"Oh, no! I am not asking that, of course. But, well ... Do you have any hints?"

At this, all the sisters, and Anna, Judy, and Ruth laugh heartily.

Josie has come to greet them and hearing Kelleth's question responds, "I can offer you a hint." All of the Maidens gather quickly. "What will happen is ..." there is a pause filled with joyful anticipation, "one will be chosen," and she laughs.

"Oh, Josie, that is not fair," groans Andra. "But it is true," and she, too, laughs, throwing her head back as she does. Her laugh is so light and beautiful that it causes all to laugh along with her. "Truth is like that, is it not? Always the best thing. Sometimes not what you want to hear but, still, it always turns out to be better than anything one might conjure up. Right, Josie?"

"Well, I suppose I have to agree with that, for it is a foundational aspect of what you have learned. And if I were to disagree with it at this point, merely hours before the ceremonies, how would that leave you?"

"Oh, that would leave me quite strong," Abigale answers with a beautiful smile. "For I know that truth so well that no words could dissuade me from it at this point."

"Well, it is good that you are saying that," replies Josie, "for life has a way of bringing us wonderful opportunities wherein we can prove that to ourselves. And I have no doubt, sweet Sisters, you will have an ample supply of those opportunities, as shall we all." She glances at Judy, Anna, and Ruth. "Come, come now. Let us prepare you. Let us try on those wonderful gowns."

Excitement is everywhere. Each disappears into chambers especially erected for her. The other sisters are busy doing this and that, some bringing special ointments and balms, others bringing flowers and such until, finally, all twelve are gathered in their raiment, bedecked in beauty.

Each one reaches down to hold the folds of her garment. Some bend to look at the garment on a sister, stroking it with smiles and compliments.

"These are just beautiful," Little Sophie whispers in wonder. "They look like they are all made of the same wonderful cloth. Where did we get such a quantity of this beautiful material, Ruth?'

"It has been collected carefully. The wool gathered and stored, cleansed and re-cleansed, softened and re-softened for a very long time. We shall remember to offer a special blessing to our herdsmen who provided it."

"Yes," adds Judy, "and to all those who processed it, cared for it, cleaned it, softened it."

"And those who wove it," Anna continues, "and those who have prepared it to match perfectly that which lies ahead. Let them be blessed by the smile of God's sunlight."

The elders are gathered in the inner circle, along with the seers, the prophets, the healers, the practitioners. Surrounding this circle are the many messengers and those in training or study with those whom they serve, awaiting instructions.

There is another circle of the other maidens, and behind them, the elder sisters. And others yet, who are of various works and walks and labors of the Expectant Ones.

A small pathway is the only break in the circles, and even that is only temporary, for the symbol here of the circle within the circle within the circle, and so on, is very important to the Expectant Ones, who know from the teachings of the School of the Prophets its ancient mystical power.

Now, Benjamin begins to slowly ascend the stairs and, behind him, several of the other elders. As he approaches the altar, he turns, raises his hands, and asks a blessing, recognizing Enos, who is in his last days, as so many know, then all of the others. Finally, he offers a prayer to bless all who are present and to strengthen them in the journey ahead. Gesturing, he summons a figure from the rear.

The narrow aisle through the circles of Essenes widens, and a strong stride and bright smile tell all present it is Jacob. Naught can be seen of him but his joy as he turns to smile and wave a greeting to all he sees. When he reaches the top, he approaches the altar and is received with a warm, stout embrace by Benjamin and the others with him.

Finally, Benjamin nods and Jacob turns, a staff glistening in his hand. "Sweet brothers and sisters, many have given all they had that this day, this ceremony, and that which lies ahead could be possible. They live in our hearts and spirits. We speak their names in our prayers.

"I have brought this staff with me to this gathering, as inappropriate as it might seem for this time and place. It is sacred to me, for it was taken from the hands of one of our fallen guardians who gave his life that one of the Maidens you will see ascend the steps could survive to be here this day. I, Jacob, ask the Lord to bless this staff and the one who bore it in His Name." He holds it up, turning slowly that all can see it glistening in the rays of the sun's light.

"Now, I shall give it to Benjamin for his keeping, that when the Messiah comes, it shall in its appropriate time be given unto Him. So do we honor all those who have given so much that He could bear the Word of God to the world." Turning, he strides to Benjamin and hands him the staff.

Benjamin accepts it and leans forward to kiss it, passing it to his left and then his right, that each of the revered elders with him can do the same.

One comes bearing a beautiful cloth woven with rainbow bright colors, and brings it before Benjamin, holding it up. The staff is carefully wrapped in it, then Benjamin holds it up again. "We have embraced this staff in all the colors we know, for all whom we know will hear the message of God's

Promise through His Son." He hands the wrapped staff back to his ward, who turns and strides away.

Jacob, bright again, calls out, "Let us sing! Let us celebrate," and begins a song in a deep resonant voice.

All rise and join with him. Reaching up their hands and clasping one another's fingertips, they sway this way and that. From the oldest to the youngest there are smiles all around, for a great journey has been traveled, and a destination has been reached.

And now those upon the altar descend.

In bright raiment, with bits of brightly colored ribbon interwoven into strands of their hair, Anna and Judy come to the forefront beneath the altar.

All kneel.

Anna and Judy clasp hands and raise them. Judy speaks in her clear, beautiful voice. "Lord God, we are filled to exception with joy as we present to You, Your Daughters."

Humming comes first from the elder sisters, picked up next by the young voices, and then by all the elder ones, enchantingly beautiful humming, a rolling, mesmerizing sound of honor and truth, of love and compassion. It is the sound of the Promise held in the hearts of these humble people.

In the center of the altar is a single illuminated lamp. Next to it, on either side, many small scrolls containing a myriad of prayers, thoughts of hopefulness, and joy have been placed, all blessed by the Essene priests and priestesses. Each one of the peoples has been offered the opportunity to place their spirit's light upon the altar of God to welcome these Maidens, and to be a part of the path ahead.

And now, they come.

Their pace is slow, but deliberate, as they ascend the steps in single file. The sun's light shines brightly, making them look even brighter than their fine garments and radiant smiles and spirits cause them to be.

Up they move, twelve steps.

The first reaches the altar.

Some of those gathered can no longer contribute to the wordless prayer, the chant, the humming, so deeply touched are they. For each of these Maidens is so radiant and so beautiful that the mere sight of her, and the awareness of the life to which she has dedicated this moment and all that will follow, could overwhelm even the stoutest of hearts.

The ascension continues.

Suddenly, the sky darkens and great sounds roll across the heavens, first off in the distance. Many turn this way and that, startled. *Why is it that this sun-filled afternoon is suddenly swept away and replaced by darkness, thunder, and lightning?*

An opening appears in the midst of the swirling clouds. Rumbling and lights flash all about.

The opening grows, and a great finger of light thrusts its way through the darkness and illuminates the one called Mary.

Some gasp as they struggle to continue their humming, chant-like prayer.

Mary, impacted by the light, seems to labor and, yet, Her face aglow, She takes another step, and another.

And the light grows.

The great rolling sound is now directly above and behind the altar, and a hand reaches down.

Mary looks up. In awe, She receives the hand of the Angel Gabriel.

Now, the only sound is a strange, curiously enchanting movement of sound all throughout, not one created by these peoples, but seemingly, descending upon them.

She turns as he leads Her up to stand before the altar.

As though from his very essence, he reaches up and places a mantel of light upon Her, bends ever so slightly to kiss the top of Her head, and is gone.

The darkness remains, but the light now shines upon Her.

Those whose hearts had been weary with labor and loss, now gladdened, weep and call to God, *Praise God!*

Judy and Anna embrace, weeping with joy, for they knew in their heart of hearts and shared with one another that it must be She, and now they see it is so.

They turn and move up the steps, aided by Ruth and Josie and many of the elder maidens.

The other Eleven are gathered to stand in a semicircle, with Mary at the center.

One who is from the School of the Adepts rises before the altar directly in front of Mary, entreating, "Bless us, My Lady. Bless us."

Mary looks down upon this one. A great smile comes upon Her as she sees Her dear friend, and friend to all of her sisters, Isadore. Slowly, illuminated in light, Mary raises Her hand, palm facing Isadore, and nods, smiling.

Isadore kneels and bows.

Mary turns, as though Her hand were reflecting the light of God which shines upon Her to all She beholds. As She meets eye upon eye, face upon face, She does not waver. Her gentle smile is constant, the light shining from Her eyes unmistakable.

Each is touched. She turns and turns, and not a one is overlooked. But She speaks not.

She turns to look at her Sisters, whose tear-stained faces also shine with great joy. Walking unto them, embracing each one, exchanging whispers of love shared perhaps by only Her and that one or that group alone.

They hug and hug, and kiss each other's cheeks. Some touch Her face. All pledge their presence with Her to the end of the journey.

Finally, Mary summons Judy, Anna, Ruth, Josie, and the others ... and steps forward.

All fall silent.

She stands with Judy on one side and Anna on the other.

In a soft but clear voice She states, "These are those who have made the Way passable to the now. I accept that which is given unto me by our God. I give in return unto God my eternal love. And I give unto each of you the same.

"These are our sisters whose hearts are strong, whose dedication unto God is as the rocks upon which we dwell ... timeless. I know that there is much ahead, but I wish to thank God for the presence of each and every one of you. And I ask of you, pray often that we have the strength and wisdom to follow that which is aright. That we are open, each day the greater, to become all that we are. And I ask you to remember all those who have gone before, as sweet Jacob has stated, for surely they are gathered here even now as I speak to you.

"But this last prayer I ask of you from the heart which is in my spirit: Open yourself to receive Him. Be of great joy. We know the prophecies, but this is the Gift of Life that comes. I thank each of you that I am here, for you have made it so. And now I dedicate myself and my life eternal to His service. May God's blessings ever be known in your hearts, in your minds, and in your lives. We thank you."

The activities following the ceremonies cannot be described in mere words. It is as though these are a people for whom there is one cause, one work, one path, at least for now. Even those who diverged from that believed to be true believe what has occurred this day, for all they have seen and heard in their lives until now is no measure for what they have experienced here.

Yet, each must meet that which is in accordance with their highest and best. Some of them may drift. Some may hear a call that is not always in such beautiful harmony and oneness as it is this day. But so shall it be that those who are one with this Promise, this Work, will grow stronger, more purposeful. And they shall overcome.

"Oh, Mary, I knew it had to be you," squeals Hannah.

Little Sophie laughs lightly. "I, too. The way the energy of God comes up from the earth and spills all over you. Who else but you?" Delighted, the other Sisters laugh.

"Mary," Abigale offers, "anything that is within your sight to be done, tell us, and we shall fulfill that."

Zephorah giggles. "It is so exciting!"

"It is not just exciting," Andra insists, "it is … Well, did you see him? I mean … an angel! *Here!* Who could ever imagine that we, here in the wilderness … Oh yes, I know as well as all of you everything that you could say back to me." She throws her head back and laughs her wondrous laugh. "But, I mean, to really, really see an angel!"

That is all it takes for the Maidens to giggle and laugh, form a circle and begin to dance, singing a song to which each one makes up lyrics to contribute. It is a song to celebrate the choice of Mary as the vessel for the Promise that shall come.

"Incredible," Joseph begins softly, "purely incredible!"

"How so?" Elob asks.

"I mean it is spellbinding, what took place! Who besides those present will ever believe it?"

"What does it matter?" Jacob responds. "*We* know it. We have the light of it in our spirits from here to evermore," and he laughs easily.

"Oh yes, I know that. But hearing about it, reading about it … Well, you know. Having been told about the ancients with the angels is one thing, but to be in the presence of one, that is quite another." And Joseph, too, laughs.

"Many things will come to pass. Of this I have no doubt," Elob begins, adding, "some of which will touch many present here." He glances around the large group, but his eyes rest upon Joseph, only for a moment but many notice this.

"Some of us," he continues, turning to glance toward

Benjamin and several of the other elders, "will be called upon to serve in ways that we could not believe in this moment, but they shall, nonetheless, come to pass. And the call will come. It is good for us all to begin a work, just as these young Maidens shall, with vigor. We must strengthen our faith. We must build our honor and our truth into bastions of support. And we must claim righteousness, which shall be tested, which shall come to us in guises so familiar so as to beckon to us *Come this way* or *Go that way.* But we must not. Let us all pledge for a moment or two in prayer that this shall be our ideal: that we shall be unwavering in our faith, in our oneness with each other and with our God." And he speaks no more, but bows his head.

The adepts that surround him, men and women, do the same. When he looks up again, the others seem to know and do likewise.

Once again, his eyes fall upon Joseph. Then he turns to glance at Zechariah.

Turning again, he speaks to Nicodemus. "There is much to do that few of our people can do. You are one of them."

"I am ready, as are my brethren. I know the prophecy and I know what is needed. When we depart, we shall make the preparations."

"It is perhaps not well for you to return here," Elob cautions. "For if it is known that you are among us at this level, your standing, your credibility may well be questioned."

"We understand, and we are ready. Our spirits are strong." Nicodemus glances over at those with him, including the other Joseph.

"This I see." Elob smiles. "As we have planned and discussed with you, we will communicate with you, of course, as often as need be in the matters as we have agreed."

"And we shall be with all of you in our prayers, in our visions, but most of all, in our hopefulness of Him who comes and the Promise He bears." Rising, Nicodemus gestures warmly to all present, embracing several of them, stopping to speak to Joseph, Zechariah, and several of the others. Then he, Joseph of Arimethea, and their entourage depart.

"Well," states Jacob, "if there was a question in any heart, I pray it has been answered this day. For if not, the immediate journey ahead will be challenging to them."

"Who could not hold that light within them forever?" responds Joseph.

"Some hearts need a continual light given from without," Elob begins again, "for they have not found the pathway that leads them to their own light. Thus, whatsoever is given them from without is all they know. As they continue to search there for that which is within, their journey may take them this way or that. You hold the candle of God's truth within you, Joseph, as do all of you who are gathered here. But some have not learned to illuminate this candle, and thus they walk by the light of others."

Elob looks down for a moment. "But I say to you all at this time, we are with you unto the journey's end. We are here with you in spirit, utterly. Even if we are not present in our physical being, we can hear your call. So, no matter where any one of you might be," he adds, slowly turning his gaze about to take in all present, "call out in your prayer, at the very least at the celebration of the day's arrival and at its departure. We will always be listening, searching, looking. This we pledge to you."

He then raises his arms and gestures in the curious way of all the adepts present.

"Are they finally asleep, Judy?" Anna asks quietly.

"I think so, but it is very difficult to tell for sure. Most of them keep tossing and turning. I am certain that on the morrow, our discussions of their visions and dreams will be lengthy." She smiles, laughing gently.

"Look at Her." Anna's sweet matronly smile, for which

she is noted, radiates warmly from her as she gazes in Mary's direction. "Of all of them, look at Her. She is utterly at peace. And see Her face? It still glows."

"I imagine that will never go away now."

Ruth has moved up quietly to join them. "Quite a day, you two."

Judy sighs deeply. "It is the beginning of the manifestation of the Promise. In many ways, it is only the beginning of one part of the journey. Now we must get them to truly know themselves and to know they are one. Let us pray for this."

Any who might be upon a journey, seeking, questing, looking for that which is of strength and righteousness to give them support and purpose in life will come to that time wherein there is a gift offered. That gift shall be, in so many ways, similar to that which you have just read.

It is perhaps only the preparation of the one who is seeking, the one who is upon the journey or quest, which makes the difference between seeing the gift, seeing the answer to one's quest clearly, or not.

For as it was given, some hearts do not have the candle of God's light illuminated within them, so they believe not unto themselves but only unto the light of others. Indeed, they may not know that the light of God is already within, merely awaiting them to illuminate it.

Chapter Six

His Living Light

At this point along the headwaters, the stream is barely wide enough for perhaps two or three of the Maidens to stand shoulder to shoulder. But down somewhat from here lies a beautiful pool that has been made by barricading the water's movement downstream. This pool is the favorite of the elder sisters and, of course, the Maidens. They are gathered here, purifying themselves in anticipation of the day's events.

There has been the giving of self in spirit, heart, mind, and body to the beginning of a new day, the calling forth of the opportunity to strengthen and enlighten each in her own uniqueness, regarding her own purpose and path.

"May I still splash you with the water, Mary?" Zephorah giggles, knowing the answer to her playful question.

Glancing over, head tilted with a soft smile upon Her face, Mary just bends and swiftly scoops a handful of water, then sends it hurtling into Zephorah's shining face. "Perhaps that answers your question, my sweet sister."

Then they all laugh and begin to splash one another.

Above, near the edge of the great outcropping that protects this small hollow, sit the elder sisters, talking joyfully.

"With the clear indication now that the work begins in a new direction, so to say, there will be great joy at today's ceremony and perhaps a moderating of some of the emotions the others must be experiencing," Anna begins softly.

Judy, her eyes fixed upon the young Maidens below, simply smiles and nods. Without turning, she answers, "It is difficult to look at these beautiful Maidens, and then to hold in my heart and mind all the others. It is important that we remind them all of the teachings … that not one is lesser than any other, that each one's work is a gladness to her spirit and perhaps, indeed, a choice of it." She now turns and smiles at her beloved sister Anna. "I affirm with you, dear Anna, that it shall be glorious, indeed. And I know that they understand within. It is only the outer mantle of emotion and flesh that may lament a moment or two."

"Some are well at peace with it," Ruth interjects. "Most, in fact, are. For everyone has known all along that there would be different works and different purposes. But as you say, Judy, it is important that we emphasize this."

The Maidens have concluded their ceremonial and somewhat mirthful purification process of bathing, purifying, and releasing any limiting thoughts. Just as one washes away that which accumulates on the outer body, so have these Maidens been taught to wash away inner limitations that might mute or dull the true beauty of God's light within. But in these times, the elder sisters have encouraged them to bring even more joy into this ceremonial process. Not to diminish the sacredness of this bathing, but to embrace the joy that is ever thought among these peoples to be one with God.

This morning's meal has been specifically prepared. Some of the elder sisters have done so with the understanding that this is the first day's light to shine upon the Decision. So, each Maiden can sense, even taste, the deliberate sweetness and love added by the elder sisters and elder maidens whose hands have lovingly prepared this food for them.

They are now seated around a small fire, passing an assortment of biscuits and various foods, the hot tea being continually refreshed in the bowls the Maidens hold.

Seeing them from a distance, a small circle of young women barely at the threshold of womanhood, smiling and talking gently, one would have no idea of the magnitude of what now lies before them.

"I dreamt that I was before a bright shining figure, mostly golden. He looked upon me with such sweetness, such kindness." Abigale looks down, a lone tear falling into her bowl. Swallowing hard, she looks up and glances around at her sisters, who have paused and whose hands now rest in their laps, devotedly, lovingly listening to their sister recount a vision. He came up to me and put his hand on my shoulder, here," gesturing to her right shoulder, "and said, *How sweet you are, Miriam.*

"And I answered, *But Lord, I am Abigale.*

"So He continued, *You are that, and you are the sweetness of the past. And in the past I have known you and I have walked with you, and I called you Miriam. It is honorable that you should know this. And it is honorable that you shall hold this as the truth of your love, and claim it, that you might return it to me when we next meet.*

"He smiled for a moment ... his eyes soft, sending a light of warmth to me. Then I tumbled and swirled. The light was all about me, and I sought it. I reached out to claim it and I grabbed wisps of different colored lights. I took them up here," placing her hand upon her bosom, "and each one felt different. There were twelve in all. But one I cherished and could not release."

"What was its color?" questions Ruth attentively.

"It was ..." she glances about her, "like the new morn's dew on the rose. It was like the rays of the sun's last light, promising its return on the morrow."

Ruth glances directly into the eyes of Judy, who smiles broadly.

"This is a very special gift, dear one. How are you with it at this time?" Anna asks.

"I feel strange. As though something has been illuminated here … right where I took the beautiful rose-colored light and held it close to me."

"And who do you think the golden one was, or is?" probes Anna.

"Oh, there can be no question. It is He who comes." She looks over at her sister, Mary, adoringly. "He whom you will bear."

Mary smiles happily and looks down, placing her palms upon her abdomen. "Through God's grace. Pray with me sisters that I am ever worthy."

"You *are* worthy." Abigale reaches out to lovingly touch Her. "We all know that. Nonetheless, we shall ever be with you in prayer, and in spirit and body. But please, my sisters. What is the meaning of this vision? Am I to be someone from the past? Am I to look upon the beautiful rose light as something I am, as He said, to *bear and return to Him?* How do I do this? What is the nature of this vision? I am Abigale. Am I to be Miriam, as well?"

"No one is ever apart from all that they have been," responds Judy. "Everyone is always the sum of what they have been, what they are, and what they can be. It is our choice to believe that which is most true within. Then, once we believe this, to cleave to it forever, so it becomes the rod upon which we lean, that by which we measure all else, that which has ever brought you joy, Abigale … also called Miriam." Judy smiles at her. "It is a question that can be answered in the heart of hearts.

"But it seems evident to me as I look upon you," Judy continues, "that the light around you is His. And that His call to you is meaningful. You would not, as you contemplate this moment," looking into her as well as at her, "diminish the honor to your name by also claiming the name which He, our Lord, has called you. Perhaps He will choose for you. Perhaps in a time ahead, you might even ask Him that question."

All of the Maidens begin to *oh-h* and *ah-h* at the contemplation of being actually able to speak with Him.

"When do you think He will come?" questions Hannah, glancing over at her beloved Mary. "We are as young trees, as you have taught us," glancing down at her own body, "not ready to bear fruit, and certainly not the fruit of this Promise. Is it a great distance ahead?"

"The journey through life is one filled with promises," answers Isadore. "It is difficult when one looks ahead at them and then measures the distance between now and their manifestation. It is like looking at the seeds I have shown you and anticipating the birth of that contained within them: seeing them when they break forth from the warm earth and speaking to them, calling them to come forth and bear fruit, and surrounding them with the prayer of our love, recognizing what they are … gifts of God's Spirit in the form of nature.

"Then, when the time of birthing comes and we go forth to gather the leaves for medicines and herbs for teas, when we search for the roots that nourish and the grains that strengthen our endurance, if all the while, we envision the seed, its sprouting, its bearing fruit, and the joy of our harvest, then we see from the sight that is good and clear and open.

"I tell you this now, Hannah, and all of you, sweet sisters, that you might ever remember this moment. For it is the beginning of the manifestation of the Promise, the time wherein the seed is prepared and you recognize that you are the good gardeners of God's Promise. As you nourish and nurture that which you, *Miriam*, have been given by Him (and all of you, as well) it becomes the treasure within. It becomes the gift of nurturing which, when He joins us, you will be ready to bear to Him as your fruit … all of you, all of *us*. No matter what our choice of work, no matter how the joy of service might manifest for us, we shall be ready. Thus it is good to hold the vision of completeness even as you anticipate with awe and excitement, sweet Hannah, that time ahead."

Hannah looks down, weighing these words by focusing on the earth beneath her, contemplating the magnitude of this teaching. "Thank you, Isadore," she says, looking up again, her eyes shining, "but it does not answer my question."

All of the elder sisters laugh.

"In its season, all things are given. Look you upon your bodies. Listen to them. Hear their call. See the movement of the force of life within you. If you do, you can and will answer your own question."

Eyes focused upon Isadore, Hannah goes within, as all can see. After a brief moment, a warm smile fills her face, and her moist eyes glisten with the joy of her discovery. "Thank you." Then she begins to look at her sisters one by one. "It is three to four more years. This I deem from within." Her final gaze comes to rest upon Mary.

Mary smiles expansively, and nods in agreement.

The excited chatter among the young Maidens begins again as they return to finishing their morning's meal. Some giggle and laugh. Others, more serious, question a sister about a certain thought, a certain perspective.

"I rather like the sound of Miriam." Andra leans into her. "It has a sort of charming ... a sort of timeless ring to it."

"Well, it is new to me." She looks down. "What would *you* think, Andra, if someone changed *your* name?"

"If *He* changed my name, I would rejoice." Andra leans back and laughs heartily, attracting the attention of all, young and old, who cannot resist the lure of her laughter.

"Besides, what difference does it make?" Kelleth asks Miriam. "Unless, of course, you feel it makes a difference."

"Well, I still feel it. I feel it strongly, like something living, something alive, has been placed into my body." She glances around to see who is listening and notes that most are.

"It is His light," Mary offers. "It is holy, and it *is* living," she continues, smiling.

"Is it what *you* feel, Mary?" questions Kelleth.

"Yes. It is very much as you describe it, what I feel when the energies move up and spill down all over me."

All laugh quietly, reminiscing about a past event.

Outwardly, the ceremony appears quite similar to the one just prior, when Mary was chosen. This time, though, all of the other young maidens are aligned in rows upon the altar, and are bedecked in beautiful garments not unlike those given to the Twelve.

The attentiveness of the elder sisters, the seers, and prophets is as reverent as in the previous ceremony. Upon the altar, the single flame burns brightly once again and as though to honor these young maidens, the sky is filled with billowy white clouds, unique for this land in this season.

Glancing up at the beautiful clouds, Judy murmurs softly to the elder sisters gathered, "I think it is a symbol of God's joy. I think it is clearly a sign."

"Indeed," Anna responds, following Judy's gaze and then looking back at the children gathered on the altar. "How sweet they each are. They know not, even though they have gained much, the magnitude of what lies ahead for them."

Ruth sighs. "Yes, many only see that which is immediately ahead. As much as we have recounted to them, it is the glory of His coming that is predominant in heart and mind."

Their conversation is hushed, as they see Jacob, Benjamin, Joseph, and many other respected elders of the tribes arriving at the steps.

It is Jacob who steps forward before the altar to begin the ceremony. "We greet you all joyfully. And we thank you, sweet Maidens," smiling gently upon the Maidens standing to the forefront of all those gathered, "for your prayers honoring those who have gone before and all those who are gathered here … especially you." He turns to smile warmly upon the beloved children behind him on the altar, who utterly adore this man of Spirit they call Jacob. "This is a celebration," he continues, turning back to the entire gathering, "in a manner which is perhaps beyond my humble words to communicate. Nonetheless, I call forth mine own spirit to speak on these things, and I invite my brothers and sisters to do the same."

All bow their heads in silence for a moment following Jacob's lead, for all gathered here realize that he is now coalescing, unifying himself in that special way that he has mastered. His head rises abruptly and his face is aglow. The warmth of his smile, so typical of him, shines upon all gathered.

Some strike their breasts. Some make the Essene gesture of utter devotion and dedication unto God. Some kneel and bow their heads. For what they see in their brother Jacob is the very Spirit of God shining through. They not only see it, they believe it and they hearken unto it. Silence falls. Jacob's gentle gaze sweeps across the gathering.

Slowly, he turns again and looks into the eyes of each of the children now being honored on the altar, reminding them, so it would seem, of a past hug, a previous kiss upon the forehead, a gentle caress of his hand upon their brow or cheek in time of need, the refrain of a song of joy, a celebration in the form of sacred dance. All these and greater rush to the surface of their hearts and overflow into their minds and bodies, making each one glow in the presence of his gaze.

Finally, he turns back to the gathering and speaks. "We are the children of God. This land is holy. We have prepared ourselves and the land for the arrival of God's Promise. And now, we are of knowledge sacred." He gestures to Mary in the midst of the young Maidens standing below the altar to honor their sisters now chosen.

"It is a part of the work that each should know themselves. Each should know the glory that is God's gift within them. And each should know that this gift from God is to be honored, to be held sacred, in the knowledge that He knoweth the greatest that can be given unto each one.

"It is the nature of the Earth to call out, *Is this fruit greater or sweeter than this other?* And upon tasting the fruit, one might adjudge that it is not sweeter or greater, but beautifully unique and different. So is the gift of Spirit within each of us beautiful and uniquely different. Ever must we, God's children, hold to the forefront that who we are, what we are, that what we have to give to the Way is the greatest of all because God giveth this to each one. Then, as we honor God and the Spirit of God in all, we honor ourselves. To do less than this is to question His wisdom and glory and that which He has set before us as His beloved child.

"So now," he raises his hands and turns to look again upon the rows of beautiful children on the altar, "I, Jacob, son of God, call upon each of you to bring to the forefront of your minds and hearts, now and forever, that which thou art and that of which thou art the bearer. Honor it as you honor God, Himself. Never do less than this, lest you do less than that for God. Rejoice in that which lies ahead. As you see Him who comes enter, and as you are honored to witness and participate as your Sisters nourish Him and call Him forth, hold that which you are to the forefront above all else. And when He is called unto service in our Lord God's name, bring that, for He will have need of it and of you.

"You will understand this the greater when He looks upon you, each one." He gestures to all of the children gathered. "His eyes will reach into your heart and embrace you. He will embrace you in a manner you cannot conceive, nor can I begin to express. Then you will know the truth of what I speak to you this day.

"The gift you have to give to Him, and to the Work, and to the manifestation of the Promise, is one which only you can give. Do not measure it as the Earth would tempt you to do. Do not weigh it out or call upon it in comparison to another's, for to so do is to allow the shadow of the illusion of finiteness to fall upon the beauty of who and what you are. When He calls your name and sends you forth, remember me. I, your brother, Jacob, am ever with you."

He bows his head, raises his hands, and speaks gently. "We, Thy humble servants, Lord God, give thanks unto Thee for the fruits of Thy Promise here before me. We give thanks for the honor, the privilege, and the joy to have walked with them in their time of growth and discovery. So do we ask, one and all, that Thou strengthen and purify us, that Thou guide us that our foot falls aright upon the paths of righteousness, that that which we have to give shall grow and flourish in Thy sight to be the very best. We pray this in the name of the King who comes, and in our love and service to Thee.

"Bless them, Lord God. Strengthen them in their times of need. We rejoice. We rejoice in their presence, and in the forthcoming Promise, and in the glory of life eternal. I, Jacob, ask this of Thee."

The day's activities are filled with celebration, dance, song, and great banquets of many unusual and rarely available delicacies and foods. Once again, those from the School of the Prophets have gathered to honor those who will be among the workers sent forth by the Lamb of God.

Many elders and seers tell wondrous stories of the ancients, recounting to groups here and there, children and elders alike, stories which have been repeated over and again: Here, the story of how their Elder Brother entered in the time of discovery, that time in which the Promise was formulated in the consciousness of Earth; there, of those times when all peoples walked in absolute freedom; and over there, of times when so many had subjugated their will to the dominion of others, whose intent diverged from the original Promise.

They recount gloriously, joyfully, the movement of many of their elders through the times when He was called Amelius and when the Promise was given universally to all who were with Him, and they took it within, in the Holy of Holies of their own spirit. They recount how they promised to hold it until it was again needed, and that this is that time, as they point to this one and that, to the wonder and giggles of the children, and to the awe and tear-filled joy of the seers and prophets identified by name from those ancient times.

Among one of these groups is seated that one called Elob. Glancing at the Maidens, he bobs his head up and down. His eyes close. To his right and left are several of his adepts. His eyes open, and his face warms into a brilliant smile of love and discovery. "Who is it here who is to be called Miriam?"

The young Maidens gasp with wonder, and Miriam begins to weep. Several of her sisters, including Mary, come to her. Some stroke her hair, others embrace a hand, some kiss a cheek, but all place their prayer and love around this, their beloved sister.

Raising her bright, tear-stained face, she responds reverently, "I am the one who has had a vision wherein the Golden One called me Miriam."

Elob smiles and nods. "And you have been in this time called Abigale, have you not?"

"Yes, I am the same. You honor me for knowing this."

He laughs gently. "I know each of you. I know each of you perhaps better than you even know yourselves."

"Do you know me?" questions Kelleth.

The sisters soften and even Miriam begins to laugh a bit. "Indeed, I do."

"What do you know about me that I do not?" Kelleth continues, her face quite serious.

"I know many things."

"Will you share them with me?" She smiles now, in an engaging manner unique to the Maidens, taught to them eloquently: that a request given in utter love, in sincerity of spirit, is one that is difficult for anyone to deny.

"You have learned well. The power of your love is felt by all here. I can feel it calling to me. Indeed, I shall share this with you, but not in this time, nor place. When you take your sacred journeys, I shall meet with each of you, as shall my brothers and sisters, and we shall be with you. We will offer you our strength to add to your own. We will offer our visions, our insights. What is the rod against which you measure all of your life, sweet Kelleth?"

She straightens up, gazes at him, and looks around. "The rod against which I measure all else is compassion. If I cannot feel oneness with each thing and understand its needs, its wants, then how can I serve God? If I know not the source of the sorrow or joy of a thing, be it a creature of the Spirit of God, or a brother or sister in the Earth who knows not the Way, if I do not know these things, how can I serve God?

"If I cannot measure the pain that underlies the actions of one whose deeds are wrongful, how am I able to bring them the truths of our people's teachings, the enlightenment of our sweet sisters who have given their very lives to us, and the truths of the ancients unless I have the compassion to feel what they have felt and know that which has taken them awry. The rod against which I measure all in life I call compassion. Some call it oneness. Perhaps it is both."

"Then if you look upon compassion as you see it in others, what does this do for you, Kelleth?"

Glancing around, her eyes become fixed upon Mary. "She has the light of God within her shining forth. Oh, yes … I know we all do. But in Her, it is unique. I find my pattern for compassion flowing from Her, through Her."

"Are you saying," probes Elob, "that you both have the same rod against which you measure life within you?"

"Yes, I would have to say that is so."

Mary's face is aglow with a warm smile.

"But She is … I don't know, different somehow. I guess that is why God chose Her. She has compassion that is universal. She has compassion for everything."

"Would you not say that you have the same?"

Straightening herself, her eyes flicker and close for a moment. She opens them again and her face is radiant. She looks at Mary, each connecting with the other through their eyes, smiling. "I would. Our compassion is the same."

The elder sisters and maidens, and all of the adepts, including Elob, smile and murmur softly. Some laugh with joy.

"Well done. Very well done, sweet sister, "commends Elob. "In your sacred search, I will speak all things to you as God giveth them to me, as will my brothers and sisters."

"I will await this." Kelleth responds with a strength that is almost amusing, and with a demonstration of patience, not something she is particularly noted for.

"Who knows what purpose such a rod, a rod against which to measure all else, has in the times ahead?" asks Josie.

Zephorah raises her hand, "I do."

"I, as well," responds Hannah.

"We all do," we hear from Little Mary.

"Well then, could one of you speak it?"

The Maidens glance at one another, giggling, one pointing at this one, and the other pointing at that one.

Hannah stands. "It is the truth of our spirit, which nothing can penetrate, or weaken, or weary, or tire. It is that to which we turn in times of challenge and that which lifts us up. It is the gift of our truth given to us by our God, against which naught can prevail."

"But what will you do with it, sweet sister?"

"I will live it."

"For what purpose?" Josie continues to probe. "If you have it within you, if you know it, if it gives you strength and all the wonderful things you say it does, to what purpose will you live it? To what work would you apply it, and how?"

"I would let it shine forth. And others will come to know that they, too, can look into the future with anticipation rather than with doubt or fear. I will let it be that which lifts up those who are fallen from their joy. It will give them the ingredients with which to rebuild hope, to restore ease where the shadows have darkened it. I will hold it in my hand," she outstretches her young hand, cupping it upwards towards the sky, "and let God fill it again and again, and each time it is filled, I will give it. And as I give it, God's Spirit will flow through me and become a part of that one to whom I give."

Hannah turns and glances at her sisters. "I know each of them will do the same. Together, we will have given the Twelve Tenets of God's Holy Truth. And once this is done, righteousness will emerge."

"Unto Him who comes, how will you give this?"

Hannah's hands rush up to cover her face at the mere contemplation of this, and each of the Maidens bows her head, each silently contemplating the question, for it could well be asked of her next.

Rubbing her face gently, Hannah brings her hands down to cover her heart. "I will offer it openly for Him to take of it, as you would offer a cup of warm special tea to one who thirsts or has need. Not that He will have a need, but that we are to be the reflection of all these qualities that, as you have taught us, my sweet teachers, He will bring into the Earth.

"It is my prayer that, as I hold the joy of my expectancy out, He will find it good. Of course, He will amplify it many times over, but that He would know I am ever here if there is a need, a work, to which my truth would find good purpose. This is God's gift given to me to bear, as He would will it to be so, but first I will surround Him with it." She turns to look at Mary, whom she so loves. "Upon His birth, as one would robe a new babe in a garment, so will I robe Him in the joy of my love for Him. In the expectancy of the Promise that He carries, so will I wrap Him in my heart and, here, in my mind." She touches her forehead. "And I will ever stand at the ready to any need to which I am honored to respond."

Josie speaks not, but smiles and nods. Glancing about, she looks from one shining face to the other. "All of you … All that you have learned to this point that my sweet sisters," glancing at Judy, Anna, Ruth, and many, many others, "have given to you is only the beginning. Now, the path is set before us. Now, your foot shall take its first step. In this meal is the completion of your childhood. This first step is upon a path which is of a magnitude that even we, all of us together, the greatest of all seers and prophets hallowing those who have gone before and the one who established the holy Spring of wisdom, cannot truly know nor express the wonder, the glory of, of what lies ahead."

"There are, as I see it, two ways to approach this. For one, your brothers and sisters from the School of the Prophets could assume identities and be placed in appropriate positions, that when the time arises, there will be the shelter and the answer to the needs."

Nodding, Elob agrees. "Some of this, Joseph, as you well know, is already done, and they are in place, as with your own peoples that you sent forth. Have there been messages from them?"

"For the most part, all is proceeding as anticipated. But there are those areas wherein there are great struggles, where the forces seeking to limit us are manifesting powerfully. It is as if they seem to know, as do we, of that which approaches."

"Oh, that would be quite understandable," Elob answers unhesitatingly. "Though I do not wish, through my word, to create a greater power than what they believe they have at present, it is foolhardy not to recognize what is. Even more foolhardy not to speak of it, in order that understanding can be had among us. And from that, to evolve a knowing of how to proceed, what our choices are. So that is the one path. What is the other you speak of, Joseph?"

"It is not clear to us. But Zechariah …" he turns to look

at his beloved companion, "has seen it in a vision. It is as though one would have a garment around them wherever they go that repels any shadows or limitation. Zechariah saw it, in a manner of speaking, as a cloak of sorts." He turns to look deeply into his brother's eyes, inviting him to speak of it.

Zechariah picks up the cue. "It is, for the most part, as Joseph has summarized it. I saw our people going forward as a singular light with the Messiah in the midst, surrounded by layers of light that looked like garments. And wherever this great sphere of light moved, with its wrappings of layers of light around it, the shadows would fall away. It was as though the sphere of light could go wherever it was sent or called and fear naught."

"So," Joseph interjects, "that is the other path. But we ask of you and your brothers and sisters … Can you help us interpret this?"

"That we can do." Elob glances at Benjamin, who nods.

"We, as well, shall pray and meditate upon this. But I think it is of several meanings. What thinkest thou, Elob?"

Elob looks to his right and left at some of his colleagues, who nod. "It appears we all agree."

"Well, Zechariah," Benjamin continues, "my perception is that it is a message for you individually as well as for us and the Path. It is a message for you to surround yourself with the twelve tenets of truth, for if you look upon the vision again, I suspect you would see twelve such layers of truth."

Zechariah's eyelids flutter but he does not go there at this moment. His reverence for his beloved Benjamin is too great.

"Think you on this." He looks over at Elob again. "And I believe it to be a message even beyond this for Zechariah. What say you, Elob?"

"I have seen this for some time, Zechariah. I have mentioned it here and there, but only lightly, to see if your spirit might hear and validate and bring truth to what I have seen."

Joseph turns to study Zechariah. The rising energy within

him causes his body to pound. He feels a tingling all through it, and the thought arises, *Can it be Zechariah, whom I so love, who is my brother? Shall he be the caretaker of our sweet Lady?*

Zechariah appears impervious, having become immersed in some very focused thoughts or energies. "I know I am not he," Zechariah states suddenly, to the surprise of Joseph.

Joseph ponders, *Did he hear my thought? He is a great spiritual leader and teacher. And he knows the Law, the teachings of old. Perhaps he has seen into my heart.*

Once again, as though he heard Joseph's very thought, Zechariah turns and gazes at him, the wrinkles of time etching the smile on his face. "But I am ready to serve in whatsoever way God asks of me. Greater than I, however, shall lead the Way, if my heart and spirit are understanding what is being discussed here." He looks at Elob and then Benjamin.

"Nonetheless, there is that which lies ahead which will test you, Zechariah," responds Benjamin, his countenance grave. "Witness your vision and the light of our people being tested by the shadows of limitation and illusion. And look you and hold in your heart, as the Promise … They did fall away.

"My heart," Benjamin clenches his fist and strikes his chest, "is with you, Zechariah. For what you have seen, and what I now know, comes to you on your journey through life. But you are the greater, and I shall be with you in spirit each step of the Way, as is our Lord God."

Chapter Seven

Joyful Expectancy

Two solitary figures are outlined in the campfire's light against the darkened sky. They speak not, but gaze down into the flames of the small fire.

"It is remarkable, is it not my brother? Here we are, guarding and watching, and within the interior, our people begin the work, the journey." Then with a more serious countenance, he looks up. "How often my heart calls out unto God, *What more might I do? What other works, what gifts could I give?*" His voice trails off.

His brother ponders for a moment, offering a smile and a nod. "I, too, often have these thoughts. I suppose it is true of all our peoples. The mere contemplation of that which is within our embrace, that which is ahead on our pathway, does at times seem staggering, humbling, and from an outer perspective, almost impossible. Yet, you and I know within, as do our people, that the Promise is true, and the Path we walk upon is that which He will walk upon."

After gazing into the flames again, the first guardian looks up at the night sky. There is no moonlight, but the stars are radiant, brilliant, some twinkling here and there. "Sometimes when I see these beautiful stars I think of them as our brothers and sisters who have gone before us, looking down and smiling on us. See this one over here?" He points to a particularly brilliant star. "I think of that one as my own brother who gave his life that the Promise could continue."

The other guardian sighs deeply. "So many have given so much."

"Then let us celebrate. Let us receive from them that which is their gift, and the very gifts of God from life itself, and hold them for a moment in our thoughts and prayers that our hearts will overflow with the beauty and abundance of that which has been given unto us." He reaches an out-stretched hand to take his brother's. "We hallow Thee, Lord God. Look within us and see our joy of service. We know that we are not two here keeping the watch, but many. We send our spirits forth to embrace all of the faithful. And we ask that You come into us and let Your Spirit illuminate our beings."

Around another campfire a tight circle of young Maidens sits, looking into the flames. Occasionally one places a bit of fuel upon the fire.

Walking around the periphery of the Maidens are the elder sisters, the teachers, the seers.

Anna is speaking. "If you look into the flame and allow your thoughts to flow freely from you, you will find that it is calming, soothing. Do not think about what you have learned, nor about that which puzzles or troubles you. Think only of the flame."

The Maidens are silent, their faces illuminated by the dancing color of the fire. Their knees touch one another, and their hands are clasped, each to the other.

"Now, close your eyes and see the flame within," Anna continues gently, with a mesmerizing tone. "If you cannot see it, open your eyes again and look at it, then close them and see it within."

The elder sisters and the others continue to move silently around the outer periphery.

"Are there any of you who cannot see the flame within as you see it without? If so, speak, and we will help you."

"I see it," offers Zephorah softly, "but it is different. It is not like the campfire. May I open my eyes, Anna?"

"Of course."

Upon Anna's permission, many open their eyes and look from one to the other.

"What is the difference between the flame before you and the flame you see within, Zephorah?" questions Anna.

"Well, the flame within me is not of these colors."

"And what are the colors?" Judy inquires.

"They are blues, purples, lavenders. They are not the colors of the flame that is before me."

"I, too, see them differently," Editha interjects.

"How so?" asks Judy.

"It is not actually that the colors are different. They are mostly yellows, golds, and oranges, somewhat like the flame. But they are … well, different."

"What, then, distinguishes your inner flame from the outer?"

"Well, as I look upon the fire before me, it feels warm, and I see the flames rising here and there, and little wisps of smoke and an occasional spark. With my eyes open, I feel the fire outside of me. My back is cool, but my front is warm."

The Maidens giggle, for they truly understand. The air is chilly and the fire is, indeed, warm in front of them.

Ruth smiles at Editha. "How does that differ from your inner flame?"

"The inner flame? Oh-h, it is warm all over, all through-out me, not just in front or from one direction."

"Yes, me, too," Zephorah agrees.

Off to the other side, Hannah adds quietly, "And I."

"Who else feels the flame within in this way?"

Virtually all the Maidens respond. But Mary, the Chosen One, is silent, Her eyes fixed upon the flame.

Josie moves to stand beside Her. "Mary, you have not spoken. Is there something you wish to share?"

Mary straightens herself, and all the Sisters gaze at Her expectantly. Her gentle eyes look over to meet Little Sophie's. "I see the beauty of you in the flame first. And I wonder, is it because you are directly across from me?" She turns to Josie. "Is that the reason? Why would I see the beauty of Sophie singularly? I hold the hands of others of my sisters, and we are all one in our sacred circle, so why is it that I see Sophie?"

The elder maidens glance at one another. There is an air of expectancy. All nod to Judy.

She brings her hands up, blessing her own being with them. All present know that she is seeking guidance from God from within. She then comes 'round to seat herself off to the left of Mary, where She can turn and gaze at her while the circle remains unbroken.

Judy reaches out to place her hand atop Mary's head. "Sweet sister, when the out-of-the-ordinary occurs, when there is the unexpected, it is good to pause and ask God, *What is the meaning of this?*"

The presence of Judy's hand on Mary's head seems to have a reassuring effect upon Her. Her eyes flicker and close, as She knows the intent is that She seek within.

"Speak what you experience, Mary, and share it with all of us. I will help guide you as God guides me."

"I see Sophie again."

"In what way do you see her?" Judy asks softly.

"I see swirls of light around her."

"Describe them."

"It is like swirls of yellow moving all around. They move up the sides, and seem to almost dance around her head. Some of them are trying to get into the top of her head."

Sophie is transfixed, her eyes wide.

"What are you feeling, Sophie, right at this moment?"

"I feel strange … Like a part of Mary is inside of me."

The other sisters glance quickly at each other in wonder,

for they know that this is significant.

"How do you know this? Do you feel it?" asks Judy.

Anna has moved around the circle. As Judy is to Mary, she is now positioned similarly beside Sophie, and places her hand on Sophie's head.

Sophie's eyes flicker, blink, and close. "Oh! I see you. Sweet Lord God, I see Mary. I ... I want to weep."

"Why, child?" questions Anna softly.

"I see Her, only ... Her body is older. She is walking a path alone. I want to be with Her."

"You are with Her," Anna gently reassures her.

"But She looks alone."

"Look at Her carefully. Do not dwell in the emotion that you feel but go beyond it. Claim the sight of your own spirit."

"I am trying." The struggle is evident in Little Sophie's body and in her voice.

Anna's hand still rests firmly but gently upon Sophie's head, and she now closes her eyes. Those who can see, see the glow of golden light begin, first barely perceptible, and now glowing brightly around that hand.

"Oh, thank you. I feel your love passing down through me. Now I see Her! And She is not alone. But ... It is so dark, so ominous." All of the elder sisters, the seers, and the great group gathered glance at one another, nodding, knowing the child is seeing the future.

"And what are *you* feeling, Mary?" questions Judy.

"I, too, feel strange. I see my sister. I feel her. But there is something else ... like a voice I cannot hear, yet know is there."

"I hear it!" Sophie answers. "It is calling your name."

"Oh yes, thank you. I do hear that."

The silence is now intense.

"Speak what you feel, Anna," Judy invites her.

Anna, with her hand still upon Sophie's head, nods, "You are seeing the completion, sweet sisters. You are seeing that which is the fulfillment of the work."

"Oh-h …" Sophie's voice chokes.

Now all the other little Sisters have bowed their heads. Some are swaying a bit, as they have been carefully taught to do to align their spiritual centers, to relax and calm, and transcend the physical, mental, and emotional. Some are bobbing their heads. Others are clearly in their spiritual consciousness.

"Must it be as prophesied?" questions Sophie, her voice breaking.

"This is the Will of God," Anna responds gently. "It is purposeful. Some see it as the end of a journey. Those who have the wisdom of God's sight see it as the beginning."

"I feel helpless. And I feel a great loss," sobs Sophie.

Some of the other Maidens also are tearful.

Not Mary. Mary is beginning to glow.

Judy slowly removes her hand from Her head. "Speak to us, Mary, of what you see and feel."

She breathes deeply and begins with a firm, steady voice filled with gentleness and love. "I see a light breaking through the darkness. In the light, I see a figure dressed in white descending upon the shaft of light. I see Him walking towards us, His hands outstretched, smiling."

"What does it mean to you, Mary?"

"It means there is no darkness of death. It means that there is only change. It means, as we have been taught, that we are never apart unless we believe it."

Sophie is straightening her body. Her shoulders go back as she turns her face upwards.

Anna removes her hand as Judy has done from Mary.

Several of the other Maidens have also turned their faces upward, the glow of understanding filling them.

It is Little Mary who speaks now, very quietly. "I know it is as Mary says it. Why, then, do I feel such sorrow?"

Now Josie moves around to be near Little Mary. "Look

at the sorrow. See it. Name it."

Little Mary adjusts her body as though to relieve some discomfort, perhaps from a bit of scratchy garment, or to move away from a small pebble's pressure under a leg. "I see swirls of color, as my sister said, flashes of different lights."

"And what is their essence?" Josie asks.

"They feel bitter. I can taste them. They do not taste good, and I feel them as though they are irritating my body."

"What do you feel in your heart?"

"Oh, Josie … My heart is filled with such heaviness."

"Then you do not feel it as your sister, Mary, just said?"

"Yes. But She is Mary, the Chosen. She sees, and knows, and understands. I do *not* understand."

"Then you must look at it," Josie urges. "Can you?"

"I think not. It feels as though, if I do, I shall perish."

Gasps come from some of her sisters.

"No, no!" counsels Judy. "Do not join her. Do not claim nor endorse what she has spoken."

Little Mary is tearful. "I am sorry. I am so sorry."

Josie instructs her, "No, do not add your sorrow to speaking your truth. You will diminish your truth if you surround it with sorrow. Remember?"

"I do, but I feel so lost and alone. And I feel such grief."

The elder sisters are looking at one another, communicating without word.

"Listen to me," Josie continues in an authoritative, strong voice. "State aloud your name."

Moistening her lips, moving her jaw, a soft voice speaks, "I am Little Mary, Daughter of God."

"Again," Josie commands.

"I am Mary, Daughter …" She begins to weep.

Across the way, Josie sees Judy shaking her head and Josie nods.

Ruth comes over to seat herself behind Little Mary. "We are with you, sweet sister, and we are greater than the illusion," she begins softly. "It is important for you and the work that you face what you are experiencing."

"But I am only a child. I do not know how to face the sorrow, the grief, the pain that is in the *entire world*. And that is what I see and feel."

"Why do you think you are seeing and feeling this?"

"I think it is because of Mary, the Chosen."

Across the way, Mary's face is serene, up-tilted, glowing. She remains silent.

"Open your eyes, Little Mary, and look at your Sister. Do it now."

Blinking, a flood of tears bursts forth as she opens her eyes to see before her the sweet compassion of love and peace emanating from her Sister. "Oh, thank you. Thank you my Sister, Mary."

"It is my joy."

Little Mary glances around the group, as though to reassure herself that she is here now, in the company, the safety and embrace of her people, her beloved sisters and brothers.

"Do you feel better? Stronger?" asks Ruth.

"I do."

"Then close your eyes, take this with you, and go back."

Little Mary straightens herself. "I can do this. I *can!*"

Smiles appear here and there among the other Maidens, who all have upturned faces now, aglow with the power of the faith of their teachings.

Taking several deep breaths, Little Mary closes her eyes and tilts her chin up just a bit.

"Speak aloud, and tell us of your journey. Take us with you, that we can be a part of what you are doing."

"I should like that, Ruth." There is a pause. Then, "I am surrounded by a great luminous circle. I am moving within it and I feel the light of God's Spirit all about me. I am walking. I do not see you, but I feel you. Oh-h! Now I have reached it again. It is sour-tasting, and it is abrasive."

"Feel the sweetness of your sisters and let that take away the sour taste. Hold the thought of your sisters now."

A shudder passes through her body. "I have done that now. I do feel your sweetness."

"What remains?" Ruth asks gently.

"It is like voices shouting at each other, coarse things rubbing against me, outside. But they are more distant now."

"Speak to the voices."

"What shall I say to them, Ruth?"

"Tell them of your love for them."

"But I know not these voices. How do I love what I do not know?"

"Oh, but you do know. If you think for a moment, you will remember in the oneness of God, that these voices are of Him, given through His gift ... the right of Free Will, free choice. True, they are expressing according to that which they choose. But remember the oneness."

"Oh-h. I see the flame. I see the beautiful flame, blue and white, the flame you told us to see. It is the flame of oneness. I love you all. I am Mary, Daughter of God. I love you."

Again, a silence so intense it seems to have substance. It seems to encase everyone here in a moment where time does not pass, where all things stop in their progression, in their movement, a time when this young Maiden, called Little Mary, speaks to the darkness in the voice of God. "I and my sisters give you God's blessings. We pass on to you the holy grace of God."

A small sound is heard off to the side. One of the adepts from the School of the Prophets, seated cross-legged in a position of reverence and attunement, has begun to express a small, incredibly pure, beautiful tone.

Little Mary's eyes are still closed. "Oh-h ... It is you, is it not, Isadore? I hear you. I feel the power of your faith. Oh, Editha, Mary, I see you both. You are walking hand in hand towards the One who has descended the path of light. His hands are up-stretched, and He smiles. And, Andra, here are you, as well! And Miriam," A tiny smile appears on Little Mary's face. "There are you, too, and Hannah. And here am I, and all of us. Oh, it is so sweet!" She smiles, tears streaming profusely down her face, and down all of these young faces as well, save Mary.

"Tell us what you see now, Little Mary," prompts Ruth.

"We have surrounded Him, and we are embracing Him. He touches us and bends to kiss us. And He hugs one, holds the hand of another, and we are smiling and laughing happily. He lives on! Oh-h … I am so joyful."

Now another pure tone comes from the elder Sarah off to the side, and another to the other side, and another, and another, and they are all swaying. Soon the air is filled with beautiful tones, each one reaching out to embrace and augment the other.

The young Maidens now hum their tones, their hands squeezing each other's, their shoulders leaning this way and that. Of course, it is Andra who begins to laugh, and then the others. Soon laughter is all about. As they turn to look upon one another, they excitedly share their visions, each one with the other.

After a time, Judy steps into the center of the circle. She turns 'round and around to look at each young face, her hands thrust within her garments. "What is the meaning of what we have just shared, my sweet sisters? Who would like to tell it?"

There is silence as each one smiles, looking to another, encouraging her to speak.

"I think it would be very best if our Sister, Mary, were to speak it," Hannah suggests quietly. "Through Her eyes and heart there will be the clearest expression, for She is Chosen."

Judy studies her. "Are you not also chosen, Hannah?"

"Uh … yes. All of us are. But She is the Chosen *One.*"

"Do you think that Her sight, Her understanding, Her heart is greater than your own because She is Chosen?"

"Well, in a way, we all know this, do we not?" She glances around at the others. Receiving nods of support and agreement, she looks back at Judy. "It seems apparent to us. She is the one to whom the angel came."

"We can add a great deal to what we have learned here," Judy continues, turning to look at all of the faces. "We can add a wonderful strength to what we already have if we understand the foundation of what Hannah has just spoken, with which you all have agreed. If you follow the path ahead comparing and analyzing, equating, based upon what is in the outer, you will provide an opening for the outer to come within and dwell in you."

"I do not understand," Andra interjects. "Forgive me, but I do not understand. I agree with my sister, Hannah. Mary *is* Chosen. It will be She who will bring forth the Messiah. Of course, we will be at hand. Of course, we will support and encourage Her. But She will bear Him forth. And that is my truth," Andra asserts, smiling broadly, for all know Andra's | truth is Truth.

"Well spoken, and, of course, well founded. But you miss the spirit of what I say to you." Judy answers directly, much in the manner of Andra's own demeanor. "It is the nature of reality to invite you into its bosom. It is the nature of life here in the Earth to call to you to believe it as that which *is*. And yet, you know in your own truth of Truths, Andra, that it is God that is the Source ... that God offers all of creation its right to exist. Therefore, the reality that we exist in, called life, and all those within it, are always of God ... expressions. But not *God*! Not *the* Life."

"Well, I know this. I feel it. But I also feel what I said. And I would love it if you could help me understand that, so I do not feel both things at the same time. It is very confusing."

Some of the little Sisters giggle, but not certain it is appropriate, they attempt to suppress their giggles.

Glancing around, Judy smiles. "No need to stifle laughter. For laughter is an expression of joy. And God is joy."

With that, Andra begins to laugh heartily, inciting the others, as always.

"To answer your question," Judy continues after the laughter subsides, "is to answer something so foundational that it can empower you beyond belief. We have spoken of it many times, taught it to you, shown it to you in diverse ways. Now I speak it to you on your own terms, Andra. I speak it to you in the spirit of the Truth of God."

"I like that," Andra interjects, smiling.

"We all know that, Andra," Judy retorts, and then explains, "If you believe unto that which is here," tapping her foot lightly upon the earth, "and you subjugate what you believe here," patting her chest with the palm of her hand, "then you are as a house divided. You are as a peoples with two beliefs."

"Oh, yes! And that is precisely what I feel. Help me." She looks down. Her sweet, childlike countenance is such that some in the group find it difficult to keep from rushing across to embrace her. Her head comes up, but her eyes are closed. "I am listening, my sweet teacher, with all of my being. Speak to me of this truth."

"Sweet sister Andra, you are likened unto two Andras." Judy pauses to glance around the circle, "This is, likewise, for each of you." Then she refocuses on the Maiden before her. "One Andra is the being that tastes the foods, that feels the wind, that sees the stars in this evening's sky, that feels the warmth of the campfire before her. And then there is the eternal Andra. She perceives and knows all these things as well, but she knows them also from the perspective of eternity, from the perspective of all of existence, everything, everywhere, always. It is the Andra that you go to in your dreams, and in your deepest prayers and meditations in our sacred ceremonies. It is the Andra who infills you and gives you the light that we all see. It is the Andra who loves the Truth of

God, and seeks it in and for the outer Andra every moment of every Earth day. … Look upon me, Andra."

Andra opens her eyes and looks at Judy.

"I hold up my hands now." Judy turns that all can see her hands raised to about the height of the top of her head. "Look you upon my hands. These are the hands of the Judy you see before you. Now I call upon my eternal being, the spirit eternal which is ever one with God." She pauses, bows, and nods her head ever so slightly, almost imperceptibly. Her eyes close for but a moment, and then she opens them with a firm, strong gaze at the little Sisters. "Now look you upon the hands of my spirit. Look from your spirit, as well as from who and what you are in the physical."

Very quickly there are *oo-o's* and *oh-h's*.

"Look now upon the love of God, which I radiate to this world we dwell in."

More bring their hands up to their cheeks, and sigh and *oo-o*, for the rosy-red glow all about Judy's hands is clearly evident, seemingly illuminated from within.

"And now I call upon that which is your truth, Andra. I ask God to let it be seen in my hands."

As though she is stone, Andra sits transfixed, steadily gazing upon the upraised hands of her great teacher, Judy. There are no words, only the air being pulled into her body as though breathing in the brilliant white light that now surrounds Judy's hands. Only after a prolonged moment in the stillness that follows is there the audible sound of Andra's releasing the deep breath she has taken in unknowingly. As though that has surprised even her, she begins to breathe rhythmically, with deliberation, recognizing that she, too, has stepped out of her physical form and, for a moment, even forgotten it in a curious sort of way.

"Very good," Judy continues. "Now, Andra, release your sisters' hands, and raise yours as I have."

Those to Andra's right and left relax their grip, realizing

that it has been firm on one another.

Andra raises her hands, imitating Judy.

"You do it now, Andra. It is, after all, your truth."

All are in awe, for the authoritative tone from Judy is undeniable. It is the great seer, the great prophetess, the great teacher, who now speaks, not simply one of their beloved elder sisters. It is a spokesperson of God who now commands their sister Andra to demonstrate her truth.

Without being asked, Andra rises to her feet. Her hands are up. Her eyes flicker. "I … Andra … Daughter of God … call forth Your Truth, Lord God. Let it now be one with me."

Instantly her hands are aglow with the light of God's Truth. Again, a murmur of wonder passes throughout her Sisters. But she does not stop. "I am Andra, Daughter of God. I bring my Truth, Your Truth, Lord God, to all of my Sisters." She steps away from the circle and begins to walk around its outer periphery.

Ruth, Anna, and Josie are looking at each other, tears of joy streaming. For here, one of the Maidens is claiming.

"I give you the Truth of God." Andra's hand now rests upon Hannah's head. Hannah bows and thanks her. "I give you, my sister Editha, the Truth of God." On she goes around the entire circle. She stops not, but walks up the gentle slope, blessing everyone with the Truth of God.

Finally, she turns and lowers her hands, placing them over her heart. "Have I done well, my sweet sister, Judy?" she questions, her voice soft.

Judy swallows hard, her own hands now resting upon her bosom. "You, Andra, have done very well."

"I think what we have learned here," begins Mary softly, "is something I will always cherish. I think what you have given to us, Andra, is an eternal gift. For I now promise God I shall strive to see through His eyes of Truth. I promise that I shall not waver, and follow the call of the shadow of illusion. I, Mary, Daughter of God, claim this and promise Thee, God.

This I shall bear through eternity, and I will always bless you, Andra, for what you have given us this evening."

They make room for Andra to sit beside Mary. They kiss each other and gather up one another's hands. The circle is perfect again.

"I, too, thank you. I thank you all," Little Mary adds. "I feel like a bird just set free from a cage. I can feel myself soaring. Thank you."

Each one, then, offers an insight, a comment, something that she has gained that perhaps was not addressed in the past, or not completely released.

"I feel my truth now, as well, all throughout," Editha offers gently. "I hold your hands and feel the pressure of your knees against mine, but I also feel the oneness of understanding that will help me be compassionate in all things."

The others all nod.

"Is this why Mary saw me, Judy?" questions Sophie.

"There are, perhaps, many reasons. But if you remember, as we were giving to you, when you encounter that which is out of the ordinary, different from the normal, look at it. If you look at it in the truth of joyful expectancy," Judy explains smiling at Hannah, "then you empower it to give you its gift. But if you look at the unfamiliar, the unknown, that which is out of the ordinary, with apprehension, doubt, or even fear, then it is like covering up the light within it and the gift it bears. See the difference?"

"Oh, I do!" Hannah responds vibrantly. "I like to look at things as though they are magical. I like to see things and ask myself, *I wonder why God has given me this? I wonder why God put this here on my path for me to discover?*"

"And how would you apply this," asks Ruth, "were there to be an unseen stone upon your path, and you were to stumble over it and injure yourself slightly?"

"Well," Hannah laughs softly to herself, "at first I would grumble a bit, and I would probably chastise myself for not looking where I was going. But if I fell upon the earth, perhaps injuring my shin, first I would rub it. Then I would look about, and say to myself, *Hannah, what is it that God wants you to pause and see on your journey through life?* When I have had such an event, which is not too often since I usually do not stumble over stones, you know," and the others chuckle, "I have usually discovered some very nice things that I might not have otherwise found."

"Like what?" Andra asks.

"Well … like flowers, pretty stones, interesting plants. Once when something like that happened, it was not a pebble, it was a hole in the ground," and the others chuckle again. "I just sort of laid back and I felt the warmth of the earth. As I glanced at the sun, I remember saying to myself, *Hannah, look at this.* When I put my hands on the warm earth and gathered up some handfuls, I could feel in it a little wiggly worm, and I set it free. I said, *Remember always, lots of life goes unseen, lots of beauty and warmth can be missed or forgotten.* So now, when I am not falling and I am just walking around, I remember this, and it makes me joyful because I know that the Spirit of God is bringing life to all things, all the time, even if I do not stop long enough to see it."

"Well, you see?" Ruth interjects, for, much to her delight, Hannah is obviously prepared to go on and on with examples. "It is a question of how one sees, is it not? It is the power of knowing that you have the choice to see things this way or that. True?"

The young Maidens, whose attention span has been saturated, nod, but their restlessness is beginning to show.

"Well, then, let us conclude for this evening, but not without some joyful dance." She rises swiftly to her feet and claps her hands, turning about this way and that.

This is all it takes for the Maidens to jump up as their laughter fills the air.

Some of the elder maidens begin to sing and clap their

hands, as others produce rudimentary instruments and add those tones and sounds to the joyful dance that follows.

"Is it not amazing," the first guardian comments to the second, "how transforming it is when we choose to go within to call upon God?"

The second guardian is rocking a bit, smiling, his hands upon his crossed knees, the glow of the campfire illuminating them with its beautiful multi-colored light. "It truly is. You know, while we were in prayer, I felt as though I could actually hear the young Maidens singing."

"I, as well. And right now, if I close my eyes, I can almost see them dancing. Who knows, maybe they are."

"Deep within the spirit and life-essence of each entity is a wilderness. It is the journey to this wilderness that is a part of what I call a *sacred quest*. We who have gathered together in our School as it is called, though it is not actually so, are each upon a journey into that inner wilderness because we have heard a call from within it."

The elders and seers who are gathered with Elob and his entourage are either gazing off in a different consciousness, or nodding gently as they gaze at the flames of their fire.

"I think," continues Elob, "it is the call that comes to us as a people, the call which inspires us to embrace the Promise and to prepare for His coming. I think it is the call that He hears from His present position in spirit, in oneness with God. And I think it must be His intention that His journey will lead Him to answer that call, a journey from the light into the dark wilderness of definition, a journey from the utter embrace of unlimited love, compassion, and perhaps most powerful of all, from the unwavering grace of God into finiteness."

Pausing, Elob looks around the group before his eyes fall upon the two seated across the fire from him. "I say unto you, again, Joseph, you will hear a call. Prepare yourself. And you,

Zechariah, have seen your vision, but you will hear it and know it in a way which will test you." Elob glances around the group broadly, then continues. "It will test each one of us to the core of our being. Therefore, let us oft be in joyful prayer and oneness that as one of our group is being tested, we shall know of it and journey to be at his or her side, spiritually and figuratively, so naught in the darkness can sever the bonds of our love for one another.

"I speak on behalf of my brothers and sisters, and add this to the prophecy as we have seen it of late: We have but three cycles left of the movement through the seasons, and He shall come. He will enter not here, and not in the embrace of our holy place, or in the sanctity of the Spring of Elijah, but in the wilderness itself.

"Those who are chosen must ever know that wheresoever they shall trod, wheresoever the path of life will direct them, just as we are seated here by the warmth of this flame, so is the warmth of our love ever with them. And so does it embrace Him forever. You must go forth now and you must prepare. Perhaps I shall not speak to you, nor see you with the eyes of my physical body for some time. But if you speak my name, asking of God, I, too, shall ask of God to be sent to you, and to minister unto any need and to give to it as it is mine to give. So sayeth we all."

Closing, Elob gestures broadly with his arms to include all his brothers and sisters of the great school.

Perhaps it is a curious choice of words to think of the journey through life in the consciousness of Earth as a journey into and through the wilderness. For all about you are those trappings that are creations of beauty;

all about you, as the Maidens pointed out and as Hannah stated, is the expression of the Spirit of God giving life, offering it, warming the Earth, creating that unto the need of everything. Then why call it a wilderness?

It is perhaps a good thing to reflect upon. We are not offering this here to be a question unanswered, but rather an invitation to be explored. For if you can look within your being and bring that which is greater than the wilderness from within self into the outer, then you can look upon the Earth in its entirety and say: There is wilderness here not; only the gifts of God giving life and birthing joyful expectancy.

Chapter Eight

Into the Outer World

Several months have passed. It is one of those early evenings wherein the celestial bodies have not yet made themselves known to the Earth, and darkness is all about. Surrounded as ever by the elder maidens and to the periphery by the guardians, the Maidens are speaking in low, hushed voices. The preceding weeks have been very intense, and have invoked within each of these beautiful young women a sense of self.

As is so often the case, the elder sisters, those holy maidens who are the primary mentors to these young Maidens, are offering insights.

Anna is speaking. "In this moment during the transition from day to night, when looking upon your Sisters and in the distance, the guardians, evidence of the life around the body physical is very visible."

The Maidens turn this way and that, some twisting their faces a bit as they tilt their heads and squint for a clearer view of what is being taught.

"Do any of you not see this life-force?"

The light is very subdued. No fires are present, only the scant illumination of the day reflected in this moonless sky as a curious light.

Anna, Judy, Ruth, and many others are studying the faces of their young wards.

The Maidens, too, look at one another and smile gently, for all can see that which is being asked of them, the life-force around each.

"I will now," continues Anna, "ask those who have what we call *sacred sight* to invoke it. As they do, little Sisters, look at them and see the differences in that which is the norm compared to that which shall become their light, their energy." Glancing about, Anna nods at several of her elder sisters to begin. Straightening themselves, they close their eyes.

Soon, some of the Maidens murmur quietly as the light around this one or that grows.

The elder Eloise is perhaps the brightest at the moment, having already entered into the sacred silence. The light around her is glorious to behold.

While Judy has not yet moved into this altered state of consciousness, she is nonetheless connected with the Spirit Eternal. She looks around at her companions (the elder maidens, the elder sisters, the teachers, the seers) and silently gives thanks. *I see the goodness, Lord God, in my sisters and brothers. I see the beauty and uniqueness of Your Spirit as they have summoned it from deep within. Let this and mine own light be a gift to those whom You have chosen to minister unto our Lord. Let this be a light eternal, carried within each who will partake of His teachings, His gifts. And let each of us be a part of that which we shall give unto Him who comes.*

"Have you any questions or comments, sweet sisters?" Anna asks quietly.

The Maidens are looking about, surrounded by many of their own people, barely visible in most cases and invisible in others, for they are at the outer periphery.

Little Sophie, also called Sophia, raises her hand timidly, a bit of glowing light moving upward from her body.

Anna nods to her.

Sophie points to a summit. Though it is bit of a distance away, it is clearly visible, dimly outlined against the growing light in the night sky. "Could you tell us about his light?"

All turn to look, and there in the distance stands a solitary figure. It is the guardian who is called Nathanael.

"That is the light of one whose life, whose heart, whose mind is in utter oneness with God and God's promise unto all of existence."

"I do not see much inconsistency in the light around him," Sophie continues. "His light seems to be so even. As I look at our elder sister Eloise, hers billows with beautiful colors, swirling, almost dancing on the inner light of her being."

Eloise is smiling, her eyes still closed, nodding, knowing that she has made that connection aright.

Anna studies the form dimly silhouetted, illuminated more by his own light than by any external source. She knows that Nathanael is absolutely alert, scanning the horizon, listening for any sounds of possible danger, and yet is all the while in a constant state of peaceful, joyful prayer, a state of awed oneness with God. She turns back to look at Sophie. "It is the nature of their spirit to cleave utterly, totally, unto God. So much so, perhaps, my sweet sister, that naught differentiates them from their oneness with God."

"Are you saying that that is what God would look like?"

Smiling very broadly at Judy, Anna looks down, greatly delighted at Sophie's question, and then replies. "Perhaps it is so. It is the light of God which shines through and is eternally one with this son of God we call Nathanael, who has claimed it. So in the sense of that, yes, your statement is true."

"Oh-h." Shaking her head in wonder, Sophie unconsciously reaches out with both hands to grasp the hands of the two sisters seated at her right and left. "He is so beautiful."

Again peering in the direction of Nathanael, with a deep sigh Anna affirms, "That is a truth. He is indeed beautiful. What you see around Eloise is the same, but you also see many other colors, do you not?"

Zephorah chimes in boldly, "Oh, yes. I see many colors. I see colors that are not in the Earth, colors that are majestic, perhaps like the colors God would choose to fashion a garment He might wear, maybe like the colors of life itself. For, look over here." She points to the right of Eloise.

"See the beautiful greens, and how they intermingle with the yellows and golds? And up over here, rose and beautiful blues. Why are they so different? When I look up at Nathanael, I see none of this. What is the difference?"

"Perhaps Eloise can answer that for you," offers Anna.

"Really? Would that not … you know, make her colors go away if she speaks?"

"Is that what you think, Zephorah?"

"Well, when I am in prayer and meditation, and I speak, things change. I would like to be able to speak and hold that focus but each time I try to do that, something changes."

"Well then, we shall move past that right now, Zephorah. Tell us, Eloise, what it is that is creating the beautiful colors we see around you. What are you doing? Where are you? Would you explain this to us, please."

Eloise's gentle smile and nodding head are precursive to her announcement of something the Maidens know is significant. They hold one another's hands very attentively.

"I have gone to the temple within myself," she begins. "There, I found my light, the light that God gave to create me. I claim this. Through that light, I returned here to look upon you in my heart and spirit. What you are seeing about me is the thought of you, my sweet young Sisters, and the thought of the beautiful gifts that each of you shall offer in nourishment to the life-force of the Master."

There is a stunned silence.

One of the Maidens begins to weep, and then another, and another. Soon, all are sobbing, not really knowing why, yet knowing the truth that is being given to them by an elder sister. They take it unconditionally, without question or doubt, into their own being, whereupon, as they have been taught again and again, they test it upon the table of their own truth, comparing it to that which they most honor.

Finding it to be aright, each of them begins to glow, and as they have been taught, they close their tear-filled eyes.

The clasp of one another's hands becomes very strong as they bow their heads.

A light surrounds, and encompasses them, then begins to swirl, causing many of the elder sisters to gasp, awed by the beauty and majesty of those whom God has chosen.

He stirs the embers of the campfire slowly, his eyes transfixed upon its glowing coals. It is evident that his mind and consciousness are elsewhere. With a deep sigh, Jacob looks up at the fire-illumined faces of the many who are gathered. "Unquestionably, we are approaching the threshold whereupon we must begin the involvement of some of our sweet Maidens in the outer world."

Many of the elder Essenes are obviously filled with hesitations and doubts. "I still disagree with this approach," one protests quietly. "I honor you all, but several of my brothers and I do not feel this within us to be a righteous path. My heart is heavy with the potential of what could occur. The risk to the Promise of God seems too great."

Uncharacteristically, Jacob's face is almost stern. "Then what say you, my brother, as an alternative? We have discussed this often in the past. The seers," glancing up to acknowledge their presence, "have said it must be so. How can we do one and not the other? How can we honor that which they have seen and that which is the prophecy, yet also do as you are proposing? Explain this please, dear brother." Jacob's gaze is neither threatening nor aggressive, but truly penetrates to the core. It is as though his eyes see all that one is.

Yet this brother returns a gaze equal to Jacob's. "Why

can it not be that the prophecy is honored, but on a different path? Is it not possible to bring the truths and righteousness of the Maidens into focus without making them vulnerable?"

"They must experience the outer world," Joseph explains, "in order to truly know what lies before our Lord. To best prepare Him, they must understand the contrast. Look you about, Bartholomew. See you any such contrast here?"

Jacob's eyes have not left Bartholomew. While he sees this not as a challenge, he does sense within that the pathways here still are not fully united. The pathway being proposed by Bartholomew, while born of truth, love, and the celebration of oneness with God, carries with it the essence of fear. This concerns Jacob, for he knows that the seeds of fear are like the weeds in the fields. They can grow quickly, spread, and take root deep and long. Knowing this, he seeks to forestall their growth, even to eliminate them, at whatever cost.

"It can be taught," Bartholomew argues. "We can bring those from the outer world here, and it can be taught. We can create an environment that is, in effect, a simulation of what exists beyond, and all the while preserve our sweet Maidens in the absolute security of our embrace and in the strength of those who watch over us. Out there," he gestures with an arm pointing off to the horizon, "they are vulnerable."

Jacob keeps his eyes fixed upon Bartholomew. "How many of you feel as he does?"

A number of hands come up here and there.

He glances at some of the elder maidens. "And you … What say you to this point?"

Ruth, whose eyes have been closed and whose face has been upturned slightly, blinks and levels her gaze upon Jacob, then Bartholomew and the others. "The faith of the Maidens is powerful, as is ours, my brothers and sisters. It is not that I, Ruth, would usurp your loving concern, brother Bartholomew, but it is that I would point to the prophecy and honor our holy seers and elders. It is clearly written in the ancient scrolls (praise God that we have recovered those) that He shall come into the world within the embrace of the wilderness. And in the words of the prophet Elijah, He comes to save those who are lost. Well, *we* are not lost." She looks up, offering a silent prayer of thanks. "We must summon our courage. We must strengthen our faith and our resolve. Above all, we must honor the prophets of old, the prophets of now, and the prophets who shall come. I feel, as do my ..."

"Sorry to interrupt," Bartholomew breaks in, causing a bit of a stir (for it is not oft done among these peoples), "but I think it is important to speak to those points before you continue on. Is it not also written and taught, dear brothers and sisters who speak and see in the Name of God, that we are to use all that we have, all that we know, as well as honor that which has gone before? Mine eye and ear see and hear that which is against us in the outer world. My mind weighs these, and even though my spirit-self is strong and sings a constant song of faith, my mind insists there is a better way. Thank you for hearing me, and I apologize for my interruption. It is not meant disrespectfully. It is meant to offer a fuller picture of that which Ruth presents. Please, continue."

Ruth is smiling that incredibly warm and beautiful smile so typical of her. "I hear and see your words in my heart. But, you see, we do not fear. We know that the prophecy is true. We have found it given in so many diverse ways which you have not had the great honor, joy, and privilege of experiencing first hand, sweet Bartholomew. Each of these Maidens is prepared, I assure you," she continues in a warm, awe-filled tone. "They are as twelve aspects of God, and yet each is complete. Though they know it not as yet, soon they shall. I say unto you I, Ruth, daughter of God, believe that we are to follow the path that has been given. If we stand aside from it out of concern, concern and fear become the seeds which we will sow."

Jacob turns to look directly at Ruth. His faint smile, a

characteristic of his commonly recognized, appears once again. As their eyes embrace, they both know that they have held the same thought: Seeds of fear and doubt cannot be sown in the garden of God's Promise.

Turning to fix his gaze upon Bartholomew again, Jacob continues. "You are truly honored, dear brother. To all of you brothers and sisters," gesturing about, "who share this concern, I say unto you, I, Jacob, have no fear. I shall go forth with them, and I shall give all that I am to their preservation. Now, it must be that a decision is made. Final. We can have no more differences in agreement, even subtle ones, upon the path and the one ideal. How say you, Bartholomew?"

Bartholomew's sigh is so heavy and so deep that all can hear it in the silence that follows. His head bows, and he looks down, obviously going within for a moment, for he is well versed in inner works. Moments later, with another deep sigh, his head comes up. The soft glow of the fire's flame highlights the glistening drop of moisture in the corner of one eye. "I am not complete with this, Jacob. I cannot find it within to be in agreement. A part of me calls out that there is a better, safer way. I honor all of you, but ..." turning to look at the seers and prophets, "I must speak only in truth, for this is a work of God's truth. God seest within me. If I speak not my truth, then I blaspheme against Him."

Jacob's gentle smile reveals his honor for Bartholomew.

To the surprise if not shock of some present, with deliberation, almost laboriously, Bartholomew stands. He clenches the fingers of his right hand, outstretches it and brings his fist against his chest, striking it repeatedly. Then, he brings his arm out, opens his hand, and stretches the palm up to God. "I give my heart to Thee, Lord God. All that I am is Thine. I am Thy instrument. I pray Thee that it ever be so in my actions, words, and deeds. I must depart, Jacob, as thou knowest." Jacob nods. "Any of my brothers and sisters who yet hold this doubt within, I call to you ... Let us not remain and be that which in any degree minimizes the agreement of our brothers and sisters here. For their work and their path are great enough without their having a moment's doubt that all with them are as one in the ideal, the intent, and every facet of the plan and work before them.

"This I say to all of you, my brothers and sisters: I journey to the outer world, but I am with you and the Promise. I pray unto God that in the outer world I be guided, strengthened, and purified to be totally one with that which you hold. As this is born within me, I shall return. But until then, I shall stand aback, ever with you and always only a call away. I shall be as another pair of eyes and hands of God, watchful that no harm shall befall those who will nurture the Promise." He brings his hands together and bows, first to Jacob, who nods, speaking not, and then to Joseph, Zechariah, Benjamin, and all the others.

Not another word is spoken. Bartholomew turns and strides off, his presence absorbed into the folds of darkness lying beyond the periphery of the small flame's light. Almost inaudibly, several others rise, gesture in the manner as has Bartholomew, and also move off into the darkness.

Silence with an intense sense of loss and grief permeates the night. Many are seated, heads bowed, hands together. Some are moving their hands to and fro as though to bring the Spirit of God into the center of their being. Several of the elder holy maidens have clasped hands and are rocking.

The silence continues until broken by Elob.

"If you feel a sense of loss," he begins with quiet deliberateness, "then that is an illusion. For that which you hold in your heart in utter love can never be lost, lest you never truly loved it. If your love for another, for a work, for an ideal or a purpose, is complete, it cannot be broken. Even though a loved one might depart in what would seem as disagreement, they are not gone. If you grieve to any degree for their absence from you, then you begin a journey upon a path that has at its destination many things that are not of the light. So must we all in these very moments rejoice, not grieve."

A small voice comes from one of the elder sisters seated off to the side. "I know the truth of your words, dear brother Elob. Yet, there is pain here," she gestures to her chest, "for these are my brothers and sisters gone." She looks down.

"Look you upon the past," Elob continues, fully comprehending and feeling what this sweet Essene maiden feels. "Have you not a sense of loss for it? Do you not long to stand before those who have gone before and hear them and see the incredible light of their souls as they delivered unto us the prophesies that we honor and follow this day?

"Only a short walk from this very place is where our elder brother stood and taught and gathered others and shared with them the truths of God. His Healing Spring yet brings forth the pure waters from the wilderness of life. Inexplicably, they flow today as they did then. We can only suppose how this could be so. If you see with the eyes of spirit, you will see that water as one and the same with the waters of love that embrace you and your brothers and sisters who are now departing. Insofar as one cannot stem the waters of Elijah's Spring, neither can the waters of your love for Bartholomew, and all your brothers and sisters departed, ever be stemmed, lest you make it so."

The maiden nods, her face somewhat softened, comforted. For Elob's words ring true within her. "Thank you. It is passing. I know that we shall all be together again. I guess it is the call from … well, I do not know, the call from something within that finds joy and comfort in oneness physically, as well as in oneness eternally."

Elob smiles and nods. "Ah-h. We will teach you to transcend that, as the holy Maidens have already been taught. The doubts of Bartholomew and the others have validity in the sight physical. Even as their sight spiritual and eternal tells them not to be concerned, they yet struggle. And they know, which is testimony to their utter oneness with us and the Promise, that the waters of God's Promise must flow pure and unobstructed if they are to manifest in finiteness as they do at their source."

"Are we all prepared?" questions Joseph of the sisters and maidens who are busily gathering those things that are needed for the journey.

"Well ..." Anna scratches her head pensively. "I suppose when we are an hour's distance on our journey, I will remember something," and she laughs. "But as best we know, we are more than prepared. We are sumptuously prepared." She laughs again.

Judy has just walked up, and hearing Anna's laughter, smiles broadly. She glances over at Joseph. "Greetings on this beautiful new day, brother Joseph. Are you well?"

"I am well, but as some of your little Sisters would say, I have some *fluttery things* inside."

All near Joseph laugh at this commonly referred to saying that the Maidens gave to all of their people.

"Fluttery things are sometimes good," Judy responds. "They bring one to see what is and to see what is not. Do you not agree, dear brother?"

He smiles widely, knowing full well not to carry this any further, for the prowess of the great teacher Judy is known throughout all of the tribes. "I accept your great wisdom." Sighing deeply, he looks around. "I did not really think this day would come. But I guess it has."

"It is a beginning of a sort, would you not say?"

"It is, indeed, a beginning, Ruth," laughs Joseph. "You know, it is like having nursed a motherless animal, raising it to a point where there comes that day you know it must go forth and be what it is. Still, there is the concern. You want to stand and watch and protect it. You can quickly forget that you gave it strength to endure, that you have taught it how to fend for itself, how to see danger and deal with it. As with such a hand-raised creature, the question arises: *Is there something I forgot? Something I could have done and didn't?"*

"I like to call that a circular path of fruitlessness," Jacob interjects with a bold laugh. "You can go around in a circle of question and doubt and preparation until you are deep in a hole that you have dug yourself by repeating the same things over and over again. I personally like to stride forth and to find what is needed, given by God, at each turn of the way. And I need not remind you, Joseph, of the power of that kind of thinking."

Joseph nods at his dear brother and laughs with him. "Ah, yes. Well, I have not forgotten the comments from Elob, Zelotese, and many of the others. I do not as yet understand them, but I have seen the truth in Zechariah's dreams and visions. He is so at one with God and so knowledgeable of the teachings, it is wondrous! I thank God for his presence. But what shall *I* give here other than, of course, that which is what we all give? I mean outwardly."

Jacob laughs again. "Well, I suppose if we go meet the experience, the experience will tell us. And perhaps, God has gifts awaiting us, properly positioned along the path ahead if we would but walk upon it." Jacob smiles, shifting his grasp upon his shining staff.

They walk along slowly, the dust from the dry earth swirling up and collecting on the hems of their garments. They are in a long file as they head towards the Great Sea.

Anna speaks gently to Jacob. "It is always a fluttery thing to be heading off into the outer world. You know, no matter how much I have seen and learned, no matter how many times God gives me His great gifts, I know that at the end of this journey lies the application and testing of those gifts."

"Ah, yes. And the opportunity to serve, too, great teacher Anna."

Anna laughs as they shuffle along. "Yes, that is true, and I know there will be opportunities to serve aplenty."

"Do you remember any of the city? Can you remember … I mean, you know … any specifics?"

Mary closes her eyes briefly as they walk. "I can remember some. Some I see in my prayers. Do you not, Zephorah?"

"Yes, in my prayers, but my mind has only dim pictures anymore. I do remember voices and sounds and smells, though, and I am excited to see if my memory is correct."

Mary looks at her with a loving smile. "I am sure it is. You have such a keen memory." She reaches across to take Zephorah's hand reassuringly, and so they walk.

Much like the first, another column is moving to the east along a different path, so that there shall not be too great a number in any one entourage.

"What do you see, Judy? Are there visions given to you that you could share with me at this time?"

She glances over at him. "Many, my brother, many. But in of all of them, I see a time of … She pauses. "I guess what I am attempting to convey is that we will have to work some to adapt to what they in the outer world consider to be normal ways of living. Also, when we do meet, it will need to be in secret, being very guarded."

Judy notes the presence of one guardian some distance from their group, trodding silently alone at the periphery, keeping watch, and to the other side, another one. She knows that to the front others lead the way. Inhaling deeply, she turns to look at Joseph who is looking straight ahead. She thinks in her heart, *This is not only a journey to bring some of the Maidens to their proper position, but it is a journey for you, Joseph, as Elob said … to bring you to your destiny.*

Ruth busies herself, but there is an emptiness, not just because of the physical absence of so many of her beloved brothers and sisters, but because her participation in the present unfolding of the Promise is not as active as it has been in times leading up to this.

Her hands are busy cleansing the utensils from the midday meal. In her spirit, she sees the groups moving along their pathways. She can feel the anticipation, the questions, and all that which each is holding. She is so close to her sisters, Anna, Judy, and the many others, that when she blinks, for a moment she believes she sees as they see, and it gladdens her heart in a curious way. Yet, she knows her time is passing. Her gift to the Promise is coming to an end.

Turning to place the pot she has cleaned with the others, she is nearly nose-to-nose with a wondrous pair of deep brown eyes. "Greetings, sister Ruth. Is there joy in your day?

Startled, she drops the pot before she can speak, but Zelotese moves in swiftly and recovers it. "Joy is rather like that, is it not? One moment you have it in your hands, and the next moment it is gone. But you see, here?" He extends the pot to her. "I return it to you, just as I know you can return to them whenever you so desire."

"Thank you, sweet brother," she responds quietly. "It is as the journey, itself … No matter how much one knows, no matter how much one's spirit cleaves unwaveringly to the Spirit of God, some of the sweetest moments in the journey through this wilderness called life are those we would ever hold around us. And when portions of that sweetness are removed from us, there is the after-effect such as I now feel."

"I, too."

"You?"

"Yes, I, too. For we are in the instrument of God's plan, this physical body, and that instrument is intended to feel. Just as our bodies give us experience through smells, sights, sounds, taste, and touch, so is it the beautiful design of God's plan and will that it be so. And we, as His Children, make it so. If we paused not to experience through these gifts of God, what purpose would there be to the journey? All about us, even as we speak, sweet Ruth, are those who are without the instrument of manifestation called flesh. Yet, they walk with us. Thou knowest this to be true."

Ruth nods.

"Then let us be their instrument," Zelotese concludes. "Let us be that through which they, too, can in this moment feel, and know, and see, smell, and taste ... and be."

Ruth's smile is such so as to melt away the hardest heart. She says naught, but the softness of her eyes causes him to raise his arms, and she walks the several paces between them to rest herself in the embrace of the warm love and tender caress of this brother called Zelotese.

His stride is unmistakable, its surety and bearing announcing, *Here is the guardian Nathanael.*

The entourage slows, and Jacob comes to the fore.

"We are close," Nathanael tells him. "It may be well to make our encampment here that we can enter in the light of pre-dawn."

"Is all well before you?"

"It is well. From what we know from our brothers and sisters who are already in place, there is a general sense of ease. There does not seem to be any cause for concern or alarm, though we note that there will be a few challenges in acquiring facilities and such. But several of the adepts have already begun the process of this acquisition. God's blessings upon them and our thanks to God for their presence."

Jason has walked up to stand beside his brother. Picking up the conversation, he reaffirms to Jacob and the others that all appears to be well, and that, just over the rise, there is a wadi, a sheltered place where the encampment can be made.

To the east, the same is unfolding. They are gathering together, sharing foods and such, and resting their bodies.

"I wonder what the others are doing right now."

"They are well, Joseph," Judy assures him.

"Have you … you know, seen them?"

She blinks her eyes slowly and deliberately. "I have seen them. I *am* seeing them."

Joseph smiles broadly and nods. "And the Maidens? How are they?"

Judy, too, smiles, a warm stirring light beginning to glow within as the thought occurs to her, *On some level, he knows.*

"These must be quarters which have protection on three sides," Elob directs several of his brothers and sisters. "And make them down the way, over there. He'll need a place where He can do His work and become accepted. So, separate chambers will be needed for the living and separate for the works. Look you. Along this way, I see in my mind's mind that there is a potential here."

The adept nods. Gesturing to the others, they stride off soundlessly.

"Make the way passable that they can procure according to their need."

So, Elob continues. Finally, glancing about, confident that he and his brothers and sisters have done all they know to do, he turns to several of those closest to him.

"Let us go to the temple. Let us celebrate in the presence of the ancients. Let us give honor to the teachings of old. And let us rejoice! For in a time not too distant ahead, He, Himself, will walk upon the stones of that temple, and speak the Truth of God."

As one walks upon a pathway and knows not what lies ahead, there is always the question: What shall become of me?

To the extent that one has made all things aright within, then that question begins to fade. In its place come the questions: What gifts can I give? Where can I be of service? And the prayer thereafter might be: Lord, guide Thou me to hear the call, to see the need that I might gift unto it in the joy of service in Thy Name.

As you have seen Mary approaching the altar of life itself, not unlike the altar of the temple upon which She stood when the light descended on Her, so is it also true that the light will descend on Her as She stands in the midst of what has been called the wilderness, and becomes an island of light. And with those who gather about Her, and who hold equally the joyful anticipation of the Promise's manifestation, so is there ever cause to rejoice.

Though the way may be hard, the path difficult, it is the journey's end that one does well to ever hold in mind and heart. And if at that end there is the opportunity to serve but one, all that has been endured is purposeful and righteous for that one.

It is a good time in the Earth to begin to think much in this same manner: I have looked into my heart and spirit, and seen the good-

ness of God therein. I have explored this. I have learned of it. I have strengthened it. I have lived it. And now, as I journey into the expression of finiteness called life, I am filled to exception with joy for the opportunity to give of it.

Bring forth that which gladdens your heart, and celebrate it. And as ye find a brother or sister doing the same, clasp their hand and celebrate together. For one voice can sing out and call the Spirit, and that is good; but many voices joined together in song can call the Spirit of God into manifestation. So is it, here, that we have joined our voices together. We are with you as you do the same.

Chapter Nine

Joseph Is Called

To Zephorah the first rays of light all seem different as she views them coming over the tiered rooftops of the city.

It is evident that there is a longing in her, yet it is equally evident that she is striving to balance with this.

She feels the touch of a warm, gentle hand upon her shoulder and turns to gaze into Elizabeth's smiling eyes. She knows Elizabeth is aware of what she is feeling. Then she hears Mary's soft voice as She offers a prayer unto God as though reaching out to call the new day into being, to call it into birth.

In the preparation that follows, there is much discussion, and many of the Expectant Ones come and go, for the celebration of matrimony is a momentous event, of course. But this celebration is moreso, for Zechariah's vision is now being fulfilled and underscored. Having visited the Holy Mountains and having conferred with the seers and such, it has been confirmed: He is to wed Elizabeth, who has been in training in one of the other encampments to the north.

The joy that follows as some of these Sisters of light are reunited after this long absence is remarkable. Excitedly, they speak of many things. They speak of the light of God as it shines upon them and manifests in so many unique ways. They delight in exploring their capacity to call upon their own spirits to manifest many wondrous works. Yet there is piety, reverence, and the knowledge that this ability is not merely for their joy and amusement, but is a tool to be contributed to the work that lies ahead.

As Mary and Zephorah question Elizabeth and the other Sisters who have returned from the distant encampment, they compare much that they have studied, and find it to be the same. Their laughter can be heard all about as they discuss their discoveries and the many little journeys into what might be called awareness.

The elder Josie comes to stand before them, smiling, arms outstretched. They rise swiftly to their feet and rush to her for her embrace. She wraps an arm about Elizabeth and gives her a hug. "It is so good to see you all together again, and to see the Promise unfolding right here and now."

"Oh-h!" responds Zephorah, holding Mary's hand in hers. "We are so joyful to be with you again. We have oft spoken of you. Your visits were so few, but we hold them within as jewels in the crown of our love."

Jason swiftly joins Nathanael as the approaching group is detected.

Leaning upon his stout staff, Nathanael watches, his eyes intensely focused upon the group, discerning whether or not to call out to his brothers, the guardian warrior priests, or whether these men are merely travelers.

As the group comes more into view, he notes that to the forefront is Bartholomew and some of those who had departed with him. But several others follow behind.

An expression of concern crosses Nathanael's brow. He glances at Jason, who nods, indicating that he, too, does not recognize the group following Bartholomew.

When the distance between them has shortened enough, Bartholomew gestures the Essene greeting to Nathanael and calls out. "Greetings, my brother. It is I, Bartholomew, and these with me are of the Zealots, whom we have brought for council. It is a passage of peace, not one to cause concern."

Again, Nathanael glances at Jason who looks quickly at him, then back at the group, and nods at Nathanael, his face softening.

Soon they are all gathered beside a small cookfire, which has been quickly prepared. As they sip a warm drink, Nathanael and Jason listen to Bartholomew.

"In the many months since we have departed, we have had opportunity to explore, to listen and to learn much, and we have discovered these, our brothers, doing much the same." He gestures to the group seated around them. "It is our intent to ask the elders for permission that the Zealots and we might form a group to watch over the work being done in the outlands, specifically to serve with you and your brothers. Since the Zealots are integrated into the community quite comfortably, well accepted, they can be of great service to the Promise, and we can be of service to them."

"What would be the request of our service?" Nathanael's eyes are clear and penetrating, as he looks over each one in the group, as though his spirit somehow reaches out to feel the essence of each.

To his left, off just a bit, is Jason, doing much the same, both of them cradling their stout staffs in their laps.

"They, too, follow a promise of a sort," responds Bartholomew. "They believe, and their seers tell them, that there will come a leader and that he will help us, God's children, to drive off the invaders, to cast away that which desecrates the Name of God."

"Is it not true that they seek to do this by force?" Nathanael gazes so strongly at Bartholomew that it causes him to shift his weight, though he knows very well that Nathanael is a priest first and a warrior second.

"It is not, perhaps, best for me to speak for them." Turning, Bartholomew gestures to one in the forefront with a youthful-appearing body, but whose face and countenance seem aged, evidencing that there have been many struggles. To his side is a young lad, perhaps seven to eight cycles.

The Zealot brings his hands together and nods in a gesture of devotion to God, different from the Essenes, but, nonetheless, obviously honorable. As though a reflection of his father, the young lad does the same.

Nathanael and Jason, in respect, gesture in return to the Zealot.

"It is purposeful for us to understand one another," the Zealot begins. "And it is purposeful for us to align ourselves wheresoever we can to support and encourage the Name of God as it is to be reborn in God's own lands."

Nathanael pulls his staff up in the crook of one arm and presses the length of his other forearm and hand upon it, as though the connection with this instrument, which, to the guardians is a near holy symbol of service, somehow also enables him to make a more complete connection with God. With his chin upon the back of the arm that rests on the staff, he nods. "Please continue."

"We are well established. We are many in number, and yet others come from the distant villages. We believe that we shall bring forth a leader who shall be of such stature and strength so as to unite our peoples. I remind you, we are not distant from you. Though our beliefs have taken us on different pathways, we nonetheless hold the same basic tenets as do you and your peoples."

"What would you have us do?" Jason interjects.

"We do not expect you to join us in the literal sense, for we know and honor your prophecies. All we would ask of you is that you understand and know ours, and that you would see us as kindred souls. That as we have occasion to serve and protect one another, perhaps giving shelter or aid, we might be permitted to so do."

"You do not ask of us, then, to serve with you in conflict?" questions Jason further.

"No. Bartholomew has clearly defined to us what your purposes and works are."

Both Jason and Nathanael quickly focus their gaze upon Bartholomew. Their unspoken question being self-evident to him, he subtly shakes his head in silent response. *No, I have not given away any of our truth. I have betrayed nothing.*

Jason and Nathanael cast a quick glance at one another, but it is as though they have conversed at great length, for as they turn to face the group before them again, they are different. It is clear that they are of one mind and purpose.

Nathanael begins. "Our path is clear. Our service to God is long-standing, and we are joyful that you know our standing and the singleness of our mind, heart, and spirit in service to God. And we speak for our people in this regard, that insofar as we serve those who are in need whom God brings to us, so do we offer ourselves; that, as there is a need or want that we can attend to in the work of healing, or prayer, or service that does not bear an arm against another, so shall we do. This we give to you as our pledge. We ask naught of you, and what we offer to you is that which we offer universally in God's Name. That this might be clear: It is not a gift given in barter, or trade, but our universal pledge of service in God's Name. I believe that you know this of us."

The Zealot nods. "This we do know. We do not ask you to rise when we rise or to serve in the manner in which we will undoubtedly serve. But there may be that occasion when one in our group is in need of shelter, of nourishment. We gladly accept your offering of healing and prayer, for we know the power and wonder of what you offer. Will you also provide sanctuary for those of our group should the need arise? We know that you have positioned some of your people within various communities, that you have dispatched others to the east and north. We, too, are there and, thus, we offer our services along those routes and in those places. We ask only, will you give us sanctuary should we have need?"

Again, Jason and Nathanael look to one another.

"We shall need to confirm this, of course," states Jason, "but I believe we can do this though only to the extent that so doing does not place in jeopardy any of our own works or those we have positioned, in particular those we know you are aware of ... those who shall nourish the Promise."

"Good enough," the Zealot nods. "We seek only to serve God. We seek naught for ourselves in the sense that the outsiders do. We do not wish to dominate, but to free our peoples. Unto that, we give you our word."

"There is the potential for great loss," Jason begins, "and many years of conflict. We must caution you in this regard, for my brothers and I have seen this often. In our meditations, we have seen the cloud billowing, rolling towards us. Since we have asked of God and our prophets, we know your intent and that there is the potential that you will cause much strife. We would ask of you to be cautious in the lands that we shall identify to you, for these will be places of holy work. Be sparing in your activities where we have positioned our Maidens and those who are to guide them. Will you grant us this?"

An authoritative air has come over Nathanael and Jason such that many of the Zealots look at one another, for the underlying ferocity is unmistakable; these two and their brothers will defend what they are saying. An essence emanates from them like a spring storm forewarning those around of its approach: Be at the ready, the power comes.

Nathanael and Jason are fully aware of this reaction and in the greater sense have called it forth. For while the abilities of their bodies (which are of notable stature) seem limitless, so complete are they in service to God and their people that it is almost as though what one sees first in them is the very intention of the Word of God; as though were they to speak it, all before them, person or otherwise, would immediately submit. Such is the intensity that these warrior priests can command. And the Zealots have now seen it.

There is a brief conferring among what appear to be some of the Zealot leaders. "We agree," the lead one responds, turning to smile at the guardians.

"Then it is done. As we said, we shall confer with the elders to confirm this and then dispatch someone to communicate it to you, Bartholomew, and you can relay it to the Zealots."

Bartholomew nods.

A few of the Essenes have come down from the Holy Mountains, as is typical at this time in the day's transition. Somehow having known of the greater number gathered, they have brought added foodstuffs and are busily proceeding to serve all those gathered.

"It shall not be me," Mathias states, "for I am called to return to our own village."

Nodding, Benjamin looks at the exhausted figure before him. "We have seen this, Mathias, and we honor you. It is our prayer that the movement of you and your peoples," gesturing to them, "will be a separation only in the physical sense. That having explored the Promise together, we now hold it as a light in our hearts, and because of this we shall be as one no matter where we might each be dwelling physically."

Mathias smiles and glances around his people. "It is not that we hear a different call. It is, as we have so oft discussed, that we see it as having some differences in its manifestation."

"Understood." Benjamin then turns to the seer, Zumada, and asks her to speak.

Rising, she comes over to where these revered elders and seers are gathered and kneels with two handmaidens, one positioned to either side of her. She reaches her hands out and takes one of each of theirs in her own. "I and my sisters have done as you have asked of us, Benjamin. We have looked, and we have seen the paths move. Enos is to be followed by you, Aristotle. And Mathias, we have seen your light leading your people into goodness.

"We have seen, as well, that when the Promise is manifest here, and our Lord is walking upon the Earth, there will be great times of testing among our people. The patterns move and show us the movement of other energies crossing the lines of light as we cast them. We consulted with Elob and the others of the great School and, to the greater extent, they have confirmed this vision." She glances across the group to meet the eyes of Elob, who has been seated silently, as though his consciousness is only partially present. An impressive array of his people, brothers and sisters who follow the light of the prophets in the great School, is gathered with him. All their faces are aglow with an energy, an excitement, yet there also seems to be a hint of crosscurrents.

Zumada nods to Elob, who blinks an affirmation. His body, though evidentially relaxed and comfortable, is positioned in an attitude of reverence, clearly connected with his spirit self.

Glancing about, still holding the hands of her sisters to her right and left, whose heads are bowed, Zumada continues. "It is important for all of us, we have seen, to oft revisit our oneness and, in those times, to set aside anything which would call to us to be separate. Like artisans each having their own talents and abilities, such as the one who makes the bricks and the one who hews wood for the roof, would see themselves as brothers and sisters called together unto the common purpose of construction, so would we all hold foremost that through which we see all else: the joy, the hope, the wonder, of the Promise to come."

There is absolute silence.

Now Elob begins. "One path has already been seen and is now opened, given unto him in vision, in dream, and, humbly given, in consultation by us: Zechariah has taken unto his household the maiden called Elizabeth from the northern tribe. As many of you are aware, having known her during her visits here to the Holy Mountains and the Sacred Spring, she bears the light of God and is as equally skilled and trained as our own beautiful Maidens.

"There remains yet the proclamation of the Path, and we are at the ready to offer it. Anna is knowledgeable of this, and has returned from her journey to bear it. But we are honored to speak it to you, and we do so now that there shall be the gifting of our love through prayer and meditation, that this can surround them and the glory of God that is to be born through them:

"I have previously spoken to one (though his spirit already knew) that a time shall come which shall test him to his spirit. Some of you have seen this, as well, in our brother … Joseph." As Elob glances about, some eyes flicker, some brighten, a few faces smile softly, for most have noted the growing bond that Joseph feels for the young Maiden, Mary.

"He shall form a covenant with God as he claims his own spirit's light. Anna shall journey, guarded by some of our group and the guardians, to announce it to him, though we have been told that God shall send His own messenger. Anna, our sweet sister," turning to raise a hand in a gesture of respect to her, "finds this to be so. Therefore, all is aright, and the Word has been honored in the Earth once again. We speak it to you here now, that it will bring the truth of our words and the righteousness of our oneness with God to the forefront of your minds. And we ask you, as you see it unfold in the days ahead, to let this be the staff, the strength, upon which you rest when you are challenged." Elob nods, indicating that he is finished. His face becomes peaceful and serene, his eyes soften, and most know he is back in communication with the light within.

Rising, Anna gestures to all. With her hands upon her heart, she looks warmly upon Mathias and his people. "Oh, how I long in my heart," she begins softly, "that I might always be with you, physically walking at your side, hearing your words in my ears, singing songs together and dancing arm-in-arm with you. But as with you, sweet brother Mathias, and all of you, my brothers and sisters, I have a call. As brother Elob pointed out, on behalf of the great School and on behalf of the Promise, I will bear the prophecy, though I know he will have heard it before I arrive. Then I shall remain in the outland to serve as our God calls upon me, that I might offer the gift of confirmation when He is brought to mine temple.

"Many of you, these eyes," gesturing to her face, "will never behold again. Let me drink in the love of you." Gently, with an aura of brilliance around her as she does so, she raises her right arm and hand, the fingers loose, her other hand upon her heart, and directs her hand to point to each one present. Slowly, her eyes connect with each brother and sister. In what seems but a moment, she lowers her arm, placing her other hand over the first, upon her heart.

"I am one with you all through eternity. We are all one with the Word of God. The work that lies ahead must be seen as joyful. Let us all oft celebrate it, as we honor the new day. And as we revere the coming of oneness with God at the edge of night, let us sing the song of praise that our God has so graciously given unto us all … that we have the opportunity to open, without limit, our hearts, minds, and spirits to one another. What a treasure! And here," she pats her chest, "I hold that treasure of you forevermore."

She bows her head in a silent prayer, then brings her hands up to gesture the Essene maiden's gesture of oneness. Then, she steps to Aristotle, bending to place a hand upon his head. "Thou art a bright light, my brother. Guide well, ever from the wellspring within. Call that forth. I am with you."

He reaches up to clasp Anna's hand and gently kisses it. "The strength of your spirit, sweet sister, is the line of light that shines upon my path ahead. It is straight and bright. I pledge to you, I shall walk along it, and it alone."

Stopping to pause a moment before each of the elders, seers, and prophets, Anna turns to stand before Zumada, who reaches up her hands, and they clasp, smiling.

As she turns to stride down the hillside, several from the School rise to their feet silently and fall in behind, sworn to guide, preserve, and protect her. To the periphery, a guardian can be seen taking long strides, his gleaming staff catching the rays of the mid-day sun, another guardian to his far left.

They are lifting the garments up and down in the water, folding them, turning them, rubbing them against the rocks, speaking softly as they do.

"I miss them so much," Josie confides.

"I, too," responds Rachel.

"Well," Kelleth pats her heart, "they are in here."

"This we know," replies Hannah, "but I should like them to be right here for a little while." She pats the earth beside her. "It is wonderful, though, is it not, to have some of our sisters from the other tribes present? We love you so much, Eloise. We glory in God's name that you have returned."

Smiling softly, Eloise nods. "How many times have I seen your faces and smiled." She turns to glance at the other Maidens who are gathered, washing garments at the stream. "So many times, I and my sisters spoke of you."

"And we of you," Hannah responds.

"It is strange, though. All the while that we were exploring the strength that is the Light within each of us called our truth, there was always this curious ... Well," Eloise continues, "it was almost like a sound, but it was more a knowing that sort of hovered right up here somewhere." She raises her hand and wiggles her fingers above the back of her head.

Hannah laughs softly. "Yes, and sometimes right here," wiggling her fingers over her stomach.

"But now," Rebekah chimes in, "it really has begun. Zechariah has fulfilled his vision. Who would have thought that our sister Elizabeth would be given unto him?"

"In these past years that she and I spent together in study," Eloise comments, "I know her spirit to be so beautiful, so bright."

"We agree with this," replies Kelleth. "It is only that there is something different here now, something I did not understand before. It is rather like being told again and again what lies beyond that mountain over there. Until you go see it for yourself, you do not truly know it. Now I feel we are truly knowing it."

"What was it the seer said?" Eloise asks softly. "And now, more than a cycle has past! What do we have remaining before He comes? One cycle? One and a portion?"

Looking down, Little Mary comments, "I think it not even a full cycle, personally. I feel it, here," striking her chest.

"Oh-h, and our sweet Mary!" adds Hannah, "What must She be feeling? What must Her thoughts be?"

"Each of them is in their proper position," Jacob begins.

"Are their needs met? Do they have any wants?"

"No, Nicodemus. As best I can perceive, all is well and complete. There has been considerable visiting between the Maidens and their parents who are in the villages and towns, and the parents have visited those who have been kept in the sanctuary of our holy place."

"Well, what is it I sense about you, then, Jacob? You seem unlike your normal nature."

"I have, I suppose," he answers pensively, "heard a call inside. I will journey on the morrow to visit Joseph. I think the time is nigh."

Nicodemus seems to drift away. His eyes become still, glassy and fixed. Then, he takes a deep long breath. His eyes flutter closed and he looks down as he exhales. "Oh, my brother Jacob ... I pray we have done all we know to do. I cannot help but on occasion visit the complete prophecy. I have had a vision of late, of pleading for Him. Mind you, my resolve is not weary, but, Jacob, I know whereof you speak. It is as the foods prepared which are both bitter and sweet, which challenge the one taking them into their body, could this truly be good or is it bad? How can a thing be bitter and sweet at one time?"

Straightening his shoulders, Jacob becomes erect. A gentleness comes over him as he looks lovingly at this brother of his who has been so separated from all the gladness and joy, from all the celebrations and wonders, the laughter and song that he, Jacob, has been privileged to share with the sweet Maidens along with their brothers who soon will begin their own individual soul work. "I have no words to tell you how much I admire and love you, Nicodemus. You are often, as you have always been, in my prayers and heart."

Looking up and smiling, Nicodemus leans over to take Jacob's outstretched hand. "Well then, my brother, we now know that we share a mutual admiration, for my love of you and my prayers for you are, just so, the same. Now, to use your own words, might we have a bit of song? And I have prepared a special meal in your honor." He turns and claps his hands. Several come bearing foodstuffs of sweetness and goodness, as Jacob's rocking body and smiling face foretell the coming of his melodious gift of song.

Seated upon a small stool, cradling his face in his hands, Joseph is moaning softly. "Oh-h ... oh, Lord God! Can it be true? Was it mine own mind, or Your messenger?"

Hearing a sound at the portal of his abode, he looks up to see his sister Anna standing in it, bright-faced, and behind her, several others. In a single, fluid motion, he leaps to his feet and rushes to embrace her.

When all have come in and are settled, and warm teas and a bit of foodstuffs have been offered, along with prayers, Anna and Joseph move to the nearby courtyard.

"And what new light is in your life these days, dear brother?" questions Anna softly, her beautiful round eyes encouraging him, embracing him with anticipation.

Joseph fidgets, moving this way and that and looking all about.

Finally, he straightens himself, summoning up the kind of strength that his position holds among his people, one of authority, one of respect. "A messenger of God has told me … I, Joseph … am to take Mary to wife."

If that which is found on your path of life exceeds what you expect, would you contemplate your worthiness to accept it? Or could you, in that moment of reflection, evolve a decision that this is given of God?

Can you with equal surety, pausing in the path of life to, in God's Name, lift one who has fallen and lies injured upon the earth with naught beholding her, accept that which is given of God to thee, thyself, that is greater than you think possible? The majesty of the gifts God ever offers is boundless; thus, it cannot fully be known. For how can you know a thing that has no boundary?

What would you do if a messenger of God came unto you and called your name, stating,

*'Rejoice, for a great gift is given unto thee.'
Would you be of stout heart and good cheer,
and fall not into the shadow of doubt or question? Would you cleave only unto the light and
goodness of the gift of God? Unto each, dear
friends, is given according to that which can
be received.*

*If you open your spirit and the sight therein, you will be able to see that far greater gifts
have been offered to you than you have been
able to conceive of. A time just ahead is one of
these. If you know it, and you await it, you
create a path for it to flow to you.*

*Regardless, yet shall it come unto those
who do not. Unto thee it is given as a part of
His Promise. Be, then, as Joseph: filled with
joy and expectancy.*

Chapter 10

Anticipation

Zechariah is seated across from Joseph, elbows upon his knees, hands clasped, eyes looking intently, but gently into Joseph's. "To a degree, I understand. And I know only too well what you are feeling, Joseph."

Smiling, knowing that this brother has, indeed, walked upon this path shortly before him, Joseph gazes upon Zechariah and nods, his eyes somewhat glazed but his smile one of joyful expectation. "I am grateful for your reassurance and support." There is a long pause, then, "After all these years of watching them grow from childhood to their current state, now here we are, you and I, a goodly number of years past theirs, yet we are chosen!" He speaks with incredulity.

"Well, who among our people would hold them in greater reverence than we? Who among us would offer them that which they shall need in the years ahead? I know you, Joseph. I know your strength. I know your faith, and I also know both are being tested this very moment." Zechariah smiles broadly.

Joseph nods and bows his head. "Will you pray with me?"

Zechariah extends a hand, resting it upon Joseph's shoulder, as they offer a few moments of silent prayer.

Joseph then lifts his hand to place it equally so upon Zechariah's shoulder, and they study one another.

Finally, Zechariah states, "It is time."

"It is time," Joseph responds.

They stand, embracing for several prolonged moments, patting one another upon the back in gestures of support before moving off to join the others.

Anna comes to accompany Zechariah to the temple.

The ceremony is simple, entirely in accord with the law. Few are present, yet there is the feeling of an immensity of unseen entities and forces. The prevalence of the Light is unmistakable, shining upon them … embracing them, so it would seem, in the Light of God, Itself, as Zechariah and Elizabeth are joined in oneness.

A curious stillness is upon the desert, the sun not yet giving any indication of its birth into the new day.

Their number is great as they walk two by two in a long file, heading towards the Sacred Springs.

"It is difficult for me to comprehend that the time is nigh."

Elob, striding in long steady paces, glances down, then up, looking all about the predawn sky. "Oh, Zelotese. It is majestic, is it not … all those who have gone before and given so much to make this time possible. And those who are out there," gesturing off beyond the distant hills, "even so do they give each day, separated from the source of that which they love and cherish, yet holding it so brightly within that they are able to sustain and endure the energies of the outer world in order that they can be in place when called upon."

There is barely another sound save that of their footsteps falling upon the ground beneath them.

Upon their arrival at the sacred Healing Spring, a ceremony is held in the tradition of the adepts from the School, celebrating and honoring the ancients who have gone before, and even Elijah himself.

They make themselves ready as they anticipate his coming, his birth, unto Elizabeth and Zechariah.

"Look you how he makes his fingers into fists," Rebekah remarks to Andra, "and look how he furrows his brow."

Elizabeth smiles as she looks down upon her son. "He does seem determined, does he not?" She strokes some hair from his brow.

"I think it is more than determination. It looks to me like there is a will of stone, unyielding!"

The fingers open and close around Rebekah's, who, receiving a nod from Elizabeth, scoops him up.

Time has passed swiftly, and the Essenes have made all the preparations they know for this One who is to come.

One of their own, who has become an innkeeper, hears the knock and directs them across the way to the stable and manger therein, as a flicker of something from his childhood passes fleetingly across his mind. It is a memory dimmed by many years in the clouded, misty collage so typical of life in the outer world. But there is a moment's pull somewhere within him as he slowly closes the door of his inn. A shudder passes through his great form before he turns to the inner chambers.

There, along with several others, his daughter stands in the shadows of a candle's light.

Mustering his typical demeanor, he speaks to her in a low, but gruff voice. "Go, then! Go to them. And, here! Gather up unto their needs and take it to them."

A momentary pause, and he turns, striding to ascend the staircase to his chambers.

A small child is walking through the dimly illuminated streets of this town called Bethlehem. As he walks along the roadway, hungered and thirsting, the darkness grows greater in its envelopment around him.

His footsteps weary, but steady, he asks quietly, "Oh God, dost Thou not hear my voice? Is it too small, too weak, that Thou canst not hear me? Thou knowest my love for Thee, Father, and I shall falter not. But I am so weary, and I hunger and thirst."

Those who pass by the young lad pay him no heed. As he makes the sign to them of being in need, he is met with either a scowl or a look off to the side as the passers-by continue on their way. He sighs heavily and tightly grasps the tattered rags that are his garments, stopping here and there to adjust the bindings around his legs and feet to protect him from the cold. On and on he trods.

Finally, by the illumination of the stars above, just ahead he can see some buildings, several of them, down a little valley. Wearily, he presses onward towards them. Perhaps he can find a sheltered corner and, if no one ejects him from it, at least be somewhat protected from the elements.

As he comes closer, he can see that it is an inn, and he can hear voices and laughter. Coming to the door, mustering all his courage and the remnants of his strength, he knocks.

A very stout fellow answers it, looks about and sees no one at first, then looking down, spies the tattered young lad.

"Good sir," the lad speaks out in a shaky voice, "I am so very hungry and weary. Could I do some labor for you and gain some food and perhaps some shelter where I could rest?"

There is a pause. The stout man steps back, reaches across where the lad cannot see, comes back with a small crust of bread and thrusts it at him, saying, "Here. Do not tell the others! I do not usually do this, but take it. You can go across the way over there," pointing to another building, "and you can rest there. But be gone before dawn's light! I cannot have it known that I have wastrels here." Without waiting a moment longer, the man slams the door.

Looking joyfully at the bit of bread in his hand, the lad

turns with renewed vibrancy and goes to the building across the way.

Hearing murmured voices inside and seeing the glow of light through the cracks between the boards, he hesitates a moment, thinking, *Perhaps they will take my bread from me.* Munching a small morsel and savoring it, he thinks, *At least I'll have had this much, if they do. But I must find warmth.*

Slowly, realizing this to be a stable, he pushes the great door open a crack, just enough to slide his body in backwards, then quietly pulls the door closed. He hopes to not arouse anyone's interest and intends to find a quiet, secluded spot to cover himself with hay, eat his bread, and sleep.

But fear runs through him as he turns to walk straight into the mid-section of a very large man. Bracing himself, he slowly looks up.

The face of this tall man looking down at him is gentle, warm and compassionate, eyes majestically aglow. "Here, lad. Take my hand. Come in and be with us."

Hesitating a moment, a grimy hand slowly comes forth from beneath the young lad's tattered clothing, the fingers aquiver with the emotion he feels until, finally, they grasp the large hand of this stranger.

The lad receives a smile and a quick nod, and then feels himself being pulled across the stable to the other end, where he looks about with some wonder as he sees an array of animals, several people, and a woman heavy with child.

"What have you?" Judy asks Nathanael.

"A lost one," he responds smiling softly, looking down.

"How are you called?" she asks the young boy.

Eyes awide, the lad looks wildly about, not knowing whether or not he should attempt to turn and bolt away. *Who are these strange ones? Why are they surrounded with light? Is this ... Shall I perish here?*

As though he knows the lad's thoughts, Nathanael pulls him over gently and bends, his face very close to the young lad. "You have come unto a place that welcomes you."

Judy, Sophie, and Anna gather 'round, and Miriam, also called Abigale, comes to slip between them, bending to place her hands on either side of the young boy's face. "Who are you, little one?" she asks sweetly.

"I do not know my name."

There is such compassion as the hearts of Miriam and the elder maidens are tugged greatly.

Miriam glances up to look into the eyes of Nathanael, their beloved guardian, then back down. "Well then, here is a great name, which, if he would so honor you, I should like to call you by."

The lad looks up at all the faces smiling at him, and a tear begins to form. "You ... you won't send me away?"

"No." She kneels and reaches out to embrace him. "If you will have us, we would love for you be one of our family. And we should like to call you Nathanael."

The soft sobs of the little boy are muffled by Miriam's tender caresses.

Nathanael, honored by his name being given to this lad, glances about. It is rare to see a guardian appear awkward, but it is clear that he is beyond words.

Smiling broadly, he makes the Essene gesture of faith and love, and bends to pat the young boy's head. "I shall look forward to being with you often, Little Nathanael." He turns and strides off, closing the portal behind him.

Joseph comes to the lad, having witnessed his entrance and the exchange with the great guardian and Miriam. He leads the boy gently by the hand. "Mary, this is young Nathanael and he has come to be with us. This is my wife, Mary, and I am Joseph. You are welcome, lad. All that we have we share with you." He hands young Nathanael a bit of cheese.

The lad, having followed some inner light, never giving up, always being at one with God even though his life bore no outward material manifestation that God even heard, much less answered him, thus settles in with a cup of mead and a bit of bread brought to him by others in attendance, and the cheese given to him by Joseph.

Upon the summit of a knoll above the manger and the inn, the rolling terrain is dotted with a flock of sheep. Two shepherds have come here because in the heavens above there is a brilliance so profound as to bedazzle the eyes beholding it. And now, as though the many other beautiful stars have come to embrace this one, it shines with a finger of radiant silver-white light illuminating the stable below.

As the two gaze at the scene before them, an occasional call can be heard from one of their flock. There is a discussion between them, and they decide that one shall go to see this One who has been foretold, while the other shall remain behind with the flock.

Across the small valley, others are coming now, perhaps drawn by this same light. Or could it be that they, too, know the prophecy? The path leading to the stable and inn from this point curves gently downward. The topography is sparse, and the sky is moonlit at this sacred hour.

Hannah is kneeling, moistening the cloth in a simple but beautiful wooden bowl beside Mary's head. She wrings out the excess, the sound of the trickling water soothing Mary, and sweetly dabs it around Her forehead and cheeks. Then, ever so gently, she places the cloth beneath Her chin and in a slow motion brings it around.

Mary's eyes, which have been closed, flicker open. As is so typical, a smile that would melt one's heart appears upon Her countenance.

To the other side, Eloise and several of the other Maidens adjust Mary's hair and Her garments.

Judy paces back and forth.

Joseph, Jacob, and a number of others are seated far to the side, rocking gently, eyes closed, obviously in joyful prayer.

Nathanael steps in quietly. Glancing about, he catches the eye of Judy, who moves swiftly to him.

She whispers, "It is soon."

He nods, and with a quick smile to the young lad who is seated sleepily off to the side, turns, and exits, securing the portal. He strides quickly across the darkened ground.

"It is very near, Jason."

Jason nods, smiling, looking up. "Have you ever seen them so brilliant?"

Nathanael straightens his great form and, leaning upon his stout staff, gazes at the first stars of the evening. With a long deep breath, he finally responds. "I think there is as much light coming from here where we are gathered as there is from there," gesturing to the stars.

"One can only hope it is so." Jason smiles and places a hand on Nathanael's shoulder. "We have done well, my brother ... very well, indeed. Let us celebrate all of our brethren who have given all they had to give to bring us to this evening." They embrace each other and bend to kneel, laying down their great staffs.

Nathanael reaches over to grasp Jason's hand, squeezing it as they begin to name the names of all the great guardians who have gone before along with all of the ancients, offering prayers unto each. "Our hearts are open and singing, claiming the wonder of this joyful expectancy which is now but moments before us."

Chapter 11

⁂e Is Come

First comes the sound, that of radiant music, that of glory in a form of singing, which can be heard not with the ear but with the very soul and spirit of those who would heed same.

Through the veil of darkness that envelops the Earth can be felt, and, yea, now seen, a light, growing, becoming more brilliant.

Fingers of various hues of light seem to leap forth and gently touch all the other lights in the heavens, and we know this to be the soul which is about to enter the Earth ... He who shall be called the Christ.

Its brilliance grows, as closer it draws unto the Earth. Others perceive it now, moved by a strange but beautiful stirring from within their beings. Drawn into awareness of their senses, they glance quickly about that they might perceive what is taking place.

As they do, our attention is now drawn to these who have come to be known as the kings, whose instantaneous recognition of this light of the Christ wondrously attracts them unto the same pathway.

There, in the raiment of its growing brilliance, they excitedly and reverently discuss what it is they feel and sense, each having his own method, his own manner, of divination: one, from a source within, guided by an amulet; the other, by the casting of those things which bear the Spirit of God; and yet another, the third, by the forces sensed intuitively and spiritually from realms beyond the material.

All agree, and continue their journey together now, as this wondrous orb of light seems to be drawing them. Though dark, the night is filled with light, and the earth beneath them seems to be reaching up to meet their feet, giving them strength to go forward.

After a time, looking down from a hillside, they see before them a small village of no great renown, and upon a gentle knoll, several dwellings.

As we move from the kings to observe this scene, the light suddenly reaches out in a shaft, penetrating the stable and illuminating all within.

Near and about, the faithful have gathered to protect those of importance who have journeyed so far to kneel before Him, and to interact with those heavenly Forces, which now merge with the forces of Earth. The Angelic Host and those servants of our Father's Will are all about.

There is no sense of darkness nor chill. It is as though the entire atmosphere is warmed by the presence of that single shaft of light.

As the soul merges with the body, the Child becomes that light and they are as one.

The vision of this soul and its impending journey are such as to move the deepest emotion in even the strongest of those present.

The creatures all rise and the humans all kneel, almost in unison. As they behold the Master in this tiny body, He beholds them, and a bond is forged which shall remain throughout eternity.

In the consciousness of all souls in all realms in all lands, in each soul that exists, is the awareness of this moment. In this place or that, though one or another may, for a moment in time, deny Him or His presence, none will fail to know this bond. Though they may explain it through different practices, all are brethren unto the Christ.

As the moments pass, the light in the heavens changes from its more spherical form and now sends out great shafts of light reaching to the north, to the south, to the east, and to the west, as though the very essence of this Soul seeks to embrace the entirety of the Earth.

The etheric sounds of the spheres are all about now. Each entity is fair aglow with the wonder of its presence, illuminated at the depths of the soul, and the love in the glance of each is unmistakable: without remorse, judgment, fear, guilt, frustration, anger, bitterness; only love and compassionate understanding remain. And there is the essence that this moment shall exist in time and space for all eternity.

In the hills, many of the shepherds are bowed in silent prayer. None of their sheep are grazing, but all are facing towards the star, gazing wistfully, with the reflection of its brilliance in their eyes.

The flowers afield begin to bloom in the darkness, lending their perfume to the night air.

And then, softly it begins … the calling of the dove, and then the others and still others, until all have begun their songs, seemingly singing with the Angelic Host the proclamation of His presence.

Night and day merge into one, as though all souls have disrobed of their bodies and that which is self-limited to show for this moment in time that they are bound together in the oneness that must emerge in that finality of experience that is the latter time of eternity. They move from the heavens. First comes one, then another, and then great multitudes, descending from their spheres and the light of His soul consciousness to pay homage and to express their dedication and love for His presence and His task.

Each of the prophets who has gone before, visible only to those who can see with the spirit, lays before Him a certain gift. One brings unending patience. Another brings the gift of forgiveness. Still others bestow compassion, love, faith, and charity, and on it goes for time untold: They descend to place the most precious gifts they have to offer before Him.

Then comes the movement in the heavens.

As the alignment of spheres once again reaches conjunction, a great rent in all the spheres comes together with a surge of energy as one would feel a flow of undulating warmth over their being.

In the power of that moment's experience, all know now that it is complete: the union of His consciousness with this body and the awareness of the Christ within.

The Hope born this day is an eternal gift. For in the presence of this tiny body is the Spirit of Truth, the Spirit of that which honors all who would receive it, embraced in the arms of love and compassion ... the jewel of perfection in the crown of God's Grace.

So as ye, in Earth, celebrate this day, know that He is within thee, that the Spirit called Christ is not only made manifest in that one we call the Master, the man called Jesus, but it is within thee, as well. As ye would seek it and harken unto it, so is it yours. So as ye see this and remember it in ceremony and in all manner which you believe as your expressions of this day, then too, we humbly and lovingly encourage you, know this:

He comes again. Wilt thou not help to make the Way passable?

Chapter 12

One Ideal, One Intent

The laughter is gentle, soft, melodious, as the Maidens gather 'round to look upon Him.

Joseph is seated at Mary's head. While holding a tiny hand and caressing Her forehead, he smiles mightily.

Gentleness pervades the simple surroundings. Everyone in the great chamber of this humble stable seems aglow. A simple glance about evokes enchanted smiles and an all-encompassing love.

Wherever they can, the Maidens in attendance are touching this tiny form. Soon, they turn and smile, nodding to young Nathanael whose arm is around a wooly lamb. When they do, and Nathanael's gaze meets their loving eyes, he can only look down, feeling unworthy, embarrassed at the wonder of the event. One of the Maidens goes over to him, bends to take his chin in her hand and kisses his forehead. At this, he looks up and across the way, and sees Mary's eyes fixed upon him, smiling warmly.

She gestures to him to come to Her side. When he can finally bring himself to do so, Joseph is at Her side and the Essenes a bit to the background. She folds back the covering, so the lad can gaze upon the Christ. A tiny hand emerges. Mary nods and little Nathanael reaches to touch it. With a hint of a smile on the Babe's face, His fingers grasp Nathanael's ... the gift from the Christ to one of faith.

Those present sense that it was the Master's spirit, the Christ, who guided the boy to the stable. That it was the Christ who influenced the innkeeper, noted for his hostility and bitterness, to waver a tad just then, so the child would have shelter and a bit of food to eat. For this lad's faith was heard and seen by the Christ, Who so revered and loved him for it that He wished to honor him by allowing his presence as He entered. And so it was.

Those walking along the pathway now are of His own people, coming in accordance with that which is the plan. Others are also coming from further beyond.

One having joined the two others, three shepherds are now making their way around the side of the stable.

At this moment, the upper portion of the inn's door swings open and the great form of the innkeeper fills the doorway, the candles' light behind him. He extends his arms upwards, stretching and flexing his body, making grunting noises as he does. Then he closes his mouth and brings his arms down, rubbing his face and body here and there. But he stops with a start, for the normally empty courtyard and passageway between the stable and his inn has a goodly number of unknown travelers upon it!

He calls out gruffly, "What is this? Who art thou?" and turns to a wooden peg to grab a coarse, tattered, and soiled cloak which he whirls about his shoulders. Thrusting open the bottom half of the double door, he briskly strides down the slope towards the slightly ajar stable door.

Seeing his approach, those standing about pause. He pays them no heed, but continues his march to the door. Before his hand can reach out to touch it, two forms appear from within. Instantly, he stops, for even with his sizeable frame, these two are looking down at him, something to which he is unaccustomed. Their faces are firm yet stoic, their eyes fixed steadfastly upon him.

The innkeeper's countenance changes and he takes a step backwards. "Uh … Wh-what … I told them they must leave before dawn. It is now before dawn."

The two large men say not a word, but merely look upon him, their faces holding him in the echo of his own words.

Awkward moments pass.

Nervously, the innkeeper clutches his cloak and shifts his focus from one to the other, taking yet another short step backward.

Just then, the door opens slightly, and out slips one of the Maidens, beautiful to behold. A golden shawl is swept around her shoulders and up over her head, framing her lovely face and large dark eyes, which seem to have light within them. She steps forward, perhaps midway between the two great ones and the innkeeper. Her hand clasping her shawl just below her chin, she speaks gently. "Do not fear, sir. These two, and we, mean you no harm. We wish to secure this place for several days, for which we shall pay you in coin."

The innkeeper, somewhat startled by the sweet innocence of the face peering at him and the large brown eyes warm with compassion and understanding, finally gathers himself. "Well, I, uh … I suppose it would be all right. You have coin then?"

"Yes, indeed." She extends a hand from under her garment, holding a pouch, which the innkeeper quickly peruses and sees is generously filled. "We have need of foodstuffs."

"Well, if you can pay, then I suppose that will be quite well. How many do you wish food for?"

"Three score," replies the Maiden.

"What? You mean …" He leans to the side. "You do not have three score in there."

She smiles and nods. "That is true, but more are coming, and some will remain within while the others take their turn. Many will have travelled far and will be enhungered, and it is our honor to serve them. Speak only that which you need, innkeeper, and we shall meet that need and greater. We mean you only goodness, and we wish to honor your establishment and you."

The innkeeper, upon hearing this, straightens himself, unconsciously dusting off his garment, a slight smile of pride now evident. "Well, you certainly have chosen wisely, young maiden, for our foodstuffs are known far and wide as among the very best."

Extending his hand, he receives the pouch of coins, jingles it and tosses it about. His eyebrows arch and his face breaks into a broad grin, realizing he is being paid lavishly. "I shall attend to your request immediately. And have no fear … no one will disturb you. I will have my people see to it."

"There is no need," the Maiden responds. "We are caring for our own, as you can see." She gestures to the two huge forms standing behind her to her right and left.

The innkeeper glances again from one great face to the other, then smiles again and nods, for he sees a hint of gentleness in the two pairs of eyes before him. "I do see that," glancing to the left and right, "and I see that you have others as well. Three score, then? So be it. I must go. I must awaken my workers. We shall prepare goodly foods." He bows courteously, turns, and strides briskly back to the inn.

Rebekah turns, too, nodding to the two great ones, and they follow her into the chamber.

There is the sound of a door slamming shut across the way, and the innkeeper's voice calling out to his servants and to his wife, "You shan't believe this! We may be wealthy! This is wondrous. You won't believe what I have to tell you!"

Smoke soon begins to come from the oven fires of the inn as the aromas of cooking foods fill the air.

Inside the stable, the creatures are now resting, grazing quietly. More have been brought in, for the warmth of their bodies amply heats the entire stable.

Ceremonies concluded, the Maidens have prepared various foods. Lanterns burn here and there, and at one end of the stable a small altar has been set up, upon which rest the gifts brought by the Magi and others.

Moving between the two great ones who stand guard constantly at the passageway into the stable, two Maidens greet three new arrivals who have knelt before the partially opened door.

"Is it He?" one of the shepherds who has come from upon the knoll asks humbly, his cloak held reverently in his hands. "I have naught else, but I give this, if you have need of it. If it can be of service, please, I give it in the spirit of my faith in God, and if you will accept it, I shall be honored."

It is Sarah who reaches out to take the garment. She lifts it up, and places her cheek against it and kisses it. "Thou art blessed, good sir, and your gift is welcomed as are you all. Come, good gentlemen. Come. Look you upon Him."

The three shepherds rise. Humbly, cautiously, awkwardly, they pass between the two great Essene sentries posted at the doorway. As they gaze within, the warm embracing glow of the lanterns' light greets them, as do the gentle sounds of those who are barely audibly singing psalms and of others by the altar, offering their prayers.

"Oh-h, sweet lady," comments the shepherd who had offered his cloak to Sarah, "we are not worthy to be here. We have naught to give other than that as has been given. Might we bring a lamb to you?"

Sarah shakes her head, "No, leave them, for the Lamb of God is here. We need naught, for all of our needs are met, though this gift of your person is a good and worthy treasure. Come. Look you upon Him. You are welcome." And she leads them further inside.

They stop a number of paces away, kneel, and prostrate themselves, three abreast.

Sarah stands, smiling, looking down upon them. After a few moments to honor their intent, she speaks softly. "Please.

Come, as ye would, and look upon Him."

They rise to their knees, but no further. Their hands clasped before them, offering inaudible prayers, heads bobbing, they inch their way forward until they can see Mary's warm gaze. There, snuggled within her embrace in His swaddling clothes, is the Christ Child.

In that moment, the Child's eyes flicker open, and all three gasp simultaneously, for it would seem that the Child, even though newborn, has looked upon them, each one. They smile, and an expression of His eternal love reaches out, unseen, unspoken, but embracing them, without question.

One begins to sob, covering his face with his hands. The other two bend over as far as they possibly can to bow, their hands upraised to their foreheads in a salute of humility. As though orchestrated by some unseen conductor, they begin to inch their way backwards on their knees, repeating again and again, "Glory. Glory." As soon as they are in the shadows they rise, coming together, all three, to embrace, saying, "Praise God." They make a final bow and gesture.

Sarah comes again and touches a hand to each cheek. "Thou art blessed, for thy faith has guided thee, and He has looked upon thee and now shall ever be one with thee."

The shepherd in the center begins to weep again.

Sarah, moved by this one's obvious need, inquires softly, "Why dost thou weep, good sir? It is a time for rejoicing."

"Oh-h, it is that I weep with joy. But I also weep for my brother who has stayed with the flock that I might be the one to come. He shall not know this great gift and blessing. He has missed it and I grieve for him, even though I rejoice for our people and the world."

"Weep no more," Sarah answers sweetly. "Go. Speak to him. Send him. I will admit him."

"Oh, thank you. Thank you, Maiden." Without another word, he turns, rushes out the doorway and races up the slope, calling, "Simeon! Simeon! Come! He will see you. It is He.

He has come!'"

The fingers of the pre-dawn light reach up into the heavens, softly at first, and then grow. It is as though seven great fingers of golden red light are trying to reach out to embrace the darkness. The shepherds, now with their flocks, all kneel, and those who are still arriving pause to turn and pray at the entrée of a new day, as songs resound from great distances.

Many are gathered over on a hillside, and more in another direction. In all, many dozens of Essenes are here, come to pay tribute and to keep the watch. Along the roadway are small groups, ever vigilant, ever looking about, their cookfires sending up curling twists of smoke. Down below, more have gathered unobtrusively. The Way is secure. The Light is surrounded with the love of the Expectant Ones.

In this first day of His presence in the Earth consciousness as the man called Jesus, the Light of God is not only welcomed, is not only seen and known for what It shall become, but It is one with those who have awaited His arrival.

Within the stable, the Maidens of Righteousness encircle their Sister and the Babe. Joseph has left this inner circle, and only these Maidens and Our Lady and the Master remain. They are awaiting the arrival of others, and exceptionally so, Elizabeth and John.

In the predawn light, there is merriment and joy, the sense of expectation, electrifying. The Maidens are barely able to contain their exuberant joy. They look to one another and speak softly, a little giggle here, an expression of hope and speculation there, each one mentally reviewing what gift she shall place before the Christ, each one looking to the Sister to her left and right and across the way. The feeling of oneness is so empowering that it would seem all is but Light. The loving gaze of Our Lady moves to meet each expectant pair of eyes surrounding her with love, nodding. For all here in this inner circle know the prophecy, and all here celebrate this time … when all is well.

Sounds can be heard of others arriving. The guardians open the door and bow, and there enters Elizabeth carrying the infant John and behind her appear others of the Essenes, teachers and guardians alike.

Then come forth Anna and Josie.

The Maidens leap to their feet in eager rejoicing, gesturing, as is the custom, and then colliding with warm and loving embraces. It is of course Rebekah who takes John, kissing Elizabeth and bringing him over, so the two babes can be side by side between Our Lady and Elizabeth.

The Maidens then gather, and their prayer and song begin. In the lanterns' light, it appears that as they intertwine arms to perform the ceremonial dance each face changes.

Now others come, and other babes are placed within the circle of the Maidens of Light.

And on they dance and sing.

Outside, the innkeeper, whose motion is stopped at the doors again by the great guardians, calls out, "How do you wish this served? Where shall you partake?"

This time it is Miriam who goes to him. She and three of the others go forth to beckon to the travelers. Some then gather within the inn and others within the stable, but all are welcomed and are given nourishment.

There is a soft chanting of the adepts.

Within the chanting, comes the voice of Elob. "We thank You, Lord God. Your Light is with us. This we know. We surround them, all of them, with the power of our oneness. We send forth the light of our spirit to comfort and guide in Your Name, Lord God."

The chanting continues.

Many other sacred sounds rise up, intertwining one with the other. Contributing to the mystical essence in the background is the gentle sound of the water cascading down the

Spring where so long ago the prophet stood and proclaimed this very day.

So it is this day that the Hope of those who would seek has come to Earth.

In these times past, the Way was made passable by those who are His. There was the thought that was known aforehand, and in the knowledge of such, preparations were made. Many came to serve. All set aside that which might in anywise separate, and extended a hand in unison that there would be but one Work, one Ideal, one Intent.

Chapter 13

It Begins

*I*n the center of the caravan are Mary and our Master. To their side, also astride a small beast of burden, are Elizabeth and John, the four surrounded by the Holy Maidens. Their movement, though rather swift, is steady and the pace easy.

To the rear of the group are Jason and Nathanael.

"It is incredible," Nathanael is commenting, "how swiftly things are moving. It seems only hours ago that we were celebrating His coming, along with the others who saw the light and came to pay homage, and here we are fleeing."

"As it was foretold," Jason reminds his brother. "*He will be called out of Egypt,* and so we journey. How blessed we are to have Elob, Zelotese, and all the others, and how blessed we are to know the way, having traveled it before."

Nathanael sighs deeply, swinging his staff as he strides. "How blessed we are, indeed. The goodness of God is all about. I shall fall back a distance just to make certain that we are not followed."

Jason nods. "Signal if there is the need." He tightens his fist and brings it to his chest. Keeping the clenched hand firmly in place, leaning his staff against his body, he extends the palm of his other hand and places it upon Nathanael's chest. "My heart is with you, as ever, my brother."

Nathanael does the same, smiles, and then turns to stride

away, quickly fading into the dim light.

Towards the front of the line Judy and Jacob are walking together.

"Is everyone well, Judy?" Jacob asks, keeping his stride.

"Very well, and in good spirits."

"That is wonderful! Do you remember all this? It seems only a short time ago we were passing over these same hills, perhaps this very same soil."

"Oh, yes," she responds pensively. "I recall their faces … so free, so filled with hope. Even though we were fleeing from those who would smite them, they kept their focus upon the joy and upon one another." Turning to look back at the Maidens, who are taking turns walking beside the Master and the Forerunner, she sighs. "We are so blessed, Jacob … so very blessed."

It is a simple encampment, its structures made from placing various cloths across the ribbing: tent-like, but more substantial, more permanent. Here and there some bits of sod have been placed around to deflect the mid-day sun. The arrangement is circular, but with an entry on the north side and another to the southwest.

Some of the Maidens are singing songs as they prepare the morning's meal. Others are returning from having gathered foodstuffs from land which seems barren and harsh, yet the skills given them by Isadore and others are evidenced in the great baskets of roots and such with which they are returning. Laughter echoes from their midst as some recount stories of old.

Off to one side, Zechariah is rocking his son, talking to him softly.

To the other side, Joseph strides up to Mary, speaking quietly. "My love is with you."

She smiles and nods, extending a hand, cradling Jesus in Her other arm. "Would you like to take Him for a time?"

In a single swift motion, Joseph kneels, his arms out-stretched to receive the one called Jesus. Lifting Him and receiving a great smile as he does, he holds Jesus up high and wiggles Him, receiving the laughter only a small child can give. Cradling Him next to his cheek, Joseph strides about, greeting everyone, as Jesus looks upon them ... some with curiosity at first, and then with a warm smile.

Hearing a familiar child's laugh, Jesus leans to look over His father's shoulder and, there, held up by his own father, the thrashing arms and bouncing body of John catch the Mas-ter's delighted eye, and He laughs aloud, His own arms wav-ing in response.

Joseph moves to seat himself beside Zechariah, and the two babes look at each other and touch and grasp hands.

Their squeals and laughter warm the hearts of the Maid-ens and Our Lady. All stop what they are doing, and the Maidens come to gather 'round Our Lady, and look across the way at them.

"Oh, my goodness, can you believe it? It is real, and yet, it does not seem anything like what I had imagined," Zeph-orah exclaims. "It is like we are living inside a dream."

The sweetness on Mary's face conveys the compassion She feels as She nods and reaches across to take Zephorah's hand. "It is so true, Zephorah. How many times I questioned and asked our God, 'Are you certain I am the one chosen?'" All the Maidens laugh gently. "But here we are, and there He is. Just look at them ... like any other children, and yet, look at the light around them."

"And around their papas, too," adds Eloise, and again the Maidens chuckle softly.

"Oh yes," Hannah chimes in, "and how blessed we are to be in their midst."

"And look how many others have brought their chil-dren." Zephorah gestures around the encampment.

They glance about and note many who are about the

same age as these two.

"Some of them will walk with Him." Eloise indicates with a nod of her head to where a laughing Joseph is trying to help the Master's tiny feet take footsteps.

John is again displaying the trait so familiar to all who know him, of bouncing up and down and thrashing his arms about. The Master merely smiles and moves His feet with apparent deliberateness, looking about with His steady gaze, seeing all, knowing all, it would seem.

"Now, it is we who are the nurturers," Andra laughs. "All the gifts, all those years of dedication by our beloved elder sisters, that we might each bear our truth to Him, to nurture and to bring forth that which He already bears, embraced in an environment of compassion."

"And lots of love," Miriam adds.

"Yes, lots of love," agrees Andra. "And look at the others. Do you see? They seem to know, even though barely one of them can even speak yet."

Hannah nods. "Each is so very beautiful, with obviously some unique light. Have you noticed?"

"It is hard not to notice, Hannah," giggles Little Mary. "And similar lights in our new little sisters, too."

"Yes. Filled with the sweetness of where we are and what will follow ... filled with the Promise."

The years have passed and the children have gained their agility. A cloud of dust swirls about them as they delight in discovering little pebbles and small bits of plants and such, smelling, feeling, and sometimes tasting them, to the amusement of the Maidens, whose watchful gaze is ever present.

The Master and a number of the other young lads are gathered in a circle. He has a small twig and is drawing upon the earth before them. John claps his hands with delight as he begins to see that the Master has drawn a picture of some creature. Now He hands the twig to John, indicating to him to do the same, and so he does. John then passes the twig in turn to the child next to him, and on and on it goes until the circle before them is filled with the attempts to draw creatures that they have seen and known. Throughout all this, the Maidens come and go, two always present near the group.

Nearby is another group of slightly older children who are being told of the history of their peoples by several of the elder maidens. One in the group is not truly listening but, rather, is watching the Master and the others not far away.

"Nathanael, what say you to what I said?"

Blinking and suddenly feeling awkward among his peers, Nathanael turns. "I ... I am sorry, dear teacher. I was ..."

She raises a finger, indicating there is no need to speak, and smiles. "I know. You were watching the Master, as always. Correct?" questions Miriam.

"Well ... uh ... yes."

"You may join them, if you wish."

"I may?"

"Yes, you may." She smiles again.

Hannah, standing behind Nathanael, bends to extend a hand down to him, and he jumps to his feet as she leads him off to the Master's group.

The Master laughs and claps His hands as He first sees His beloved Hannah, and then His brother Nathanael. They kneel behind the Master, who turns and extends His arms to embrace them both. Then all the others come, wanting to do the same.

"I wonder what the rest of the world would think if they could see such incredible, sweet love?" Kelleth ponders aloud to Our Lady.

"That is my constant prayer ... that I might somehow bring that love to all peoples in all times." Sighing deeply, She places Her hand over Her heart. "Lord God, if I am worthy, let me bear Your love to all the world, and Your understanding and grace to all in need."

"I, as well," adds Kelleth. With equal conviction, each of the Maidens then states the truth that each offers with their sister, sweet Mary, to the world.

"What is the status of the pursuers, Jason?"

"From what we know, Zelotese, they are all but abandoning pursuit. It appears that Herod's days are near their end, and so, as ever, the prophecy is being fulfilled."

Zelotese nods and bows his head for a brief moment. For one attuned to such, it is apparent that he is sending forth a prayer. Perhaps it is a prayer of forgiveness, or perhaps one of affirmation and thankfulness that they know the prophecy and what lies ahead.

"Do you think it will be long," Isadore asks, "before we are called to return?"

"I think not." Judy glances up to look at Jacob, whose eyes are transfixed upon the small campfire before them.

"I agree," Jacob confirms. He straightens his shoulders and takes a very long deep breath. "In so many ways it is like a new path being opened unto us, is it not?" He continues to stir the embers around the edge of the fire.

"A part of a continuum of footsteps," Judy adds, "a part of the Promise unfolding, manifesting."

"A part of the hope for the world," Isadore interjects, "and there seems to be a curious energy building. Do you feel it, my sister?"

"Oh, yes. Each meditation, each time of prayer, seems more powerful than the previous. As we prepare for this time, clearly the Spirit of God is offering unto all who would receive it blessings, insights, knowledge, greater than any I have ever known," Judy adds smiling, "in this lifetime at least."

Jacob is leaning to one side. "It is true. I see the signs of it in my journeys, in my times of fasting and prayer. I ..." his voice trails off. "Only several days ago I was seated upon that rock." He points to a massive outcropping in the distance.

The women turn to look and then quickly look back at him, pondering how anyone could ascend it, much less spend time atop it.

"I was in meditation facing the birth of the new day," Jacob's eyes glaze over as he remembers this event, "and then it was as though something brushed against my face. I opened my eyes ever so slightly ... you know," receiving nods from Judy and Isadore, "and I could see them ... legions of them ... gossamer white, billowy, undulating wings of light around them, spires of expectancy in the radiance of God's Promise flowing to the Earth. Each of these angel-like beings was coming, all moving in great numbers towards me, Jacob, alone in the wilderness of my own thoughts. I blinked, and when I opened my eyes again, one was before me, hovering. I felt my heart leap and I heard myself gasp as I said, *Lord, why dost Thou send Thy messenger to Thy humble servant, Jacob? Dost Thou call me? Am I to return to Thee?*

"The beautiful face before me said, *No, I call you not, sweet Jacob. I am sent to walk with you, ever. As you answer His needs and the Work, be ever mindful that I am with thee. The gift of thy sight of me is given of thy Father, who loves thee greatly. I am called Raphael. I am here to serve the Promise.*

"When I could not withstand blinking again, mine eyes opened and there was naught but the golden rays of a new day. But I knew then as I know now, he is with us ... this Raphael, an angel of God, the deliverer of the Promise."

"See how He grows," Joseph murmurs to Mary. "His legs so strong and already rising to a goodly stature."

Smiling lovingly, She receives a quick smile from the Master. She and Joseph merely nod, recognizing that He may well know their thoughts and words.

A bit of a grin curls one end of His mouth, known now to be characteristic of Jesus, as the steady, transfixing gaze of His clear eyes embraces them for a moment. He then turns to stride smoothly, easily, to His playmates.

"I can do this," one is stating. "Just give me a bit of room here," and his hands cup together as he shakes the stones. He closes his eyes, mumbles something inaudible to his peers, and gently tosses the pebbles into the air.

Several moments of silence are followed by sumptuous laughter as the other children point. "Look, here, John! This one didn't even fall within the pattern."

Looking down, John shakes his head. "I will get it. You watch." He glances up to see the Master smiling at him. "Once more ... Show me once more," and John steps aside that the Master might stand precisely where he has been.

The Master steps forward and bends to scoop up the pebbles. Cupping them in His hands, He does not look down but turns to smile and fix His eyes upon John, who glances from the Master's eyes to His hands moving up and down.

The corner of His mouth turns up in the little loving smile as His hands release the pebbles. Still looking at John, He simply nods.

John looks down and throws his head back in a goodly laugh and steps forward to place his hands upon the Master's shoulders. "Mind you, I am only trying to do some of the things You have shown me. Certain of these things I know I can not do nor am I meant to ... not in this life, at any rate."

"Well," He responds in His boyish voice, though with evidence of authority and wisdom already breaking through, "is it not wonderful? Is it not perfect that we each can share the work? That if you carry your part, I carry mine ... Peter, you carry yours," and glancing up, "and Nathanael, you yours, and all of us ... that the work will be joyful and just so much easier if we are all at the ready, and all joyfully contributing that with which we are gifted?"

There is stillness as each one present realizes that a truth has been given to them.

Jesus breaks the silence. "Try it again, John. But this time, do not think about it. Simply see it as you see it there," pointing to the ground. "If you see your intent manifested, it is already done."

"Let me understand this. If I see my intention completed, then that makes it happen?"

"Yes. Do it. You can do it."

John bends to scoop up the pebbles, and stepping where the Master just stood, looks up and closes his eyes, remembering where the pebbles had only moments ago been lying upon the diagram drawn in the soil. He raises his hands filled with the smooth stones. "You know I love You, Lord. You know I shall never waver. Could You help me so that these stones do not waver either?" With a small chuckle, he throws them into the air, not looking down, only straight ahead, after which he turns to walk off.

"Where are you going?" asks one of his companions.

"I need not do that anymore. I know the stones have fallen where they fell for our Brother. I believe Him and I believe His word. I did as He said, so I have no need to look." He walks away.

His companions stand looking down, some in awe. But not the Master. He smiles as He watches John's figure stride away from the group and then looks down at the pebbles ... each one precisely on its designated point.

The Master lifts His face upward as His eyes close. "I thank You, Father, for this one whose faith is as Your light, whose will goes before me and Your Work. I am blessed."

When it is a seed, does it know that it is a tree? When it is a sapling, has it knowledge that one day it shall be mighty in size? When it has reached a goodly stature, does it have knowledge of the fruits it will soon bear, the blossoms whose fragrance will fill the air?

All these things, until they come to pass, are borne in the spirit of that which is yet to come. That is the spirit called faith, and the power of faith is perhaps the greatest, mightiest power of all. For in spite of that which would deter, in spite of that which would burden or weigh, the clarity and single-mindedness of true faith are as the rod and staff of God. So this young child called Jesus, the Master, the Christ, offered a prayer of thankfulness that the faith of John was a gift unto the Path, unto the Way, and gave thanks that this faith in God would go before Him and His work.

Through the example just given, one can find a great potential. Know ye that within yourself is this same gift. All about, the light of it shines. If you give thanks for it, if you believe unto it, then just as surely as these shiny little pebbles, each one, fell upon their designated place, so will your life and the purpose thereof fall into its rightful place. Turn away from the challenges offered to you of the world, and cleave unto the truth as the Master gave it, and gives it now: That if you look unto your intention and see it fulfilled, then you can release that and move into the joyfulness of your own faith.

And just as a small child turned away from that which could test, or tempt, or challenge him, so can you do the same ... your faith being so strong that you have no need to see, for you know, for you have created the intent and you have empowered it with your faith. So is it then evermore accordingly so.

Chapter Fourteen

The Truth Place

They are gathered in numerous concentric circles facing inward, moving slowly, rhythmically, to the melodious sounds of the Holy Maidens, who are offering their prayer and their song as they move, encircling the inner group of children, love and dedication pouring from them in their words and in their very presence.

Judy comes forward, stepping through the outer circle of the Maidens, and walks about the outer concentric circle of children within the Maidens' circle.

The children are standing hand in hand, smiling, eyes closed. Some are looking down, some are looking up, some are bobbing their heads a bit this way and that as they have been taught to so do when seeking the inner awareness of the One God.

With a hand upon a head over here, a slight grasp of a shoulder over there, Judy walks around the circles. Stopping, she looks up, raising her arms and hands, palms upward. "We who are chosen thank Thee, Lord God, for the gift of these, the jewels of Thy very crown. We embrace these children with the light of our heart's life given us by Thee, and we reach out with it to unite with their hearts, their intentions. Bless them, Lord God, one and all, that they might know in these moments that Thou art ever with them."

Her head slumps forward. Hands still upraised, she then states, "You have looked within, sweet children. Now look without."

All the children turn from their position of facing inward to the center of the concentric circles, to now face outward, looking at the Maidens and the others who surround them. Their faces are bright, their eyes aglow.

Judy motions for them to seat themselves, and so they do. She begins slowly walking around them, speaking softly. "It is good for you to ever know that wherever you might be and whatever you might face in the journey of life ahead that there is ever the sanctuary of light within, waiting to embrace, to heal, and to nourish you unto your every need. As we have so often gathered in this manner, we do so again today as we move forward into new levels of discovery and awareness. Although these have always been with you, visit them and discover them now as though they are anew."

Walking around the outer circle slowly, deliberately, as though looking for something, she pauses in her movement, connecting her glance with an upturned pair of shining eyes and extends her arm, palm up, towards the young boy. "Have you found that light within you, Thomas?"

Thomas breaks into an awkward smile. His eyes become wide as he nods affirmatively.

"Can you tell us how you know you have found it?"

He glances down for a moment as though to summon up the words from somewhere within his being, and then looks up in a strong, steady gaze at Judy. Glancing about, he sees his peers, the other children. Some are looking down, eyes closed, and he knows they are sending him their love, offering him their spirits. Here and there one has turned to look upon him, smiling. "I know I have found the light of God within because of how it makes me feel," Thomas responds. "It is a feeling of life. It is as though my entire being, physical and otherwise, is somehow filled with an energy of goodness and joy. That is how I know."

"Is there that which you see or perceive, Thomas?" continues Judy.

He nods again, still smiling. "Yes. Once I find God within, then just as you have had us do, I turn and look without, and I see as though I might suppose God would see. I see your light, sweet teacher, and I see the light of everyone. And it brings me gladness."

Nodding, smiling, obviously greatly pleased, Judy places a hand upon her heart, gesturing her love to young Thomas, and then continues walking, looking.

The Holy Maidens glance at one another, for they know these teachings so very well, having experienced this same work on the part of their beloved sister Judy so many times during their own youthful years.

Again Judy stops, and looks into another pair of eyes. "What is the feeling within you now, sweet Ledotia?"

Brushing aside a long wispy strand of hair from her eyes, she answers, "Such sweetness, that it is almost as though I can taste it."

Several of the children giggle softly, not at Ledotia but with her, for they, too, can almost taste the sweetness.

"In the center of your being, is there anything you find? Is there any gift that God gives to you when you join Him?"

"Oh, yes." Ledotia rocks to and fro, her hands upon her knees. "He gives to me something that there are no words truly to express to you." Pausing, she looks about with a long sweeping gaze at all that is around her … the somewhat barren hills embracing the group, the wispy clouds off on the horizon, a winged creature riding the wind currents far above, circling higher and higher into the early morn sky. "Perhaps I would say it in this way … The gift that is given to me is true sight. It is the sight that I have heard you, and our sweet sisters," gesturing to the Holy Maidens, "speak of often. I see the goodness, the sweetness, the joy in all that is about."

Judy turns to glance, her eyes following the very path that Ledotia followed with her own eyes. "What does all of this say to you, or give to you?" she continues, her eyes refocused lovingly but firmly upon Ledotia.

"It is like a feeling of something coming. It is as though," pointing to a distant hillside, "I expect to see someone or something rise to the crest of yon hill. Or over here," pointing in the opposite direction, "or perhaps from above," pointing to the winged creature soaring lazily upward. "And I think perhaps, as you have shown me, all of you, that I expect something to come from here." She places her right forefinger upon her own chest.

"Can you identify what it is that you expect?"

Smiling, her hands back on her knees, Ledotia rocks a bit as she answers. "Oh, yes! It is the Promise of God. And, of course, that Promise is here with us." She leans forward to look across several children and into the loving eyes of the one called Jesus.

Judy glances back and forth between them, then gestures the Essene gesture of love to Ledotia and turns to walk directly over to face Jesus, who is looking up, His face open, glowing, and completely at peace.

"Have You that which You would share with us, Jesus?"

His eyes seem to bring her into Him, and even she, the powerful, wise, loving Judy, seems to waver just a bit, to stumble under the immensity of the mere look of this young boy. She bows her head briefly, and then looks up to meet His gentle but unwavering gaze.

"What I would share," Jesus responds, "is already manifest. For you, all of you, are the true gifts of God. That which shall come forth from your combined intentions is that which will answer the call from the wilderness."

Some of those towards the rear gasp. Some of the Maidens strike their chests, for these words are nearly identical to those that another had spoken of Him not that long ago.

"It is all of you," He continues, "who will go forth to answer that call, in the reflections of that which is held in each heart here." He turns to smile and look upon His friends, the sisters, the elders, the seers, those from the School of the Prophets who are gathered on the periphery, and on and on. "For it is as you have taught me, sweet sisters," glancing around the circle, "that one who strives to give of self gives the greater gift when embracing the oneness with all who are involved. Thereafter, does the greater gift flow easily, empowered by the faith of all, enriched by the unique gifts that each holds in the chamber of oneness with God within." He says no more, but His head bobs ever so slightly, as though to affirm this within and without.

The shadows are growing longer. Here and there where the group takes a few steps behind a small summit, they are in the darkness that precedes the oncoming nightfall.

"You can tell the goodness of a plant that is being embraced by the earth by that which is shown above the earth," Isadore comments softly, walking over to the side, half in and half out of the shadow. "See this one?" She bends to touch the leaves. "Look you, how it shines. It has the capacity to reflect that which it does not need. Its leaves are created so as to take in only what it needs for its sustenance and to reflect what it does not. Now look over here. This one has barbs that can sting or irritate your skin. Does that mean that it is not offering a blessing?"

Turning to glance at the children, she sees one hand come up, and she motions for that child to come forward.

"No, I think not," Annabel answers. "I think what it is doing is preserving something very special. It is saying to those creatures that might come along and prematurely take of it, 'I am not ready.'"

A few of the children laugh, but many nod.

"Well, let me ask of it. Are you ready, little plant, to give your gift unto those who have need?" With a great smile on her face, Isadore bends her ear very close to the prickly leaves. "Did you hear that children?"

Some of them look at each other and shrug their shoulders. But one stands with his arms folded, rocking, smiling. Isadore looks at him. And he answers her unspoken invitation. "Yes, I heard it."

"What did it say?" she asks of John.

"It said, 'Take of me. I have readied myself for you in God's Name.'"

"But let me ask of you ..." Isadore continues, now straightened up, kneeling, her hands upon her knees. "If I take of this plant, will its life end? Will it perish?"

John's face straightens and he strides forward boldly. "No, it will not."

"How so?" questions Isadore, somewhat amused by his forthrightness.

"Well, as you know, for you have taught it to us, if I take of this plant, its life and mine join together, and we are the greater because of it and our service is stronger to our Lord God." He turns to look at the other children, his eyes singling out Jesus, who smiles and nods. Satisfied, John smiles back, turns to Isadore and announces, "Here, I will show you."

Isadore is amused and impressed as she slides backwards on her knees to give John room.

John stoops upon a bended knee, his hands cupped over the plant. His eyes close, and we hear him speak in a clear, loud voice. "Thank You, Lord God, for this gift of our sweet little plant. I partake of it now in Thy Name, and I give thanks unto Thy Spirit for embracing it and nurturing it unto our needs. We bless you, little plant."

He puts his hand upon the ground next to the roots of the plant, opens his fingers and slides his hand forward, easily avoiding the spines on the plant's leaves. His fingers close, and he lifts upward, smiling, as a beautiful tuber beneath the spiny leaves is now exposed. Lifting it up, he turns to show his friends and then hands it to Isadore. "A gift from the Spirit of God and from the Kingdom of God called the plant kingdom. It will bring joy to our evening's meal. Thank you, little plant," he ends, striding back to rejoin the group.

"Goodness," exclaims Sophie, "there is an essence about that one that is ... well, inspiring."

"It is an essence, all right!" Andra declares. "It is a surety born of a wellspring of bottomless faith. Notice how he sought no affirmation from anyone but Jesus."

"Oh, I saw it!"

"Well," Kelleth interjects, "no matter where that one goes, he will not want for nourishment," and she laughs.

"I should think not," Andra teases. "Woe be unto the plant that does not give unto his need." The three of them laugh as they move closer to the group.

Resuming their journey, Isadore continues to show the children again and again how to find unto their need where other eyes would see only barrenness. She brings them to a small area behind a large outcropping and points up, showing them where the growth of small plants on the side of the rock indicates that the earth beneath holds water within its embrace. Bending, she indicates a small place seemingly unworthy of note in comparison to all about it. But she indicates how there is a slope this way and that, and how it runs up to the very spot where this outcropping of rock has the tiny green flecks of life growing on it. She turns to the children. "Are there questions about this?"

A little hand comes up. "May I find the water?"

"Of course." Isadore rises and steps back.

The child comes forward, pushing up the sleeves of her garment so her forearms are exposed. Carefully, tenderly, she bends and scoops away the soil more and more. Suddenly, all can see the moisture. She gathers up two handfuls of the moist earth, and pressing her hands together, laughs as tiny droplets of water fall from beneath her clenched fingers.

"Excellent!" Isadore commends her.

"Thank You, Lord God," the child responds. "Thank you so much for providing for us. And thank You for our great teacher, who has shown us that Your light is present even in the darkness of life."

Isadore comes over to wrap her arms around the child, embracing her, and kissing her on the forehead. "It is no wonder you are called Martha, for you do, indeed, bear God's love in your presence."

"Thank you." She scurries back to her companions.

The flames of the cookfire's embers are still bright, but considerably lesser now.

Between each of the Maidens in the circle are perhaps two, three, or four of the children and still greater numbers behind them. The Maidens are talking quietly, turning to clasp a hand of one seated behind or on either side, or gesturing to some who are a bit further behind. All is light and joyful, the faces brightened by the light of the small fire.

As one Maiden stands, all the children become silent.

"When you journey through life which lies before you, sweet brothers and sisters," gesturing broadly to the children, "ever look for that which resonates within."

"How so?" asks Thomas boldly. "How would it resonate within me?"

Smiling and nodding, Andra continues, "It resonates in a place I call the truth place, within."

Thomas glances down, running his hands up and down his torso. "And where would that be, sweet teacher?" he smiles, canting his head to the side.

"Ah, Thomas, must you have a certain place for it?"

"It would help." The children laugh.

"Well then, come here."

Without hesitation, he springs to his feet and makes his

way through the children and the other Maidens to stand before Andra, who looks down at him with mirthful admiration. For she sees in Thomas the very qualities that others have seen within her.

"Here is the place, right here." She places a forefinger just above his heart.

He looks down and puts his right hand where her forefinger had rested. "Here?"

"Yes, right here." She pushes her forefinger against the back of his hand again.

"Well, that helps, but I do not feel anything there."

"Why do you think that is?"

"I do not know. If that is my truth place, why is it that I feel it not?"

"Because you are not asking anything. Therefore, you are not using it."

Placing his hand upon his chin in a manner that would befit someone five times his current age, Thomas ponders this. "Then," he answers brightly, "give me a work. I want to feel truth in this place," putting his hand back above his heart.

"Very well," Andra responds. "Is your name Thomas?"

His face is blank, expressionless, at first, but then flashes into a large smile. "You know it is."

"What do you feel now in your truth place?"

"Well, it feels warm."

"Excellent. Now, is my name Sophia?"

"No, you ... Oh, I see. There is no warmth here."

"Is my name Andra?"

"Yes, and I feel the warmth of you here now, in my truth place. Oh, thank you very much." He turns abruptly and goes back to reseat himself.

All the Maidens are giggling to one another.

Kelleth puts her hand on Zephorah's shoulder, "Is that one a humor, or not?"

"Oh, yes. And does he not remind you of Andra when

she was young?"

"I must admit, there is a strong similarity. Very forthright. Powerful and strong inside." She taps her heart.

Andra seats herself, and all the children respond joyfully when another of the Sisters rises and walks around quietly.

"What would you do, sweet children," begins Mary, "if you were in the outer world and were to find no love, no compassion? Perhaps going for many days, such that the wellspring of this within you seems depleted, and you find yourself longing for one with whom to share it, knowing that the wellspring of love and compassion within you both would, thereafter, be replenished?"

Her sweet face shines upon each child, including Her own, who is called Jesus. Their eyes are locked in a gaze of tangible sweetness. "Would you answer?" She asks Him.

Nodding and smiling, He rises to His feet, walks over to Mary and embraces Her, placing His head upon Her midsection. Her hand comes up to stroke His rich, flowing hair, Her other hand caressing Him on the back.

Jesus releases Her, and looking up into Her eyes for but a moment, turns. Much as Andra has just done, He strides about, His hands placed behind Him. "If I were in the outer world, and the wellspring of love and compassion within seemed depleted, I would stop wheresoever I might be. And I would look upon that wellspring, and I would say unto it, *Come forth, thou love and compassion, for the Source of that which flows through thee is eternal and unending. Be thou not according to that which is without, but ever as that which is within ... unending.*"

Smiling and walking about in the manner as an elder might do, Jesus glances about, first at this Holy Maiden, then at another. "You are, in the Earth, the channels that nourish the wellspring within me. Thou, Hannah, my sweet mentor, who hast been as mother unto me, as have you all ..." He turns to smile at the other Maidens and then to Mary, who nods that She approves and confirms. "From the jewel that thou hast placed upon the crown of God within me, and from that which is eternal within, have I brought mine own to become one with thine. This, in the wellspring within me, flows the joy of expectation from all I shall meet."

He strides directly to another. "Andra, in what you have shown my brother Thomas, in that of the *truth place*, ever is the presence of thy loving face. Should I have need of it and the desire to add your truth to mine own and that of our God, I will see you here and be glad of it. And it will strengthen me and thee, and it will give unto the work, any work that might come before my footsteps." So He goes to each of the Holy Maidens, honoring them.

Then He turns to face the other children. "We have a wonderful journey ahead. But the journey that is now is the most beautiful of all because we are within it, and we can give light to it that the memory of it lingers well beyond this life into many that would follow. Forevermore, we can call upon the memory of the love we share, the great gifts given us by those who nurture us and call out to us to bring forth that which is the greatest of all within."

He then goes before Judy. "As you speak to our Lord God, and He in return to you, let it be known that this is my prayer: that the memory of these times of oneness together might ever endure for us all."

A tear makes its way down her cheek, so awed is she by the sweetness of this young lad and in the full knowledge of who He is ... from whence He has come and that unto which He must journey. She reaches a hand to Him, and He quickly takes it, and moves to lay His head upon her shoulder.

Softly, Rachel begins to sing, and over here, Rebekah, Zephorah, and Hannah add their voices. Soon all the Maidens are in song, having reached out to join hands with one another. They are rocking ever so gently, their faces aglow with the joy of the Promise now awakening within their midst.

Some months have passed, and these peoples have returned unto the land they consider holy, wherein the Sacred Spring flows from the earth, endlessly.

They have come together in smaller groups to give teachings unto those who are gathered, teachings which will serve their unique needs and purposes in the journey of life ahead.

Eto, who has returned from a long journey to the east, is off to the side speaking with Zelotese and Elob. "It is wonderful how well all is being prepared."

Zelotese smiles and nods as he looks down, apparently in silent prayer.

"Are the others of our group in place?" Elob inquires. "And have you heard from those who journey to the distant lands?"

Eto nods. "I believe that at this time they are well upon their destinations and that all is being made ready. Certainly I can attest to the preparation of the routes that He will travel, and that the sanctuaries, refuges, and places of shelter are all aright. Some of those in attendance know not the specific purpose for their preparation. And will that not be a wonderful gift to them when He comes unto them, and they see, *Here is the Promise of God in our own midst, in our own abode, blessing us!* Would that I might see each pair of eyes as they realize this." Rocking, Eto closes his eyes, imagining what lies ahead.

"Well," Zelotese comments, "I must take my leave of you. I go now to bring a gift."

Elob, knowing precisely that of which Zelotese speaks, smiles broadly and taps his chest with a fist. "From us all."

Eto does the same.

As he rises to his feet, Zelotese nods an affirmation. "As ever, we are one. And tell my brothers and sisters I bear them and their intent with me."

Jacob's laughter can be heard clearly as he rocks to and

fro, telling stories, talking about Imnaz and Sophie, who have gone before, and how humorous some of the events were as she tried to convince the tribes to set aside differences and begin the journey that would bear the fruit of God's Promise into the Earth.

Here and there he emphasizes the curious barriers that separated them. "Can you believe it? Because one called it one thing and another called it another, they dwelled apart from each other, believing that their name was the better."

"Could they not feel it in here?" questions Thomas, pointing to his truth place.

"Ah, Thomas ... Perhaps they had not been given such wondrous gifts as our sweet Sisters have given unto you all. Perhaps we cannot judge them from here because, mind you, they believed unto what they believed because they thought it to be the very highest and best. Not because they had any-thing against their brother or sister, but because they believed the light of their truth to be the brightest of all."

Unconsciously rubbing his truth place, Thomas ponders this. "Well, so how does one distinguish between one's own truth and someone else's? If, as they say, sweet Jacob, they believe so firmly in their own truth that they cannot see mine, what do I do about that?"

Jacob rolls his eyes upward and tilts his face. He raises his strong hands, and we hear him call out, "O Lord God, give me the great wisdom to answer young Thomas' question. Let me answer it in Thy Name and in Thy Voice. Send unto me the means by which we can find the answer. Send me ..."

"Greetings, Jacob."

Laughter breaks out as all turn to see Zelotese standing, his face aglow.

"Ah, God answers all prayers. Welcome!" Jacob moves over a bit on the boulder's ledge upon which he is perched. "Seat yourself here, Zelotese. Since God has sent you in an-swer to my prayer, we await that which you have to give."

With a smile that evidences his love for Jacob, Zelotese sits and reaches a hand around to place it on Jacob's shoulder, and Jacob does the same to him. "Can you tell me ..." He glances about and then turns to peer at Thomas with the piercing gaze so typical of Zelotese.

For a moment Thomas reels backward, for all know that Zelotese is a great mystic, a great seer, and who knows what else. "Y-yes?" stutters Thomas somewhat timidly.

"This great rock upon which my brother Jacob and I are resting ourselves ... What is its name?"

Blankly, Thomas looks this way and that at his friends, who shrug their shoulders, they don't know. Finally, his wrinkled brow evidencing the strain going on within, he answers, "I don't know. I did not know it had a name."

"Does anyone know the name of this rock?"

Everyone is looking at each other, shrugging, questioning. Even Jesus is smiling and looking at His friends, lifting His shoulders as though to say, "I only know it as *Rock*."

"Well, then, what do you feel in your truth place about what I ask you?"

Thomas unconsciously rubs the area above his heart. "I don't really feel anything. Nothing."

"What would that tell you?" Zelotese continues softly.

"Uh-h ... Well, when I feel truth, it is warm. It is like a tingly, good feeling. When there is not truth, it is dreary, an empty, hollow, nothing sort of feeling, but mostly cold."

"And what do you feel now?"

"As I said," Thomas responds, somewhat impatiently, "I do not feel anything."

"Well, no matter what you feel, no matter what you do not feel, no matter what you see or do not see, hear or do not hear, there is a message, there is something to be learned."

"Oh. I ... I understand," Peter offers pensively. "If there is nothing in the truth place, then there is nothing in the question. Right?"

"Very astute." Zelotese gazes at Peter intently, causing him to squirm a bit.

"Sayest thou that when a question comes to you," asks John forthrightly, "and there is no sense of it within, that the question is not a question?"

"In the manner in which you express it, yes, that is so. But there is much more."

"Will you share that with us then, Zelotese?" John requests sincerely, turning to look at Jesus, who nods, smiling.

"If a thing comes unto you in life in your journeys ahead, and in your truth place you find no answer, it is not warm or vibrant ... tingly, as you called it, Thomas. And it is not cold, nor dark, nor heavy, nor any such as one of you might feel to contrast a truth of a thing, then you know that there is no truth to be sought in that which is before you."

"How can a thing have no truth?" probes John.

"That which is, simply is."

"So are you saying that the name of your rock is *Rock*?" Peter interjects.

"Yes. It is not singled out from all of the rocks about, unless *we* single it out. And we have done just that. So, now, if you look upon this great rock," patting it with his hands, "it is unique from the others because we have *seen* it."

"Oh-h ..." Thomas responds, "I am beginning to understand because of how the Maidens have taught us to see. They said if we look upon a thing, we give it energy. If we speak a thing, we give it existence, definition. Is that what you are saying?"

Smiling, Zelotese nods. "They have taught you well. Or perhaps more appropriately, they have called forth from deep within you the very gifts of God."

"If I look upon a thing," Jesus notes, "and I hold my gaze upon it, I see its vibrancy ... a sort of light that surrounds it. When I look upon your rock, Zelotese, I see the light around it and it is constant, not so much moving as the light around you and sweet Jacob. Help me to understand what differentiates these two."

"A very good question," Jacob offers with obvious love. "Do the rest of you see what your brother, Jesus, sees?"

Some are squinting. Some are leaning. To the side, a lovely young maiden leans so far over that she nearly falls into the lap of the child next to her.

Noting this, Zelotese nods to her.

She brightens and straightens up. "I see it. But, to me, the rock seems connected to all the other rocks. So that if I look at this one over here and that one up there …" pointing about, "it is the same light. They are mostly all the same. But the light around you, sweet teacher, and that around our elder brother Jacob is very different."

John turns to the maiden. "How do you see the light around where Zelotese and Jacob are seated?"

Again leaning over and almost falling, she then sits erect, concluding as she points to Zelotese, "Well, right there where his back rests against the boulder, there seems to be … It is like his energy, which is in the light around him, is dancing in and out of the light around the rock, about this far …" She holds her hands several hands-breadth apart.

"Thank you," John smiles and nods. "I just wanted to be sure we were seeing the same."

"I don't see it," Thomas declares.

"Perhaps you are not looking with the right sight," Zelotese answers, laughing gently.

"Well, which sight is that? Is it the sight I see you with, or the sight I use when I look for guidance from God?"

"Clearly the latter. However, you decide whether these are separate. Is that not so?" He turns to look at Jesus.

Jesus laughs aloud. "Thou knowest it to be."

"Well, teach me," Thomas asks, almost pleading. "I can see with one or the other, but not both."

Some of the other children laugh, too, for they know this

only too well.

"I mean," he continues, "I know what our Sisters have shown us and called forth from within me. I know how to see with that inner sight. But it is this sight," he points to his eyes, "that wants to see its own way and does not want to see what my God sight sees."

"Why do you suppose that is?" Zelotese asks gently.

"Well, that is my question to you. Why is that?"

Zelotese turns to look at Jacob. One could question whether he knows not what to say, or whether he is struggling to contain an expression of humor.

Jacob laughs mightily, along with some of the Maidens who have gathered in the background to listen.

"Why do you not ask that question of them?" Jacob suggests, gesturing to the Maidens. "Give Zelotese a rest."

"Yes, do let me rest," Zelotese sighs, feigning weariness.

Glancing around to see if Judy is present, Thomas turns to look up into the loving eyes of all of the sisters who are standing about.

There she is, over to the side some distance away, leaning back beneath a rock outcropping, smiling. She gestures with a wave to the Maidens she has so lovingly nurtured, taught, and shared with for so many years.

One of them, Miriam, rises and walks gracefully down to the children, standing between them and Zelotese and Jacob's position. "This rock does have a name," she begins. "First it was Jacob's rock. Then it became the rock of Zelotese and Jacob. Forevermore, when you see it, you will think of it as such, will you not?"

"Yes," answers Thomas, as though answering for all the children.

"Well, then, what is it about this rock that you now agree has given it a name?"

Thomas rubs his face.

Again, the little maiden off to the side raises her hand.

"Yes, Martha?"

"It is because I love them both, now I love the rock that has supported them."

"You are sweet, and you have found truth, Martha," Miriam continues softly. "And you, Thomas … You asked about your sight and your God sight. The bridge that will unite them is a bridge of love. If you look upon Jacob, Zelotese, and the rock upon which they are now seated," she steps aside, gesturing for him to so do, "you see it and them with your eyes. True?"

Thomas nods, seemingly having become a bit shy in the presence of this sweet Sister whose truth is so beautiful.

"What do you see within, with your God sight?"

"Oh, my God sight sees the beauty of these two, who are sons of God," Thomas answers, obviously deeply touched by what his inner sight perceives.

"And you see the various lights and colors around each of them, do you not?"

"Yes, I do, clearly, and around the great stone upon which they are seated, though moreso like a solid, whitish light. It has a little shimmer to it, but it is not moving very much, and their light … It moves greatly."

"How are you seeing this now?"

"Through my God sight," he asserts boldly.

"Then what is the color of the garment on Jacob?"

He turns to Miriam with a look as though annoyed at being brought from what he knows as his God sight to be called to now study something evidently physical in nature.

Suddenly the realization comes over him and he leans back and laughs. "Oh, my goodness, I thought they were separate, the lights around Jacob and Zelotese, and the color of Jacob's robe. But they are not, are they?"

"No, they are not. The pathway between them is love … being able to see through the eyes that know love both inwardly and outwardly. So now you can see the color and light of Jacob's robe, as well as the light of the rock, as well as the energies, the lights and such, *around* them and the rock."

"When I see the energy around the rock," Martha interjects, "I look about and see the energy being somewhat, if not exactly, the same around other rocks. What will happen when they get up and move away from that rock where I see the energies coming together?"

Miriam turns, and Jacob and Zelotese both nod and slide easily down off the rock ledge on which they were seated.

"Oh-h ..." she murmurs. "It is still there! Look."

All the children oo-o and ah-h, for where Zelotese and Jacob had been seated, there are swirls of color and light.

"Will it always stay there now?" Martha is in wonder.

"What do you think?" asks Miriam.

"I think I shall always see it there. If I come back here and see this great rock again, I think I will always see it."

"Yes, but will it really be there?" questions Thomas. "I mean, I think she is seeing with her memory. I can see the energy getting smaller right now."

"How so?" probes Miriam.

"Well, the energy of the rock is sort of drinking up the energy of brother Jacob and Zelotese."

"I see the energy differently, though," Peter offers. "Look over here towards the right of the rock. The energy looks like it is starting to run down over the edge."

"Look you now for a moment if you would, children, upon your brothers, Zelotese and Jacob," Miriam directs.

Several oh-h and ah-h as they see that Jacob and Zelotese have closed their eyes and are standing with their hands folded, obviously doing something, perhaps praying, perhaps something else.

"Please. Share with us what you are doing." Miriam smiles at Zelotese and Jacob.

Zelotese opens his eyes to see her nodding, inviting him to tell. "Your brother Jacob and I are imparting a blessing, a prayer, to this great rock, and to all that is one with this rock … in other words, all the rocks and the earth, itself.

"And what you, Peter, saw running down the side is our thankfulness offered in prayer to the rock, for the rock has served Jacob and me by providing us a place to rest and become one with God. The gift that you saw, and do see, of its constant, stable energy is something of which we can all partake. For the very Spirit of God is in the earth, ever offering unto us according to our need and our will to partake of it. So, Jacob and I have taken the gift of the Spirit of God, given to us in the form of this rock. And the work we just did was our thankfulness in return for that given."

"Why do I not see the gift that the rock gave you?" asks Thomas.

"Because it is now one with us."

"Where?"

"There is some of it!" Peter interjects. "See? Over his left shoulder! Look at that place and then look at the rock. It is the same."

"I can show you more if you like," offers Zelotese.

The children are wiggling with excitement.

Thomas calls out, "Yes, please!"

Zelotese turns his back to the group. "Look at the center of my back, from the lower portion of my body and up."

"Oh-h …" comes a long sigh from Martha. "It is all glowy around your … Forgive me, please. But on your … Where you sat down, you have the rock light all over you."

The other children begin to giggle but they see this is true. There is, indeed, a growing orb of light identical to that which they can see around the great rock.

It is starting to narrow itself as it moves upward along Zelotese' back. They look up to the place over his left shoulder and can see that some of it has reached that far, as Peter pointed out.

Thomas is exuberant. "Tell us what this is!"

Zelotese turns back to the group. "Think back to what you have been given ... the nourishment shared with you by the Holy Maidens."

Miriam looks down shyly.

"When you join with a thing, you have a choice. You can take of it, you can give to it, or you can do both. The latter is a state of oneness and is perhaps the ideal. Taking from it is to answer a need, while giving to it is for a service. Becoming one with it, however, empowers each to give the very best to the other. What results (if you will continue to watch) is a beautiful state of oneness of my energies and those of this beautiful rock, both recognizing our oneness and affirming that we are creations of God.

"So, when you look for a truth, Thomas, and you find naught, perhaps it is because you have not seen with your total sight. Perhaps it is because the truth that you seek is not in the form in which you know to seek it. Thereafter, must you open yourself and use all that you are. For in all that you experience, on all journeys, in all whom you meet, all things exist through the truth of God."

As you consider that which has been given, ask of yourself: How do I see that which is before me? Can I look at it through the eyes of love? Can I perceive it through the vision called truth? Can I understand it because I have the sight of compassion? Can I know it because I know the oneness of it with God?

If it shall be that your footstep falls upon a pathway which challenges you, use all of this as given and the greater, that at the point of decision it will show you that you are a Child of God and that the power of God is within you. If you take from that which is before you as it offers, and only in that manner, then that thing, be it person or event, is dominant; if you look upon it in the spirit of that given above, then you know it and its uniqueness, and the decision is yours. Thereafter, you are right-eous as a child of God.

There is much in motion in and about the Earth. Because it is so, each of you must, therefore, also be in motion. It is a motion of progression, movement forward, to give you a reference for the mind to comprehend. But it is movement in the broader sense, the expansion and opening of your awareness on multiple levels of being. Look for these. Do not fear them, nor the change forthcoming. Look for the gifts they offer you.

Chapter Fifteen

Seeds of Promise

The early light of dawn is visible only by the glow growing on the distant horizon. The last embers of the cookfire from the previous evening still glimmer. Scattered about are many little sleeping forms, and around their periphery are those simple structures in which the guardians, the keepers, and the teachers of these many children are also resting.

As we gaze from the periphery of the group of children towards the dawn's light, we see an enormous boulder silhouetted against the horizon. Atop its summit, we can see a sizeable figure, standing, smiling down upon the sleeping group. With a twinkle in his eye, he raises his arms out to his sides and begins to dance about in a small circle, a sort of shuffling movement. His eyes close, his head bobs left and right, and we can hear his low melodious voice greeting this new day.

Heads pop up here and there among the group below as Jacob's song calls them to awaken. With excitement, they jump up, here and there shouting, "Jacob! Jacob! It is Jacob!"

He answers them not, but his smile increases as he continues his slow, shuffling, circular dance, eyes still closed and arms still outstretched, singing praises to God, calling out to this new day, "Come. Embrace us, as we embrace you."

The children, all awakened now, are scurrying about the bottom of the boulder, searching for a way up, shouting in excitement, "Bring me up, Jacob. Lift me up."

Jacob's voice is rising as he moves and sways in his little dance, his eyes closed, smiling all the more.

Many of the others (the elders, the maidens, and such) have thrown back the coverings of the openings on the small shelters and have begun to gather. Some place more fuel upon the fire as others replicate their own version of Jacob's little dance, but all smile as they joyfully watch the children clamoring and excitedly calling out that they should be the ones Jacob pulls up to be with him.

Yet on he continues.

Finally he stops. He opens his eyes, his arms still outstretched, and looks down. "What a glad day, dear children. Come. Join me." He promptly sits cross-legged, looking down upon the encampment.

The early dawn's light coming from behind him seems to illuminate him, as the children jump about trying to find footholds and fingerholds.

One of them calls out. "How did you arise this great rock, Jacob? We find no pathway."

Jacob raises his hand and points a finger to the heavens. "He has helped me." He laughs heartily. Then he bends to look down at those immediately before him. "If you ask, it surely will be given." Leaning back, again he laughs, and then begins to rock to and fro, as though the raucous children striving to climb this massive boulder are non-existent. Rocking and singing, suddenly he stops and opens his eyes to look into two pair of eager eyes directly below him.

There, standing near the foot of the great rock are the Master and John, laughing. The Master turns to whisper in John's ear. John, with a great smile, nods his head vigorously, rushes to the base of the rock and bends down. The Master places a careful foot upon John's shoulder and then another, and leans, placing His weight against the great rock. Slowly, John raises himself as the Master inches His way up.

All the while, Jacob is laughing.

Finally, Jacob reaches out for the Master's hand, pulls Him up the last short distance, and rests Him upon his knee. John and the Master are looking at one another, laughing.

At first, it appears that only the Master shall be with Jacob. Then He reaches to His midsection and pulls the stout wrapping from His garment. With Jacob's great arm around Him, the Master lowers it down to John, who grasps it and easily scampers up. Re-securing the wrapping around His midsection, the Master laughs heartily, as does John who has perched himself snugly upon Jacob's other knee.

Jacob, also laughing, reaches out with a great embrace and hugs them mightily. "You see?" he calls to the remaining children who are all looking up. "They cooperated."

Getting the message, the children climb on one another, and then reach down to help those left behind. Finally, the great boulder is covered with giggling, writhing children, Jacob in their midst, rolling about as they take turns pouncing upon him.

"Tell us a story, Jacob," they plead when they've settled down. "Please. Teach us."

"Yes," the Master adds. "Do teach us."

Jacob straightens up, and the children, whose bodies fairly cover the surface of the boulder, all find some way to snuggle close to him, to place a hand, an arm, some portion of their bodies against his. So great is his love for them that not one is ever left out. He sees to it here again, and in response to this love, they embrace him in every way they can.

"As you travel through the wonderful journey called life," begins Jacob gently, "you will find many challenges such as these great stones. Each time that you do, remember this day and how we, together, found a way to rise above that which seemed insurmountable. It is only in the perception of what is before one that one has either *obstacle* or *opportunity*. If you perceive a thing to be limiting, then surely you have gifted it with the power to limit. But if you perceive a thing and know it to be a gift, an opportunity, have you not equally embraced it, gifted it, with the power to be just so?"

"But dear Jacob," one of the children to his left asks, "what if I am alone and I encounter a great stone as this? It was only upon my brother's shoulders that I was able to ascend it and be with you. How am I to do this if I am alone?"

Jacob leans back and his great laugh reverberates off the distant hills.

At the sound of his laughter, the Maidens come to the forefront, for their love of Jacob knows no measure. Several of the elders also come to honor and acknowledge him.

His laughter subsiding, he looks down upon what he calls his family, his brothers and sisters, and responds softly to the child. "How is it possible that you could ever find yourself alone?"

The child's face reflects his lack of understanding, but then brightens a bit. "I know that I am never alone, that God is ever with me, and that our great elders who have gone before are looking after us, if we allow them. But what I mean is, my body being alone. Not my spirit. It is never alone."

The children all cheer for this one, laughing and shouting praises, and the Maidens smile at this.

But Thaddeus continues. "My body is not as great as yours, dear Jacob, though I hope some day it shall be," again, garnering a murmur of laughter. "How could I possibly arise such a great stone alone?"

Jacob, changing his demeanor, straightens himself like a slender young tree. He releases his embrace of the children, his eyes close and he raises his hands. "Great Father-Mother-God, here is Thaddeus. He has met an opportunity on the path of life. Tell us, that we might know how to counsel him. How shall he meet this? How shall he obtain the blessing from it?"

Naught but silence answers him.

Jacob's hands are still outstretched above him, palms up,

as though he is awaiting the receipt of something.

Then his face brightens, his eyes pop open and he looks up. "Thank you, Lord God, for the answer to our prayer!" He brings his arms down, and re-embraces some of the children now clambering on him.

There is silence again as he looks about.

"Well?" asks Thaddeus, "Are you not going to share with us what you received from our Lord God?"

Jacob's laughter bellows. "If you meet an obstacle on the path of life that seems too great, which does not evidence its gift to you, then go around it."

"What?"

"Go around it."

"But I thought the idea was to take such an obstacle and transform it into a stepping stone, an opportunity. How does going around something like that honor the gift? Have you not taught us that everything offers us a gift?"

"Indeed so. But as you saw and heard, I asked our Lord God for the answer, and the answer is, *If it seems too great, then go around it.*"

Thaddeus shakes head to and fro, obviously puzzled.

Jacob turns to Jesus. "Do you know what is meant in the answer God has given?"

Smiling into Jacob's face, the Master nods, His face bright. "I do."

"Well, then, will you share what you know, that we all might gain from your knowledge?"

Jesus straightens Himself, emulating Jacob. "There is no such thing as an insurmountable obstacle. There are those obstacles that do not beckon unto us. This great stone with Jacob upon it called to us because Jacob was a part of it. But if there is such an obstacle that is empty and has no light, then that is not a part of your path. And the gift it offers is the knowing that when such is met, then there is no ear to hear, no eyes to see, and no purpose in your challenging it."

Thaddeus, listening intently, again begins to shake his head. "How do I know the difference, Jesus? If there is to be an obstacle before me, how do I know when I should strive to ascend it, or nay? How do I know when to go around a thing, or attempt to become one with it and ascend it?"

"You speak to it. If it answers you, it is a part of your path. If it does not answer, it is not."

Thaddeus' head is bobbing up and down. "Okay. I shall do that. Each time I meet an obstacle, I shall speak to it."

Laughter bursts from all those gathered.

Without another word, Jacob begins to lower the children, one after the other, over the side of the great rock.

He himself finally slips down effortlessly to land upon the ground before it, and the children mob him once again. Moving ever so slowly, he touches one upon the face over here, pats another upon the head over there, until finally, the children go running to the cookfire with the morning's meal upon it.

The Maidens and several of the others who are present come to greet and embrace Jacob, then stroll off together to the side where they seat themselves and watch the children play around those preparing the meal.

Jesus, standing by the cookfire with the others, has turned and seen this, and strides over, followed closely by John and two of the others.

Jacob looks up from his seated position. "Ah, children. Your curiosity is greater than your hunger, I see."

"It is so," responds Jesus. "I would have you awaken within me that which is now sleeping. Will you do this?"

"I will," nods Jacob. "And in you, as well, John, and the rest of you? You are willing to set aside your hunger to be with humble Jacob?"

"Always, Jacob." John rushes to embrace him as the others come and seat themselves close by.

"Will you? Will you awaken me, Jacob?" asks Jesus.

The Maidens who are gathered move closer to form a circle 'round this small group. Several of the elders have also come to be at their beloved Jacob's side, as well as some of the teachers and workers.

Little Sophie asks, "Please, will you teach us all?"

Jacob smiles upon her upturned face. "How can I teach you that which you already know?"

"Help me to know it, then, Jacob."

Jacob begins. "You bear a jewel of a gift of God's blessings, each of you. Because you see this in the singular sense, you believe it to be only a portion of the beauty and potential of God. And yet, because it is your gift, and because it is a part of your uniqueness, it therefore must have all else within it equally so."

Jesus presses him further. "If a thing looks like a thing and we identify it by a certain name, how are we to know that the presence of all else is also embraced within something which we see as singular?"

"Ah-ha! You have been reflecting, I see."

Smiling with some joy at Jacob's recognition of His contemplation, Jesus simply nods.

"And you, John ... Have you such thoughts?"

"I do, dear Jacob. I see in the desert that which goes unseen by others. When I speak to them, as you suggested to Thaddeus, they answer."

Jacob laughs. "Then you are speaking with the rocks and the trees and such?"

A giggle of laughter comes from the group.

But Jesus offers quietly, "I, too."

"So, then," Jacob encourages, "what have you been told by these things in the desert?"

John looks down and fidgets, glancing up this way and that.

Jesus laughs gently. "Come, come! Share with us your discussions with the creatures and the land. How do they speak to you?"

"Not in a voice as yours," replies John, somewhat defensively. "But in here." He thrusts his thumb against his chest. "Here is where I hear them."

"And here, too," adds Jesus, touching His head.

"Do *you* hear it, dear Jesus, as you hear my words?"

"No, it is without the sound. It is like the sound is inside my head, not outside."

"And you, John. How do you hear ... in there?" Jacob thrusts a stout forefinger to tap John upon his chest, causing him to giggle.

"It is not heard in the way that one hears a voice. I feel it. It is like what I feel when you sing your songs, your morning prayers to God. That, I feel in the same way."

"Ah-h. So, my morning song is heard inside you?"

"Oh, yes," giggles John, glancing at Jesus to be certain that He is going to confirm this, which He does immediately.

"And the rest of you ... Do you hear my song within?"

They nod and smile, glancing at one another.

Jacob pauses for a long time as he glances around, into the eyes of the Maidens, the teachers, the prophets, the elders, the healers, the seers, who are now all gathered. "Do all of you hear within, as these children do?"

Some look down quickly. Others meet his eyes openly with profound warmth and subtle nods.

Jacob's gaze falls upon one of the workers who is seated quietly at the outer periphery. "And you ... Do you hear and feel my voice within?"

Looking down, the young man answers quietly. "I do."

"And what else might you share with us?"

He looks up. "Your songs live on, Jacob. Your very presence is a living part of my life. These moments we are sharing here will live on in me and will be of comfort and support all throughout. This I know."

"You see?" Jacob looks at Jesus warmly. "There is your

answer. It is how we hold things. It is how we open ourselves to let the Light of God flow. Thaddeus asked about obstacles, wanting to know how to transform them into opportunities. It is by claiming the inner potential of a thought, of a word, of an intent, that it becomes a living thing. As you do this, you will, dear Jesus, awaken that which is now at rest within you. It is the holding of a thing. It is the believing unto it that empowers it, and thereby empowers you.

"But tell me, John … You hear the things of the desert. Do you speak to the insects?"

Silence.

With a troubled look on his face, John answers. "Not too well. They do not seem to be listening."

More laughter comes from the group.

"Ah-ha! Then, that is similar to our example: If you speak to something, and it answers you not, perhaps you should go around it."

"Do you think it so, Jacob?" asks John, seriously.

"It would appear so, would it not? Do they harm you?"

"No, they do not. They just do not speak to me."

Jesus laughs heartily, as do the others.

"Well, I do try, Jesus." John is again a bit defensive.

Jesus laughs again, and John soon finds the humor in his own comments and laughs along.

Jacob rises and walks among the group. All turn to watch him as he does.

Then we hear Jesus ask, "Jacob, what shall we do when you are no longer with us? How shall we have the gift that you give us in this moment in times when you are naught?"

Slowly Jacob turns to look back at Him and the other children. "Awaken that which sleeps within you, Jesus, and answer your own question."

Understanding what Jacob is intending, Jesus closes His eyes and bows His head for a moment.

The other children emulate Him.

Jesus' eyes open and He looks at Jacob. "Because I carry you in here, where John hears …" leaning to poke a finger at John's chest, making him giggle again, "because we hold you in here, Jacob, is it not so that thou art, then, ever with us?"

"What has been given here this day?" Jacob comes to sit between these two friends. "As you believe, and as you hold that belief and strive to live within it, is it not yours?"

Jesus nods affirmatively, pleased to have this confirmed.

"Can a thing pass away, ever totally pass away, if one is holding it with some intent of goodness within?" Jacob has been observing John, who has moved into deep reflection, and quietly lifts him onto his lap.

Jesus smiles at them. Suddenly, He rises to also sit upon Jacob's lap, and Jacob reaches a mighty arm to embrace Him.

John has leaned his head on Jacob's shoulder, his face buried in the great neck.

Jacob strokes him. "You have seen it. This, I know. You have seen what lies ahead, have you not, John?"

Lifting his tear-stained face, John looks into Jacob's loving eyes. "I have seen it."

Jacob brushes a lock of John's hair from his cheek and uses a forefinger to remove a small tear. "Be of good cheer, John. For the Way is open unto us. He is here. He will become the Path and the Light."

"But I cannot … I cannot be with Him."

"Ah-h, yes. Many will say this in the years ahead. Many of the faithful will come to ask, *Why can I not be with Him?* But you … You have been given a great gift," his voice becoming louder, "as have we all."

He then looks down and caresses Jesus in his other arm. "How shall we counsel your dear friend, Jesus? What do you have to teach us?"

Unaffected, it would seem, by the experience, the vision, that John has shared, Jesus smiles and speaks with a gentle, but steady voice. "As I am awakened within and I become one with you, can you not do the same with me?"

Jacob is nodding, his eyes closed, the light within emanating from and surrounding him. His arm rests behind Jesus, his hand gently rubbing His shoulder.

"It is only for us to awaken the truth that lies within." He reaches over to put His finger upon John's chest. "Here am I, John." Taking John's hand and putting it upon His own chest, He continues, "And here are you. How can we, as Jacob has awakened within us this day, ever be separate if we believe … if we hold that belief and if we let our love endure? I cannot imagine that I shall ever be apart from you."

John jumps to his feet and collides into the Master, knocking Him off of Jacob's lap. Only Jacob's great arm keeps them from crashing hard to the ground, as they giggle and laugh and roll around, so typical of young friends such as these.

Jacob sits watching their joyful play and that of the other children who have come to jump into the foray, now all rolling about, laughing, tickling and embracing each other. "Look at them." He glances at his brothers and sisters nearby. "Look at their uniqueness, their incredible beauty." His gaze falls upon young Jesus. "It is He who shall lead the Way." Then he looks upon John, "And he already knows it. He shall fulfill the prophecy and tell of his Brother and the Promise, and he shall be alone." As though shaking himself from a dream, brightening, he looks about. "But only in the outer. For is it not true, as sweet Jesus has gifted us, that what we call being alone is only the manifestation of a tiny portion of our being? And this, as we open from within, can allow oneness, no matter where, no matter what the circumstance."

The children have paused and brushed themselves off, and are seated respectfully off to Jacob's right.

Speaking to all gathered now, Jacob continues. "These are those times our great prophets and teachers … many of you, dear friends," honoring the elders who are present, "have foretold. These are times of rejoicing. In the years ahead the seeds must be sown, and these seeds are far greater than they seem in the moment. When you, each of you, and you ..." he points to the children, "are about your works, there will be those moments where you will think, *This cannot be so. This is not my Father's work. These peoples do not have ears with which to hear, nor eyes to give them sight.* And yet, so as you give it, these are good seeds and they will bear fruit.

"In times which lie beyond, which we cannot know in this moment, others like us will awaken, and they will look back upon these times. They will look back upon Him and His teachings," pointing to Jesus, "and they will do so to harvest the fruits which all of this offers them. Indeed, in that time, it may be as though they are here with us right this moment, listening to my words. Listening to yours. They may, in fact, be here now ... that as I embrace you." He turns to look with a loving gaze at all the children who have come to squeeze in tight beside their beloved Jacob. "They also are embracing you. As they tell of their love for you, it is in my words that they are empowered to speak this to you.

"Some of you may have returned in that time, carrying the seeds within you. And as Jesus so wisely said, you may then, as now, seek to awaken that which sleeps within you. When you ask, who will answer your call? Who will meet your need? Who will summon forth from within you that which is merely slumbering?"

He looks off with a distant air, then turns to look upon Jesus and John, then up at Sophie, Miriam, Hannah, then Thaddeus and all the others, and finally back to Jesus and John. "This is the beginning of a time which is the sowing of the seeds of hope, the Promise of oneness, the awakening of that which sleeps within the Earth and its peoples. It is, in so many ways, the first step of a journey that is to be of great length. Some of you," he turns again to glance about the group, "will return again and again. You will bear blessings that will nurture these seeds, that will keep them alive in the hearts and minds and spirits of certain people in those times. Then, when the heavens are in alignment, and there is harmony among the great forces, the Way will be made passable. And a great time of harvest will unfold.

"Hold these thoughts in your hearts, along with the many other joys already resident there, for as you do, they are alive … as are you alive. Believe that which is your truth, and give it honor. It will sustain you.

"Others will challenge us, will they not, Jacob?"

"Indeed, Jesus. They will especially challenge you."

"Why?" He asks innocently.

"Because your truth will reveal that which is their illusion. And they have found comfort in it. They know it. It is a part of them. Your truth will awaken their sight and their hearing."

"Will they not like this? Do they not seek truth?" He glances over at John, who nods an affirmation.

"Within them, there is ever the desire to know truth. But they are as just so many who will come and pass … striving to understand. Remember the great stone?" Jacob nods to the boulder upon which he had previously perched. "Without cooperation, without oneness, the others could not ascend. But you two," pointing to Him and John, "claimed your oneness. Where one lifted the other up, the other reached down to help in kind. Is it not so in all of existence, in all of life, that as you lift another up, so must you, as well, be lifted?

"So, yes, Jesus, they will find your truth to be difficult because they know it not. But that which is now within you (in a manner of speaking, asleep) will awaken. And it will lift them up. As it does, you will be lifted even higher. You will become known. And," pointing to John, "he will proclaim that you are the Way, in order for the truth that is within you to shine brightly. Yet, it will be looked upon by some as unacceptable.

"Dwell not long upon this, but upon the knowledge that these are the fruits of God being sown. Each seed you give, dear Jesus, will be received by some in the truth that you have within. They will carry it and give it to others, and they, in turn, to others. In the many years that will come and go, so will the seed of your truth spread. And when the cycle is complete, you will come again to claim the great harvest."

Certain of you are returned and, as Jacob prophesied, are preparing, that the harvest can be gathered. As you see challenges before you, look for that inner light of truth. And know this: You are the custodians of the seeds of truth sown those many years ago. You have borne them here and there to arrive at your current time.

The Earth and those upon it will react, as Jacob counseled Jesus that they would react to His truth. But remember his words: Let your love and your truth, first within, become that which shines forth to the without.

Chapter 16

Walk with Me

The high light of the early to mid afternoon reflects brilliantly upon the great sea. A gentle breeze stirs the luminescence of color and the radiance of light creating a display dazzling to behold.

Nathanael and Simeon are seeking further information from a family that has approached them.

"How are you called?" Simeon inquires.

"Oh, good sir, please have mercy on us. We have heard of you and your peoples. We seek only assistance. This one, we cannot tend to, for we can barely tend to ourselves."

Simeon glances behind the man and a woman huddled with a young female, and sees pressed up against them a small lad, perhaps four years of age.

"Why would you give us ... Is he your son?"

"Yes." The woman turns to gesture to him to come forth from behind the shelter of her husband and daughter.

He anxiously looks down, then up at his father and mother, and over to his sister.

His father reaches out, placing a hand gently upon his head. He leans to kiss him on the forehead and whispers, "All is well. We have spoken to you about these. Perhaps they can make your life better. Perhaps even heal you."

Slowly, the lad comes out from behind his family, his body moving strangely.

Simeon can see that he stands only with the aid of a carved branch that supports him on one side. Quickly scanning the lad, he notes that the right leg is withered and except for the toes does not even reach the ground.

With a twisted grimace of pain, the lad swings his body about moving laboriously to stand beside his mother.

Nathanael, guardian of the Expectant Ones, bends to one knee to welcome the lad. "I am called Nathanael. We welcome you. If you will have us, we will care for you and bring gladness and joy to your heart. And perhaps as your body expresses this joy and gladness, that which lacks ease within it will vanish. What say you, young lad?"

Nervously, he shifts his weight about, each time, a flicker of pain evident upon his face.

His mother has reached around to lift his chin and with her other hand strokes his hair, then draws him up against her body with obvious love and tenderness.

Tears in her eyes, she turns to look at Nathanael who is still kneeling. "Do you mean this?"

He smiles, nods, and looks up at Simeon who also smiles reassuringly at the woman.

She bends, and with her hands cupping her son's face, speaks gently to him. "Our love is ever with you, this you know. But this is the very best. These are people of God. We have heard much of them and their works. Each day, in our prayers, we will hold you as I do now." She kisses him upon his forehead and each cheek.

The lad looks at her, his face relatively expressionless, and then turns to look up at his father and sister, who each place a hand on his head. Their eyes glisten with tears of love and the loss of the youngest of their family.

He studies his sister and father, then lastly, turns to gaze into his mother's eyes one final time. With his free hand, he places a fingertip bravely upon his chest. "I have you here. I will always have you here, but I will miss you so very much."

They rush together in an embrace of such oneness that it is difficult to tell where one body begins and the other ends.

Nathanael rises and Simeon scoops up the lad, whose startled look gives way to a little chuckle as he is impressed by Simeon's muscular stature and the strength of his grasp.

"I wanted to carry him," Nathanael teases playfully.

"Perhaps if you are patient, I shall let you carry him after a time. But first, it is my turn." He looks at the lad, "I am called Simeon."

They move off. After a few moments, Nathanael, who is leading the way, raises a hand. The group pauses, turns, and gestures to the family. The family waves in return and they, too, begin their journey, but in the opposite direction, south-west along the sea.

The thunk-thunk-thunk of Nathanael's great staff provides an almost rhythmic intent, as they head towards the encampment of the Expectant Ones.

"It is not so important that one is asleep in order to be guided by God," Zelotese is sharing. "Nor is it so important that one sees all that is. What is of importance is that one observes, that one listens, and that as one sees and hears in here … " tapping his forehead, "and in here …" tapping his chest, "to know that these are the places of resonance for what is received from here." He gestures above his head.

"Must I close my eyes?" Thomas asks.

"Do you like to close your eyes? Is that how you can hear and see better? When your eyes are closed?"

"Well, yes. If my eyes are open, I see everything that is about me, and then I think about those things that I see. With those thoughts inside my head and here …" he thumps his chest, "how can I hear God's message when I am getting messages from all about me? So, yes. I close my eyes to stop the Earth messages so I can get the God messages."

Off to Zelotese' left, Jacob chuckles a bit.

Thomas glances at him, at first with a hint of annoyance but almost immediately thereafter with a warm smile.

"What do you think, Thomas? That when your eyes are closed, the Earth messages are gone?"

"No, Jacob, they are not gone. I can open my eyes and they are right there where I left them when I closed my eyes."

"Well, if you know that they are there, and you open your eyes to verify that they are there, what difference does it make if your eyes are open or closed?"

This puzzles Thomas. He rubs his chin and looks down. "I shall have to contemplate that."

Over to the side, laughing a bit, is young Andrew. "Well, the difference is, as I see it, as one is seeing with the eyes, there is a sort of *stimulation*, I heard you call it, Jacob."

Jacob chuckles. "Yes ... stimulation, indeed."

"But when I close my eyes, the stimulation is gone." Sitting very erect, hands upon his knees, Andrew looks very much like a young angelic being.

Jacob is still chuckling. "What is the difference between seeing stimulus and thinking stimulus?"

Andrew's eyes pop open. "Well, I choose what I think about. But my eyes do not have a choice. They only see what is there. They cannot make something else be there. Right?"

Jacob nods exaggeratedly. "Oh yes, that is right."

"So, Andrew," Zelotese interjects, "you are saying that your mind can choose what it sees and your eyes cannot?"

"Yes, of course," Andrew answers dryly.

Zelotese then addresses all the children. "If you would, all of you, close your eyes for a moment, please."

There is shuffling about as the children find a comfortable position, for Zelotese is known for guiding them in profound ways.

"Andrew, what do you see in this moment?"

"I see darkness, Zelotese, sir."

Jacob chuckles again softly.

Andrew fidgets as he hears this.

"Is that what you have chosen to see?" asks Zelotese.

"Well, no. I did not choose it. It was just there."

"Did you not just say that you could choose? Your mind could choose what it wanted to see but your eyes could not?"

"Yes, I did."

"Then you must have chosen to see darkness."

"No, I did not. For darkness is always there when one closes their eyes. It is just there"

"So then, you did not choose to see darkness. Therefore, your mind does not always choose what it wishes to see."

Andrew slowly brings his hand up to his cheek and rubs the side of his face contemplatively, as is his nature to do when pondering something.

"May I respond?" Thomas asks quietly.

"Certainly, if you do not mind, Andrew."

"No. I have a good answer, but I should like to hear my brother's comments, too." Wiggling about a bit, obviously pleased with his own answer, Andrew settles down, his eyes pinched closed with a little wrinkle at the center of his brow.

"I see the darkness. I think we all do," Thomas begins.

Little voices from all about answer, "Yes. I, as well."

"Then, after the darkness passes, as Andrew stated, sometimes I can choose what I see, but other times I just wait for the darkness to be filled with the light and the guidance, with the teaching."

"Is this a long wait?" questions Zelotese.

"Oh no, not long. It is very quick."

"And you, Jesus … Is this true for you, as well?"

His eyes are closed and His face has a gentle smile. "It is very much the same for me, as well. Save I oft see light, not darkness, when I close my eyes."

Seated next to Him, John echoes this. "Yes, I think one chooses whether they wish to see light or darkness."

"I think you are right, John. I think it is a choice. But I do not think it is a choice that comes from one's mind. I think it is a choice that comes from one's spirit."

"Oh," responds Thomas, "I think that is right."

"Me, too," chime several of the others.

"So, if I close my eyes," Andrew asks, "and I see darkness, I can say to my spirit, *Spirit, bring me light,* and it will?"

"Yes," Jesus answers. "If you ask it of God, He will give it unto you. Thou knowest this."

"Yes, yes," Andrew responds somewhat impatiently, to the humor of almost all present, "but it never hurts to make certain. Sometimes one can think a thing, and ... Well, believing it and doing it do not often live in the same head."

Laughter flows from all. Here and there the children open their eyes.

Zelotese brings his hands up in front of his forehead, palms pressed together, and claps once.

All the eyes pop open now, for the children know what comes next.

Zelotese is seated very erectly. Suddenly, a small sound comes from him like the letter *O,* soft, slow, gentle.

The children now all emulate Zelotese' posture. Even Jacob places his hands on his knees and straightens himself.

The *O* becomes larger and larger and soon it seems as though it fills the wadi in which they are clustered, the gentle slopes to the group's right and left echoing and reverberating the *O.*

All ponder where so much breath can come from in one body, yet Zelotese continues, the backs of his thumbs pressed hard against his forehead. Then, it begins to change.

The children squirm and wiggle with excitement, watching intently, waiting to see what will come from this.

Silence. Then another sound comes, a sound much like the letter *M,* also slow, soft, flowing as water down a gentle stream, building as a stream would, gathering strength, depth, and breadth as it moves downwards towards the sea.

Then the *M* changes, and we hear the entire chant.

"Om-mani-padme-hum."

His hands come apart mid-way through the chant. He extends his arms broadly, and his body begins to sway.

Again, absolute silence.

He begins to speak, at first in a curious voice, a language which none know.

Then a change, a bit of a trill, and his voice deepens and another language comes forth.

Still another curious sound comes, as though there is a shift, a transformation of sorts, and a voice speaks in their native tongue. "Greetings, sweet children of God. I am come to you this day to speak to you of your heritage."

Rocking ever so gently, arms still outstretched, Zelotese continues on in an almost hypnotic tone, telling each child a bit of their heritage from lives beyond the present. Speaking gently here, strongly there, lifting, encouraging, guiding each of the children.

As they hear their names called, they close their eyes and bring their hands together up, gesturing as the Essenes do, testifying that their spirit is ever one with God.

Then comes, "In a time when darkness and light sought to know one another, you were called Amelius, the first of the Sons of God to set foot upon the Earth in physical form. With you were many: great legions of brothers and sisters who became as one with you and who pledged to journey, ever, at your side, seeking to make a path of light that those of Your brethren who had lost their way might find it again. As you passed through many journeys, wore many garments of flesh and were called by many different names, so are you now called Jesus. So shall you bring the eternal Word and Promise of God and place it upon the table of humankind, itself.

"And you, John, will tell of His coming. Some will scorn you, as they shall Him. Others will call you brother, Holy

One, Prophet, the Forerunner. But you will delve not into the pot of flesh, nor into the wellspring of that which stirs the minds and hearts of those on the Earth. Rather, you shall find your sustenance, as it is evident in you now, in the Spirit of God ... that which is His to give to you and that which is eternally given to all of us. But *you* will see it and call it forth, just as you will call forth the Master."

"It is my turn, Simeon." Nathanael chuckles and lifts the lad as though he is weightless and playfully but gently jostles him a bit. "We shall have to put some food into this body. It could use a bit more weight."

Looking into the guardian's eyes, the lad sees something in this warrior priest that stirs him deeply.

"You can put your arm around my neck if you would like," Nathanael offers.

Slowly, as they resume the trek, the lad begins to snuggle his head between Nathanael's great shoulder and chin.

"What have you there?" Jacob asks, rising to his feet, as the group enters the Essene encampment.

"One who will be a part of our family," Simeon answers.

Nathanael strides smoothly to stand before Jacob and Zelotese, and the boys all rush forward to welcome the lad.

Startled, he buries his face deep into Nathanael's neck.

"Gently now, children! Simeon, will you help?"

"Children, be seated. Give him a chance. We know not how long and great his journey has been, but surely he has some weariness, and you look like a herd of mountain sheep."

The children look at each other, making faces and gesturing like sheep, but they understand and settle themselves.

Jesus is resting upon His knees, His feet folded beneath Him. "How are you called?" He asks quietly.

The lad does not answer, his face still hard-pressed into the great guardian's neck.

"Perhaps some food and drink would be good." Editha gestures to some of the sisters who have come to see what is transpiring.

Miriam returns quickly with a bowl of warm tea made of rare herbs, sweetly flavored with a bit of wild honey.

As Nathanael seats himself, the lad takes a quick about look and then reburies his face.

But Miriam moves near and asks sweetly, "Would you drink of this? I made it myself just for you. Smell of it." She waves her hand across the top of the deep bowl.

The alluring scent of herbs and wild honey is irresistible. The young lad turns to look down into the bowl and a small hand, grimy from a long journey, emerges.

She continues tenderly, "Here, let me help you. Sip slowly. It is quite warm."

The lad sips loudly and several of the children giggle, who then receive a stern glance from Editha. He begins to drink with gusto. Then, in a pause to take a breath, he glances about. "Will they not have some?"

Miriam laughs. "They are not in want, I assure you. But that was very kind of you." She gestures to some of the sisters who move off, returning with bowls of warm tea for all.

"Even I?" Jacob teases in mock surprise.

"Even you, Jacob," giggles Hannah, handing him a bowl.

"Have I ... Is there honey in mine, as well?" He smiles as he gazes into Hannah's face, very near his own.

"Perhaps so, but not quite as much as in the lad's. I think you have had a bit more honey than you need!"

Jacob glances about his body as though looking to see if it has gained in breadth, and Hannah throws her head back and laughs. He laughs as well and shrugs his shoulders. "No matter, Hannah. Just receiving it from your hands will make it sweet enough for me."

Hannah laughs again and gestures at him. "Always the tease, Jacob." She turns to move close to the lad.

Jesus tries again to engage him in conversation. "What do you know of your life?"

He shrugs and looks into Nathanael's eyes, as though to seek comfort there, his arm still clinging to the great neck.

"Have you family?"

The lad nods.

"Have you a name?"

The lad nods.

Smiling broadly now, Jesus glances at John and Peter, who have come up nearby, as well.

"Do you suppose you could tell us what it is?" John asks, canting his head to the side.

"Yes. I am called Justus."

"Oh. Interesting name. Not of our people's, is it?" John glances at Jacob.

Jacob shrugs and addresses John's penetrating gaze, "Perhaps you could tell me who our people are, John, and I could answer. I thought God only had one people."

"You know what I mean." John looks down and chuckles, having been called up short by one he so loves.

"What is wrong with your body?" questions Andrew.

He looks blankly and then re-buries his head.

"Now, Andrew, is that a polite way to greet a new brother?" Andra asks gently, but the sternness of her voice and teaching is unmistakable.

Andrew's face flushes. He looks down as did John, then up again. "I do not ask for any reason other than to understand," Andrew counters, staring directly at Andra who has come to kneel in front of him. "You and the Sisters have taught us always that if we wish to know a thing, if we wish to understand it, then we question, we explore, we ask, we seek. That is the purpose of my question."

"But Justus does not know our teachings or our ways. He is from the outland. Therefore, we must honor his ways."

"Why?" questions Andrew with obvious innocence. "Is

he not to be my brother? Is he not to be one of us? Then, when shall I let him know that he is my brother and that this is our way?"

"Perhaps, Andrew," Andra moves within a nose breadth of his face, "when he has had a bit more to drink, a little to eat, and some much needed sleep, then, perhaps we could gently share with him what we hold to be dear and sacred."

Blank-faced, Andrew looks into Andra's deep dark eyes. Suddenly his face softens and he smiles. "I understand. Thank you. Sorry, Justus."

Justus has turned to look at this beautiful woman who is speaking with such firmness, and yet, evident even to his young mind, with great love for Andrew.

"I do not know," Justus begins softly. "It has always been this way. This leg," pointing to the left, "grew. See?" He extends it outward for all to see. "But this one did not." With considerable effort and obvious pain, he lifts it.

Jesus is studying the young lad carefully, as is Zelotese, who has moved around behind them.

"Let us take you to shelter," Hannah offers, moving up to stand beside Nathanael. "Let us take you and give you warm food, cleanse your body, and give you clean clothing. May I?" She bends, extending her arms.

Justus hesitates only a moment or two. Then, looking into Hannah's loving gaze, the sunlight dancing upon her glistening, cascading hair giving her the appearance of some luminous being, he glances back to Nathanael. "Thank you." He swiftly turns and reaches out his arms.

Hannah scoops him up and hugs him. Sophie comes to help, as does Editha, who has the lad's crutch under her arm. They and other sisters move over the summit and down to where the shelters are and the great ever-glowing cookfire.

"What thinkest thou?" Zelotese asks Jacob. "Where is there sin here, that this body would be so withered? Surely not in a spirit as young as this, for how can the heart of a young lad have so grievously sinned?"

The children have gathered about them in clusters.

"Is it for me to say?" Jacob answers gently, a glint of something dancing in his eyes.

Zelotese replies, with the same essence, interested but expressionless. "It is thee I have asked, Jacob. Why not, then, thee to answer this?"

"I am a but humble servant of God. Seest thou me as a prophet of God?" Jacob continues lightly in the same tone.

"Thou sayest it, not I. Thou speakest the word, not I."

"So, if I have spoken the word *prophet*, perhaps I must search within, that I can be the hand of God, the voice of God. That I, Jacob, might use mine eyes that God could see as I, Jacob, see these things," he gestures with his hands, "from the point of creation back to the Creator."

"Well, what sayest thou, then, to my question?"

"I say greater than I can answer this, if it is His choice."

"Who might this be?" Zelotese feigns wonder.

"That one who will carry the Promise, the hope."

"Is He among us?"

The children are beginning to smile, for now they understand what is about.

"Aye so, He is among us. He is seated to your right and my left."

Zelotese, methodically, almost mechanically, turns to glance from face to face, shining bright eyes waiting, knowing that something special lies ahead.

"I will speak it," Jesus responds quietly. "It is not so much that a sin has been cast, but that there is that which can serve according to the teachings, according to the honor of those who have gone before us, and according to both of you," glancing from Jacob to Zelotese. "That the honor of your presence as servants of God might give testimony to the grace of God, and that we, together, can bring unto rightness that which has gone awry. Mark you, so shall it be."

Jesus looks down, His eyes closed. All know that He is now in prayer.

"If you look into the sky at all the bright stars," Elob observes, "you can see that some of them bear company to others. Those stars do so always."

"Why is that?" asks Thomas. "Why do some bear company to another, and others move about, seemingly alone?"

"Those which bear company to one another form the patterns which can guide, which can teach, which can bring wisdom where there is darkness or a lack of insight."

"How is that possible? Are they not jewels God has placed in the night sky to bring us joy and to give us light?"

"This is, indeed, true. But as with all things embraced in the Spirit of God, there are gifts to be given to the children of God who would look for them, who would open unto them and receive them."

Timothy questions, "What are these gifts?"

"They are the gifts of guidance. See here?" He points to a cluster. "These which keep company with one another form a creature familiar to you. Is that not so, Timothy?"

Turning his head this way and then that to look from another angle, he finally sees it. "The stinger thing!"

Elob laughs. "Yes. And over here, that which scurries to and fro on the seashore, see it? The crab." He bends to the sandy dust-like earth before him and traces the pattern of a crab with his fingertip. Then he dots it to show where the stars are, and smiles.

By the stars' light, the symbol can clearly be seen.

"Oh, yes." Thomas points to the sky. "Now that you have connected the bright stars, I can see it. I did not before."

"Unto what purpose are such patterns to us?" asks Jesus. "Do you speak these things that we should be governed by these symbols on high?"

"Nay, never," Elob replies. "For we are the children of God. We are the masters of all of these." He gestures about the sky. "They are not the masters of us." He turns to gaze penetratingly into Jesus' eyes.

Jesus smiles and nods. "I thought it so, and I thank you for your confirmation."

"Then what do you think such symbols and such placement in the heavens above have to offer to us all? What gifts has God given and placed above to shine upon us nearly each day of our journey?"

Jesus leans back casually placing His hands behind Him, turning His face this way and that, illuminated by the glowing stars above. "My heart tells me," He begins slowly, "that these are gifts of God to bring us joy and remind us that God is ever with us.

"My mind tells me that all of these are indicators. That as one enters under the fullness of one of these symbols or the other, so does it impart to them the power and gift of that particular symbol, perhaps the tools with which one journeying through life can find themselves better equipped to meet what lies before them.

"Lastly, my spirit tells me, *Jesus, look you well upon these. They are the reflections of the power of the Children of God. They are the constant reminders of the twelve positions upon the Wheel of Life, itself, a wheel which turns eternally and cannot be altered in its movement, but can be lifted up by the understanding of what is.*"

Elob has been listening, his eyes nearly closed, feeling the Spirit being offered even in this young body, the one he knows shall come to be called Christ.

"I feel stronger."

The maidens are gently massaging Justus with fragrant oils and extracts of plants and herbs.

"Look! I can wiggle my toes and it doesn't hurt. But my

other leg is still not growing. Look how much shorter it is."

"Do you believe," inquires Ruth by the campfire's light, "He could be at a point where His Spirit is so at one with His body," there is a long pause, "such that it would not be inappropriate to ask Him to bring forth that Spirit we know is His, that Justus might be healed?"

Joseph is gazing down into the fire's light, his eyes wide, unblinking. "It is not for me to say, Ruth. Better to ask this of His Mother."

"Indeed." Ruth gestures to Joseph who remains immobile, his eyes still transfixed upon the flames, several colleagues at his side. She moves slowly, deliberately. Her body is not as agile as some decades earlier, but her spirit is bright and her eyes and voice ever impart an attitude of hope. As she enters the circle, without looking Mary moves a bit to the side, as does Zephorah. They turn with a smile to welcome her to sit with them and the group.

In time, Ruth turns to Mary and begins softly. "Sweet Sister, regarding young Justus ... All that we know to do has been done, and while the pain is nearly gone and his toes move, what thinkest thou? Might we ask Him? Is it the appropriate time for His Spirit be called to the fore?"

Mary, as Joseph before Her, turns to gaze into the flame, eyes unblinking, awide, Her face serene and silent. A gentle smile, so typical of Her being, radiates across Her face.

A long silence follows. Only the soft pops and crackles of their small campfire can be heard.

Then, She responds. "Are we not taught by our elder sisters and the great ones that if we ask in His Name, He will give it?" Having said this, She turns to look, and Her eyes flutter several times. "Let us ask Him. He will tell us. And if in His heart the work is in honor to His Father, He will do it."

They have taken Justus to the Spring of the Prophet,

whom their peoples unto this day revere, and have ceremoniously bathed and garbed him afresh. 'Round and about, as is their custom, are several containers from which rise small wisps of smoke as offerings unto God to bind them, the children of God, to the Spirit of God.

Elob enters, and behind him, Jacob, arms about several of the young lads and sisters. Over and above, Zelotese and many of the others are seated.

Then Mary and several of the sisters come forth and also seat themselves.

Justus smiles in recognition of his newfound brothers and raises his hand to gesture to them. They gesture in response but do so with their hands to their hearts and upward, symbolizing the spiritual bond of the Expectant Ones.

Mary is kneeling with Her sisters nearby. She holds out a hand and Jesus comes to kneel beside Her, leaning His head against Her adoringly. He is nearly looking into Her eyes, for His stature has become significant, evidence that soon He will surpass Her in height and in breadth.

She lifts Her hand to stroke several strands of hair that have fallen to the forefront and places them back behind and over His shoulder.

"What is in your heart, my Mother?" Jesus asks softly.

Many of the Maidens have brought their hands together in silent prayer, an act He duly notes. Here and there, tears glisten in their eyes. One can almost hear their silent mantra and the repetition of *Holy, Holy*.

"Our brother, Justus … We have done for him all that we know to do. We come this day to this holy place, sanctifying ourselves in every way we know. Art thou, my Son, ready, that thy Spirit's light might touch thy brother Justus?"

Their eyes are locked, their Spirits speaking volumes, with only a sweet smile upon Mary's face and a questioning, studying look on that of Jesus.

Slowly the corners of His mouth begin to turn up into a

broad smile. "Shall it be the Spirit within that guides?"

"Ever let it be so. Thou knowest this."

"I honor you. I honor you eternally."

She leans Her forehead to touch His, and He rises to stride the several paces distance between Himself and Justus.

Though he knows not what is about to transpire, Justus has come to know and love his Brother who is called Jesus. "I know not the intention of this gathering except that they say to me, you are a Messenger from God. Are you?"

"That which is said of me is that which I am. That which is said of you is what you shall become." His eyes are shining. "Thus I say to you, Justus, son of God, be thou whole."

He places His hand upon the hip of Justus' withered leg.

Justus blinks and smiles, his face aglow.

With His right hand, the Master cups the heel of the withered foot. Still cupping it, He slowly moves His left hand down from the hip ... down, down.

There are gasps, and many sounds and calls to praise God, for all have gathered to see the Son of God bring forth God's healing grace.

For but a moment, Jesus' shoulders and head slump forward, and there are murmurs.

Then His young body straightens, and He steps back two paces, extending His left hand out to Justus. "Come, thou brother mine, called Justus. Walk with me."

In the testimony of the Akasha it is written that unto one in great need and burdened sorely, the Hand of the Christ extends itself and calls forth the purity within. That as the body eternal might shine and do the work, the body

outer falls away, giving way to that perfection within.

So is it for each of thee. According to thy belief shall it be given.

Chapter 17

In the Light of Forgiveness

The shadows are barely visible, for the light in the evening sky is minimal. Yet, as one grows accustomed to seeing in it, the silhouettes of those who are the adepts, led by Elob, Zelotese, and others, can be seen against the backdrop of reflection from the pool in the holy Spring. They are gathered, facing outward, arms intertwined.

Elob steps forward. Using a slender rod, he walks about the group, drawing a circle in the earth at their feet. As he brings the end of the circle back to its beginning, he steps back, resuming his hold of the arms to his left and right.

There is silence.

Their heads are upturned, their eyes closed. Upon each face can be seen the special blessing and beauty that is the uniqueness of a dedicated soul utterly given into service unto God, and unto that known to be the work before it.

One can perceive, very subtly at first, a gentle, rhythmic, unified motion of this small circle of adepts and teachers, first to the left, and then ever so slightly to the right.

Then a soft sound is heard from one, coming from deep within his body.

Their upturned faces respond to this pure, beautiful tone. Smiles are all about.

Another voice comes, and another, until all these beautiful souls are offering their tone to the group. Hearing this, one can envision the intertwining of peaceful, loving intents rising up, which the gentle evening breeze seems to carry even higher. We rise up and follow it, moving, moving … slowly at first, and now with wondrous rapidity.

Below we can see the outcroppings, the craggy summits surrounding and protecting the School of Wisdom, or the School of the Prophets. We see a group of small flames in a circle like the one Elob drew around himself and his companions. These flames are held in beautifully ornate containers filled with oils, illuminated with wicks that seem to float, moved a little here and there by that same evening breeze.

Here there is not one circle as at the Healing Spring near the Expectant Ones' home, but three sizable ones. All the adepts, teachers, prophets, and seers have gathered and formed these concentric circles.

Even though the distance from the Spring is great, it is as though those gathered here have heard the call of their brothers and sisters from afar. First one voice rises, all the faces upturned, aglow with joy and faith in that which they know is theirs and waits only to be claimed. The voice reaches out and seems to dance across the outcroppings of ancient stone and over to the dwellings and caves, as though it were a living light rather than simply sound. It returns and then another voice, and another, first from the inner circle, then from the second, and now from the outer, as though to symbolize that from the within to the without all things can manifest as one is open and willing.

The inner circle begins first, swaying gently this way and that with the tones, then the second and the third, their arms intertwined, facing outward as though to bring that inner light from within and shine it outward to the world itself.

The reverberations of the beautiful tones of these dedicated souls augmented by the light of the spirit shining forth from their faces is such a sight that one seeing it might well fall to their knees. For here the Spirit of God is known, seen, expressed in every way. The radiance of the light growing from within and around the group penetrates the darkness, almost inviting it, reaching out to take the hands of unseen spirits and bring them into the core of these circles wherein there is healing, wherein there is love and compassion.

It is Elob who first releases the arms of those to his right and left. In succession, each one does the same. Stepping forward one or two paces to stand upon the circle Elob has drawn, each turns to face inward and is seated.

From somewhere unseen, Elob brings forth an ornate container and, ceremoniously removing its cover, places it in the center of the group, unlit. Then he steps back and takes a place upon the circle. They are for the most part as one.

A shimmering essence begins subtly. At first, one has to look away and then look back quickly to catch a glimpse of it. Then it grows. The hands of the adepts, teachers and seers reach out in unison, palms outward towards the container. A chant comes from here, a little song from over there.

Elob, eyes closed, arms extended, palms facing the container, begins praying. "Lord God, let Thy Light be with us."

The container begins to glow and a flame appears on the wick within it.

At the School, all of these have gathered in the same manner. Their containers, considered sacred, have already been illuminated. They are seated silently, in three concentric circles, shoulder to shoulder in silence.

"They are with us," one speaks aloud.

Smiles and greetings abound from the intentions of one to another to send a message of love or compassion.

They place their hands palms up upon their laps.

"It is the completion of the three cycles," Zelotese begins. "Now the journey has begun."

Silence follows as each of these at the Healing Spring of the Expectant Ones ponders this.

"He is awakened," one speaks.

The others at the School of the Prophets nod and affirm this, for they have seen it as well.

"Our work begins from this point," another offers.

"Yes, and we must send forth emissaries to those who have gone afar to prepare the way to make ready, for His journey is not too distant."

"I make it three to four years."

"I think the latter, or a bit more," a third adds.

"Yes, it is likely," another agrees. "I perceive it to be possibly in His thirteenth year, though fourteenth is more likely."

"Then we should begin. On the morrow we shall send the emissaries forth. Agreed?"

There is agreement.

"It is too wondrous to even find words to describe," Zelotese continues, and the others affirm this.

"Could you see, as He touched Justus?" Elob asks them.

One female adept, highly regarded and deeply loved by all, raises her head and smiles, her eyes round and shining, the color and light within them beautiful. She speaks softly. "It began, as I perceived, it from within Him, as one might expect, and then within Justus. I perceived two lights from each of them coming together. Where the Master had placed His hand upon his hip, I saw it the greatest."

She smiles very sweetly. A tear of joy glistening in the corner of one eye breaks free and slips down her cheek. "It was as though the greatest among us of all of our teachers here in our sacred School and all those from the distant lands who are gathered just as we ... It was with that surety and that certainty of faith, incredible in its depth and breadth. Yet, in His three times three, His ninth year, He is awakened as a master! I saw Him bring this unified light, and I saw it from above as well, as though God had thrust a finger of light to join with the two lights of the Master and Justus. And as He moved His left hand down to join His right, holding Justus' heel, the leg became whole. That is what I saw."

There is an excited hush before Elob speaks again. "Is there another here who heard something, who will share that, as well?"

"I." One off to the left rises. "First there was a sound like many murmuring voices off beyond the horizon, as though a great throng of beautiful beings were rushing to be with us. It grew, not merely in volume, curiously, but in breadth and depth, as well. Then from above I heard the light coming, as Marta has just described. I heard it as a voice speaking from above, its words traveling down, that the Master would speak the Word. I saw not His mouth move, but I heard the intent of His Spirit clearly."

"Can you speak it?" asks Zelotese.

"Yes, what I heard were the words, *Be thou healed.*"

Afar, likewise, the seers, teachers, and adepts discuss what shall come next, what gifts they shall bear to this one they now know is the Master, the Christ.

In the preparation for this, many come and go, traveling great distances for this very purpose.

We come, finally, to that point where the Master and many of the others have been brought to the Healing Spring.

"Much has been given to all of you," Ruth begins. "Each of you will find in this that which is unique to you, likened unto a staff upon which you might lean when you are weary. Each will find in the gifts we have humbly and lovingly offered you that which will seem to reach within you and connect with something from your past.

"We are gathered here for this special time of prayer and thankfulness and encourage you to look into your visions and dreams. For God shall speak to you and guide you, anoint you, and bring you wondrous blessings that are uniquely yours as you are a unique creation of the Word of God.

"Having given our prayer at this gathering, and having made our offerings unto our Lord God and the God within, now do we, your humble brothers and sisters, open ourselves to whatsoever you ask of us. Let the thoughts of your hearts and minds be spoken. We invite you warmly, not as your mentors or teachers, not as those who care for you or guard your wellbeing, but as your brothers and sisters, for you are approaching the dawning of your recognition of yourself as a child of God in this current journey of life. Righteously, then, do we come to you without hesitation, arms extended, to welcome you as one with us."

Many of the young maidens and lads look at one another, for this is a moment that has been long awaited. Some are looking down, obviously in silent prayer, a collage of emotion visible as they strive to understand what lies beyond the doorway that has just opened.

One speaks.

"From whence shall we journey? What place do we consider to be our point of origin? Do we think, as we are about life and life's activities, that this is who and what we are? Or is it as you say, sweet sister, that it is perhaps a light shining through from deep in the past? Perhaps even from the very beginning. I humbly ask you, as we seek to measure, to know, to evaluate, as we strive to gauge our journey … Do we measure from here at this sacred Spring, or from another point of origin, a point from which we might even, some of us at least, have walked with you," he turns to Jesus, "my brother, when you were called Amelius?"

The question offered is so profound that the sisters pause. Though nothing is heard, it is as though each is catching her breath. Who would think that one so young would have such a deep grasp and perception of the nature of existence as is evident in his question? They look quickly at one another, and their eyes come to rest upon Judy and then Anna, who smiles her warm, loving smile and turns to answer.

"Well spoken, Thomas! Here is our answer to you, offered in humility. It is the nature of that in which you are engaged, that which you meet, that which is the need of the moment, that might well be your guide to determine your point of reference or origin, as you have indicated.

"Do not be rooted in the reference of who and what you are, but be as the wind ... free to move. When you meet an encumbrance, flow through it, around it, over it, under it. But tarry not long at that which calls to thee to become stationary, immobile. Each step of the journey through life ... be it this, the present, or those of the past, or even those which lie ahead ... offers you understanding and reference points. Each step offers you an invitation to come and dwell therein. If you do so, you can become as travelers whose feet are mired in the bog through which they walk. If, instead, you look for that which is of sure footing, then you will not be immersed in the mire of thought, and your journey can continue. Look you upon that which each footstep has to offer. See it. Know it. Visit it for a time. And look you backwards to see, *What have I known in the past, in this journey or another, that can contribute to my understanding of what is now before me?*

"When such a reference brings you understanding of that now being met, then embrace it and continue on. However, if there is naught that comes to mind or heart that builds an understanding of what is being met, then know that thing. Know it to the extent that you can understand and comprehend why it is before you, what its purpose and gift are. If it is a dire challenge, then meet that but dwell not with it. Speak to it, *I know thee and I claim my oneness, that thou art appropriate as a step in my current journey, but not my destination."*

"Would one hold the thought of the reference which comes to mind or heart?" questions Thomas further. "And would they hold this and see through the eyes of the past, feel with the heart that has known such a thing and build upon this? Or take from the past the power therein and use it to meet that which challenges in the present?"

Anna again draws in a long breath at the remarkable depth of thinking that this young lad continues to demonstrate. She turns to glance about the entire group, looking into the many young eyes whose light shines purely, innocently, having been held in the loving embrace of these, the Expectant Ones, and still held in the thought, in the heart, in the spirit of each of the brothers and sisters who encircles them. "Who among you has an answer for our brother, Thomas?"

"I do," one calls out cheerfully. "I believe we affirm that which we know to be in resonance with what is before us. And then we stand with the eyes of the past and the eyes of the present working together. I think that in the moment of recognizing the past and the opportunity before us in the present, we call unto the ancient ones: *Look you, sweet brethren, I, Moira, call to you. Hear my prayer. Serve with me in this opportunity that I, Moira, might give unto it the blessings of God.* So, yes. I would see with the eyes of what I have been in the past, through the eyes of the present. And I would await the ancient ones, that they would give me their sight, so through all these things together, I, Moira, might claim in the light of God and give to that which is before me."

Thomas nods, his face aglow, his eyes wide. "Thank you, my sister. You are, ever, as beautiful in your words and spirit as you are in the mantel God has placed around them, called your body."

Several chuckle softly, for it is evident that Moira and Thomas have a fondness for one another that goes beyond the relationship nurtured by the Essenes.

Moira merely smiles and nods in return, her body beauti-fully erect, her face shining and tilted slightly back.

"Well spoken, both of you." Anna engages in several more exchanges with the others, and then turns to Judy.

Judy nods, rises, and begins to walk about slowly, casu-ally adjusting her garments, bringing her hands together, stopping to bend and touch the head of one seated cross-legged here, another over there. Then she comes to stand be-fore all of them.

Seated before her to her right is Jesus. To her left are many of those she knows will walk with Him once He has returned from His journeys to the East.

She is motionless, her hands raised, upturned.

Voices begin to sing softly over here, over there. As they do, Judy begins to sway to the beautiful rhythmic cadence held by her brothers and sisters. All know that this is her preparation as she awaits the visions, the guidance that they know will be given unto this great seer, which she in turn will share on this hallowed eve.

They look upon one another as though to measure the finery that each is wearing. Their faces carry no visible fond-ness for one another. Indeed, each of these priests seems to be striving to look more solemn, more holy than the other. Their tall, fluted headwear, at times precariously balanced, looks almost humorous. They move with an air of self-proclaimed righteousness, as they are within the Holy of Holies, as they call it. Having assumed their positions of hierarchy, their so-called sacred council begins.

One speaks, who is evidently the leader. "It is being said that the one prophesied has awakened. Has anyone infor-mation to give here?"

Raising the signet of his office to indicate he would speak, a priest on the opposite side of the gathering rises slowly. "I am gravely concerned because the rumors the peasants pass about are growing. It is said that He has already demonstrated mystical powers, clearly those that would be aligned with Satan."

A murmur goes through the group. Some turn this way and that preparing to speak.

The leader continues. "Have we knowledge of the location of this evil one?"

Off to the side, another signet of office comes up and the priest rises. "To the interior, to the south near the great sea. I have heard it told there are those who seek His ... what they call *blessings*. We all know that these are spells cast upon them, for who could ever call out a demon unless they were the greater demon?"

Many murmur their agreement and recognition that surely this must be so.

"Know you more than this?" inquires the elder priest. "That is a vast area. How might we find Him and deal with this matter?"

"This is all that I have heard," the third priest replies. "However, I have a plan, if you would hear it."

Murmurs sweep back and forth about the chamber.

The head priest taps his signet of office, his staff, on the floor. The murmuring stops immediately. "Well, then, speak your plan. We must not allow this to continue. Such blasphemy, such lies and rumors! You know these peoples. They cling to anything like this. We must silence this! We stand before a time of pivotal transformation. We cannot let the voice of the One God be muted by rumors, by blasphemy. Speak your plan."

The third priest begins, becoming more and more agitated as he continues, glee in his eyes at his own cleverness as he proposes that they form a small group of peasants, yet only in appearance, ones chosen carefully. They would find one who possesses a dis-ease, who is perhaps disfigured or blind, and take this one slowly along the sea, waiting to see if anyone approaches them offering healing to the one suffering.

All agree that this is a fine plan. Surely, if there is one such as is rumored, how could he resist the bait of this trap, the opportunity to perform the work ... if, indeed, there be truth to any of it.

Anna's voice now joins the chorus, softly at first, but the clarity and beauty of her tones are unmistakable. Her song then moves into a beautiful invitation. "Come you, my sister. Speak unto us. We pray of you, sweet Father God. Here is your daughter whom we love and embrace. Let she who is called Judy speak to us in Thy sight."

In one fluid motion Judy's arms come down and her body slumps to the ground gracefully. Her legs are crossed, her arms folded in front of her body, which is erect, head tilted back, eyes closed. "Be of good cheer, my children," her voice begins quietly, "for I am ever with thee."

We can see the young lad called Jesus simulating the posture of the priestess Judy. He, too, is sitting erect, face upturned, eyes closed, smiling, a light coming from Him. Many of the other children emulate this, as well.

"Be of strength within, and know that My Light is the Light of your very life and that this Light is eternal. Know that as you take your Light forward upon the journey before you, there shall come to pass those who would seek to quell it. One such intent is being prepared and shall come to pass before your peoples in a fortnight. Be thou ready. Look upon that which seems to be, and see within it. In order that you shall know of My Light's presence, the darkness shall come, but it cannot diminish you. Rather, it will serve to make you and the Light within all the greater.

"Rise up now, My Son."

Having heard these words, Jesus rises to His feet.

"Turn. Look about." Judy is rocking slightly, her eyes

still closed. "Look you carefully upon your colleagues and remember their Light."

Jesus, eyes aglow, smiling, looking at each of the beautiful upturned faces, does just so.

"There shall come a time in the future," Judy continues, "when you will see these Lights again and call them forth to join in the joy and oneness of the awakening of My Promise."

Simeon straightens his robe. The midnight wind is cold, and the dampness coming from the great sea seems to reach within the fibers to touch his body. He laughs softly as he adjusts the folds of his garment. "A good fire would be a welcome companion to us this evening, my brother."

Nathanael chuckles, looking down. "I guess we could visualize it and ourselves being warmed by it. What say you?"

They both laugh.

"Yes, let us call on the warmth of the Light within, so naught without can affect us."

Each of them lays his stout staff to the side and positions his body so that his knees touching are touching the other's. They begin to lean this way and that, quietly chanting their sacred mantras, their holy prayers, which are utterly part of their being. Faces aglow with the joy of their service, of their opportunity, they rock this way and that.

At the conclusion of their prayer, Nathanael laughs. "Well, I could not be warmer if that flame were actually burning here. What of you, my brother?"

"I, too."

They turn, placing their backs one against the other, each pulling up his staff and cradling it across his raised knees. Seated back to back, the guardians carefully scan the dark horizons before them.

"I suspect this will be one of many times they will try to

trap Him." From the edge of the high summit upon which they are positioned, Zelotese gazes down off into the distance at a small group moving slowly along the edge of the great sea. "Look you. Even from this distance, one can see these are not just travelers, but imposters."

"Ah, yes," responds Elob. "But that one ... See? Off to their left? There is a true need there."

"Of course. How else could they bait us or the Expectant Ones? They would surely know that we have sufficient sight to know whether a need is true or false, whether an intent is sincere or only partially so." Sitting up, he reaches within the upper part of his garment and pulls forth a bit of fabric, then arm upraised, waves it back and forth.

Down below, near the water's edge, the early morning sunlight glistens off a stout staff. The staff moves this way and that to confirm that the guardian recognizes the signal that would-be betrayers are near.

The group comes to an abrupt stop as the sizeable form of the warrior priest steps forth from perhaps not ten meters away to block the path before them.

The one on the left, who is of goodly measure of body himself, gasps, for the guardian standing before them holding a great glistening staff across the front of his body is a formidable sight.

Not at all what he had anticipated, with a bit of panic in his eyes, the man turns to glance at the other two with him. Then, glancing at the withered form they have brought to tempt the one they believe is a false prophet, he regains his composure quickly and bends to a knee, raising his hands. "Oh, good sir, we are humble travelers and one of our family is greatly stricken. We have heard there is one who can bring healing light. Wouldst thou guide us unto that one?"

The guardian, as though he is not taking physical steps, glides across the distance separating them until he is only the distance of his great staff away from the one on bended knee.

"How art thou called, traveler?"

He stutters a bit with the effort to conceal his emotion. "Kotese. I am called Kotese."

"Well, then … *Kotese* … Is this one you have brought desirous of being healed?"

The withered form is an elderly woman, obviously not comprehending where she is, or perhaps even who she is.

"Oh yes!" Kotese responds. "She … She definitely wishes to be healed."

His eyes not moving from the withered woman's form, the guardian speaks in a voice that flows like the water of a stream. "You speak it, woman. Seekest thou to be healed?"

The third man of the group nudges the old woman as he supports her with one of his arms.

Her eyes blink, and she looks about as though having come from a sleep. Her eyes open wide as she sees the great glistening form, for the clothing and attire are radiant. Her eyes become transfixed upon the staff.

The guardian notes this and begins to turn it slowly in his hands, the light sparkling on its different facets.

As though awakened from a dream, the woman shakes herself and turns to look at the betrayer who has her by the arm. She pushes him away.

She stumbles, trying to move forward. "Art thou He?" Her voice shakes. "Art thou the one sent by God?"

The guardian moves not, his eyes fixed upon the woman. "Who saith these words to thee, woman?"

Kotese' movement is swift, but not so swift that the guardian's staff does not swing in time, stoutly striking his arm as he strives to pull a dagger from his garment's folds. Turning about, the guardian swings the staff to strike the other behind the head. The sound of the staff striking the head is like that of one thunking a tree trunk.

The third man stumbles backwards, crying aloud, throwing up his hands, "Spare me! Spare me! I seek you no harm.

They forced me to do this."

As he turns to run off into the distance, he crashes into the burly form of Nathanael standing before him.

Nathanael grasps him by the back of the cloak and lifts him up. "What shall we do with this one?"

"We cannot leave him. That is their intent."

All the while, the elderly woman is wailing, thrashing about as though convulsing, having fallen to her knees.

Pausing, Simeon bends, extends a hand and pulls a leather-like flask from within his garment. He gently cradles her worn, tired head in one great hand, unstops the flask and slowly begins to pour the golden liquid into her mouth, just a bit at first. "Drink thee, woman. It will bring goodness to thy body and clarity to thy mind. You have arrived. He whom you seek is here."

The woman's hands shake feebly as her eyes become gladdened with a light of hopefulness. She clutches Simeon's hand holding the flask, drinking, drinking as though her thirst was as one come from the wilderness.

Several of the other guardians have now come from where they were hiding. They take the third deceiver from Nathanael and after a brief discussion begin to head southward along the water's edge. This one shall be taken to a place afar. As they begin their journey with him, they cover his eyes and bind his hands behind him so he will know not the path of return, ever, from where they take him to the journey's end.

Nathanael nods. Simeon lifts the elderly form as Zelotese, Elob, and several of the sisters come to them from down the hillside.

"We will take her and care for her." Anna tenderly brushes back the woman's hair.

 Zephorah and Kelleth each take one of her arms, offering her small morsels of foodstuffs. Flanked to the right and left by Zelotese, Elob, and many of the adepts, they begin the journey back up to the encampment.

Leaning upon his staff, Simeon stands looking out across the water.

Knowing what is in his heart, Nathanael places an arm about his brother warrior priest. "As it is given, so must we receive it and respond. We meet out according to what is before us. Toil not, my brother, over the thoughts of what God has called thee to perform as a service. For their spirits are now free, and surely the ancient ones have lifted them up and offered them a path to the Light."

Looking down, Simeon thanks Nathanael.

After sharing a time of silent prayer, Simeon looks up, and they begin to walk slowly to the north along the edge of the sea. "It would gladden my heart so much more, my brother, if the seeds they sow did not have to be met in a harvest of like kind. What I have performed in God's Name, I have difficulty carrying within, even with thy presence, and love, and encouragement. I must go now to fast and pray that I can find my spirit's light, that I can bathe in the light of God's forgiveness ... and that I, Simeon, can forgive myself.

And so, we might all, dear friends, ask ourselves: What is the measure of that which I am willing to give? According to that which comes before me and brings challenges or opposes that which I hold to be sacred, shall I stand aside and let that which I cherish fall beneath the intent of that which would limit? Or would I stand forth, strong, resilient, as the guardians of old and the guardians of present, and meet with equal measure that which is

wrought upon those bearing the Promise?"

It is a question we have no doubt those of you in the Earth shall often labor over. It can be answered in this way:

The creation of hope, the offering of love, the extension of forgiveness and grace, are being borne into the Earth through those who hold this sacred within their spirits, their hearts, their minds, their bodies. Who, then, shall nurture and care for them? Who, then, shall be the guardians of that which is newborn and has naught with which to endure, but your intent?

Know that our prayers are ever with thee. And that greater than we comes soon.

Chapter 18

His Teachings Begin

The morning's meal has been completed, along with the prayers, the ceremonies, and other such as are customary for the Expectant Ones in preparing to welcome a new day. They have gone forth in small groups here and there to tend to various tasks, to study, to give, to share. As we move along with one of these groups, we see before us the Holy Maidens interspersed among those whom they are guiding and supporting.

"It seems a short time. Short in that each day has been a treasure, filled with the anticipation and joy of what will come. And yet, deep within my heart, each day has been met with a reluctance to release it."

"We all share this, Kelleth." Andra's response is gentle, somewhat out of her normal manner. "And even moreso, my sister, since we know that that time approaches rapidly when most, if not all, will go forth according to the prophecies, according to the works and teachings and, perhaps most of all, according to the guidance of their spirits within."

Kelleth, her arm wrapped in Andra's, closes her eyes for a few moments as they walk slowly along.

"What are you doing?" Andra asks lovingly.

"Imagining. I am trying to imagine by closing my eyes, by denying the sight of them, what it will be like."

"Why?"

Kelleth blinks and opens her eyes. "I do not know. I suppose to soften the impact of that day when it comes."

"We are, you know, to meet it with joy … and with the strength of all that we have been given." Andra draws her words out as though she, herself, is hearing them, weighing them in the inner chamber of her own soul.

The early morning light catches the glistening of a tear forming in Kelleth's eye. "It is as if a part of myself must journey on without the remainder. It is like a song in my heart that I know I will only hear by recalling it … not with my ears but only with my soul."

"Do not dwell long in these thoughts," Andra offers with a hint of admonishment, yet clearly with love, "for the call therein is one which can diminish what *is* with the concern or sadness of what *shall be* …" She finishes a bit more lightly, "Or what *might* be."

"What is the purpose of the law, anyway? Is it something that others before us have concluded is a good thing? Is the law something that was given unto our forefathers or others of authority directly or indirectly by God? Or is it just something that they sat down as a group and deliberated?" Thomas is looking down as he asks this of Zelotese.

"There are many different laws," Zelotese responds. "It depends upon to which you refer. There are those laws, of course, that are fashioned, formed, and come through experience on the part of those who have gone before us … some of our peoples who are honored elders and ancestors, and some of others' peoples. Whenever such laws have been found to be good, we have held them in esteem: those we know to embody sight (vision and oneness with God within), we have accepted as that rod by which to measure all that we are, and, of course, that which we do."

Thomas shakes his head. "There are those times when I find some of these laws to be … well, no disrespect meant but, to be without much aforethought.'"

"Have you an example?" Zelotese smiles off to the side.

"I have many examples, but I am not sure how important they are to the others." He turns to look at the group, as they have paused in their journey.

"Perhaps you would like to share one with us, and we will let them decide. How would that be?"

"Well, here is one that I really question: Why is it that that which has been done by one's ancestors (whom one might know only by name, only by recounting or legend) has impact today upon who one is, what one can do, and all that sort ... for me, for example?"

Zelotese leans back, looking up, rocking.

"Have you a particular ancestor in mind?" Jacob asks, chuckling softly.

"Not really. I just happened to have heard some of our brothers who were in the outlands talking about how structured and rigid lives are according to one's heritage, and that this determines where one can go. And they meant that exactly that way, literally! Some can sit in the higher seats in temple, others cannot. Some cannot even enter on certain celebrations. Why is that? And why is there such a difference in the honor they give to their women, when we hold ours as sacred?"

Rebekah chuckles softly as she hears this and turns to her sisters, with a telling little look.

Zephorah nods and whispers, "Our people see through the eyes of truth. Theirs do not."

"What was that?" asks Jacob lightly.

Zephorah, glancing around though not a bit flustered, states boldly, "Our people see through the eyes of truth far better than those in the outlands, I think."

Laughter pours from many of the elders in the group, then the sisters, and then the entirety.

After a time, all are silent.

Jacob straightens himself, placing his hands upon his folded knees. "This is a good question to reflect upon, my children. For when you do journey forth into the outlands, or even if you go not forth but journey within, will you not ask of yourself, *What can I see in the eyes of truth*, as Zephorah has pointed out? *Is there that which is literal as the true rod by which I can guide myself and my journeys?* It is important to understand that law is that which is agreed upon, even though not all may agree. Those who hold authority in the outlands control the law, whether they see through the eyes of truth or through the eyes of their own desires or purposes."

"Why?" questions Thomas.

"Because that is just the way it is." Jacob chuckles at his own response. "It is in our people's history to believe that which has been proven to have value and truth. Examples abound and have been shared with you all by our Holy Sisters, by the elders, the seers, the prophets, and many more. Some of you will go forth soon. And you will learn of different laws, different teachings, and, indeed, different ways to see truth from a new perspective."

Zelotese has been studying the considerable group gathered. Upon Jacob's conclusion, he speaks again. "In a short time many of you will journey with Elob and me to our sacred School, and we will gift you with that which we know and that which we see through the eyes of truth. We will give you the understanding of a different kind of Law. It is a Law that is unwritten. It is one that is, in essence, unspoken, except by those who live within it."

"What is the purpose of a law," questions Thomas further, "if it is not written and is spoken only by a few? I understood that the laws are to guide all. What kind of Law is this?"

"It is not defined because it cannot be defined, for to do so would limit it. These are Laws of the sacred teachings of Truth, the Laws of wisdom, the Laws of love and compassion, of forgiveness, and so much more."

"Who has written these Laws? Or if they are not written, who has given them?" Thomas continues.

Straightening himself and lifting his head a bit, Zelotese responds gently. "We believe these come from the One God through the expression of the Spirit of God, the foundation of all existence."

"Well, then, has God spoken these?"

"In the outward sense as you now hear my words, no. But in the sense of truth unto those who have sought His Word, His teaching ... Yes, it is so."

"If a law exists and one knows it not, and it is a law that is governing, absolute, and of (I shall call it) life itself, does the fact that one does not know it or perceive it excuse one from it?" asks James.

There is just a bit of laughter, followed quickly by a response from Zelotese. "The Laws I speak of are perfect and function always, all the time, everywhere, for everyone."

"Now? For me?"

"Yes," Jacob adds now, "for you, for all of us. They are those Laws that, even though you know them not, apply to you, and though you have no knowledge of them, will work for you and interact in your daily life."

"We are far from the Romans' law," James continues. "So, their law doesn't apply to me. Whose Law is this, then, that applies to me even though I know them not? Is it God's Law, or laws that we live by among our peoples? Or is it something beyond this?"

"It is the Laws of God expressed (as I might call it, as many of your sisters have taught you), existing in the plants in nature, in the herbs. Eloise, Eudora, and the others have taught you much of this. It exists in the flow of life, the essence of who you are, always waiting to be discovered."

"Within me?" James presses.

"And me?" asks Andrew.

"As I said … all of us. But enough of your questions. Let us move to something that will answer them without your asking them."

"I would like to see that." Thomas laughs quietly.

"Very well then, come, and you will see." Jacob gestures for all to follow.

The group begins to move again. As they do, we hear various little comments among the Holy Maidens, some with laughter, some with an eye towards the sense of completion of a work at hand.

"I am not sure at all whether the time which approaches is to be celebrated or lamented." Little Mary is now walking beside Kelleth and Andra. "I say that lightly, but I will have to ask myself on that day, *Mary, have you given all you know to give? Have you gone within and sought that out, even a small teaching that may be of import to one or the other of them in the years ahead?*"

"Why would you want to do that to yourself?"

"I am not saying I would *do* it to myself, Kelleth. I would *ask* of myself."

"Same difference."

"I suppose it is the nature of one who seeks to be the very best, to bring forth the greatest gifts, that in the process one perhaps becomes too critical, too analytical, or examines self in too great a detail."

"Who would ever think of you in that way?" Andra's laughter is heard by all.

Such discussions and analysis continue among the Sisters and many of the others as they journey along.

As they arrive at the Healing Spring and the little series of cascading waterfalls that lead up to the sacred pool, Zelotese takes a position just at its upper reaches, where he can look down upon all gathered. He gestures to the cascading water just a short distance away. "Have you ever thought of why the water falls down upon these rocks into this sacred pool and then takes its journey to the sea?"

"Well, that is the way water moves."

Moira responds with a giggle. "I do not think that is what he is asking, Benjamin."

Zelotese nods to her. "What do you think I am asking?"

"You are asking what force governs this. Right? In other words, why does it move from on high down to the sea?"

"Yes, that is the intent of my question."

"I think it is the way God created it. You know … that birds fly, trees have leaves, rocks are hard, and water flows from above down to the sea. That is just the way He did it."

Laughter flows lovingly.

Moira giggles along with them. "Well? Why does one have to complicate it? Is not the nature of God to be easy and joyful? Look at me." She taps her fingers against her chest. "I breathe all the time, in and out. I do not think about it. It simply happens."

"Have you ever had a time when your breathing was labored?"

Rubbing her chin with her hand, she looks up and then down, closes her eyes a moment, and then opens them brightly. "Yes, I can think of several times. Once, when we traveled across the great desert and the winds blew the sand and dust, I had to cover my face because it was hard to breathe. The cloth kept the dust from going in. And another time when I got the grip thing that squeezes your chest. You know what I mean? Have you ever had it?"

Zelotese laughs quietly, looking down, "I may have, but it has been so long ago, Moira, I cannot remember."

All laugh again.

"Well, it squeezes you and you have to work to breathe."

"Then, you know the difference, don't you? You know the difference between a law that people make and a law that simply flows and is easy. But even these can be impaired. By your own words, you gave two examples of something that you do not normally have to think about becoming something that you have to labor at."

"Well, I understand that, but not what you are teaching me. I only meant to say that the water flows from up above to down below because that is the way God ordered it. Otherwise, if all the water stayed up above, everyone would have to live in the highlands. Or they would thirst very badly."

After the laughter subsides again, Zelotese continues. "There is much truth to what Moira says, and to what all of you have offered here," (as many have chimed in to offer little insights). "It is a law that water flows from here," pointing up, "to there," pointing down. "It is also known to be a truth that this rock that I am seated upon is hard, and supports me. And yet, over there is the same rock in another time that has become the grains of sand that form the earth. And in that earth are found the roots of the trees, the plants, the herbs, and such that heal us.

"So all things, you see, are in motion. Even a rock such as this that appears so timeless, given the proper span of time, will change. The water, as you see it here, is pure and cool, fresh. One can drink of it as they need or wish. But down there, the water mixes with other waters. It becomes burdened with bits of other elements, soils, particles of plants, and much more. There are some places, as this water journeys down below, where you cannot take it into your body or it will cause a great imbalance, a lack of ease."

"Does anyone live in such places? If so, why?" Jessie asks.

"Many people not only live in those places, but use the water in that form as a means of their livelihood."

"What do they do with it?" Jessie asks.

"They gather from it that which is the harvest."

"Why would they want to harvest from impure water?"

"Ah-h, here is another part of the law that is not written. Because the Spirit of God provides for God's children always, everywhere. There are those creatures, fishes, that not only can live in those waters, but their presence helps to bring back its purity. Other living things take in the impurities and give off pure water as a gift."

"Are these a part of the plan of God that functions under the Law of God?" questions Jessie further.

"They do. They do, indeed. But this law is a living law. It is a law which flows with the need, which moves according to the intent and need and will of those who dwell within it."

"This seems very complex," Thomas interjects.

"I do not think so," replies John. "I do not think it has to be complex. I think one only has to be aware of it and not get in its way ... to more or less flow with it, and sense it. In the sensing, then, being a part of its good intent and taking from it according to one's need. What say you, my brother?" He turns to look at Jesus.

There is a hush as all wait for Him to speak.

His eyes gently look about the group. "I am reminded of your loving teachings," indicating Judy, "wherein you said to us, *It is our expectation and our belief that fashion what we experience and are to live.* So I think that there is much truth to what you say, my brother." He turns to look at John, jostling him on his shoulder. "But I think much more is being offered to us by our dear brother Zelotese. I think he is saying to us that if we look within the happenstance of all that is about us in each day, we will find the truth of God's Law alive, vibrant, ever offering us gifts unto any need and understanding unto any work that comes unto us."

"I would ask you ..." Jessie speaks quietly, but clearly. "We all know what has been foretold for the most part. What say you about the prophecies for you, dear Brother Jesus?"

The hush is intense such that it is as though time has stopped.

The elders, the Holy Maidens, the teachers, all are statue-like as their eyes and spirits reach out to know the Promise of God at this youthful stage.

"I am come, as are we all," Jesus begins softly, "as you have commented on, Thomas, from the heritage which is eternal of all of us. It is the living light of life itself that lights my way, and the way for all of you as well. When I am one with it, and flow with it, it lifts me up. It gives me strength and peace. It swirls around me. As the woven blankets of our sweet sisters embrace me during sleep, so does this embrace me during my every waking moment. It is a blanket that comforts me, made ... yes, perhaps even woven ... by our Lord God especially for each of us. I have mine. You have yours, sweet Sister Jessie. We all have that which comforts and gives us warmth and unto our need.

"And to answer your question, when I look upon those things foretold, there is that which passes through me, have no doubt of this. As I know for each of you, there is that which does the same when you contemplate it. But I know of it, and accept it, and claim it, thanks to the loving support and encouragement of those who have brought me to this point. So I can now give of it, unto you ..." He turns to look upon Justus, "and unto those who would be guided by God unto my hands, my heart, my spirit, and the light within. So, therefore, why should I labor for that which is not, when I have the joys present about me of that which is?"

Jessie, studying Jesus carefully, begins to smile then leans her head back to laugh, glancing over at Andra, who is her mentor and her idol, as well as her sister.

Andra laughs, too, then, and the others, as well.

Jesus, smiles. "Well, it appears I answered that question quite well. What say you, John?"

John looks down, then up. "As always, with authority and completeness." Then he, too, laughs.

"What has happened to Him, Mary?" questions Joseph.

"I think He has gone with one of the sisters."

"To what end?"

"I know not, but my heart tells me He brings His Word to the outer world."

"How is it that you, young lad, speak with such words?"

"I speak these words because they live within me, not without. Not as ciphers upon a page, but because the living God is within all of us."

"We are the emissaries of God. Knowest thou this not? From whence comest thou?"

"I come from that which is the One God, as do all of you. But you see it not because you believe unto that which is about you and not that which awaits you."

There are murmurs and many shouts of "Blasphemy!"

"Believe you that because I speak that which is alive, that which is whole and complete within me, that thou must weigh this upon the scales of that which is not alive? Which cannot give unto the need of a passerby but, rather, asks of him? I ask of you naught, but offer to you all. What do you ask of those whom you serve? Do you not levy tax against them? Are you not expectant that they should give tribute unto your office? Do you not wear those robes that exalt you above others? You say you speak the words of God and you speak them as though God speaks directly to you. Yet I hear not the love of God in your words. I see not the compassion and the embrace of God in your deeds. Rather, you sanctify yourselves and that which you hold to be your edict, not God's."

"That is blasphemy, young lad! Clear and simple! How do you speak such here, in this temple of God?"

"It is here that I find the greatest of ease to speak as I do, for these are the words of God. These are the teachings of the One God, not the separation of God defined in those comfortable purposes as you have. Look you upon the ancient teachings and you will find the truth of my words, and far greater."

"Then name those teachings!" a priest calls out.

Without a moment's pause, He reiterates them one by one, quoting their position, indicating their intent, on and on.

The shock and amazement of those who sit on high is evident.

"And so I say unto you now, test my words against these laws, these teachings."

"Who are you and why have you come here? Why do you challenge us?"

"I am that One that I am, and I come because it is my Father's Will that I so serve. I do not challenge you, but I come to awaken you that you might know the way which is aright and the path that will serve, not only those you are intended to serve, but will serve you. For within, we are all one. It is the outer we must look upon and see: *We* manifest this, not God; we choose what we are. Just so as you, Rabboni, have chosen the garments you wear, the signet of office upon your head. But what is the signet of your heart? What is the gift of light that you allow God to give to others through you, and the beauty which is your uniqueness?"

"How can you say this unto me? Thou knowest me not."

"Aye, I know thee. Thou art the son of Mesichiah, is it not true?"

His eyebrows arch and come down. "That is true, but many know this."

"Thou art born of the Hebrides, and lived long there but not always, journeying here that you could come unto the laws and the elders through your uncle who was a priest before you. Is that not also true?"

There are gasps among the group, for few, if any, could know this in the populace, for the heritage of the priests is kept from common knowledge to insinuate that they are somehow mysteriously anointed by God.

"And if I know these things of thee … and *you* as well,

whose mother died when you were of seven years," and there is another gasp, "and *you*, whose father was imprisoned for doing a work on the Sabbath."

On and on the Master goes, revealing facts which could not be known, certainly not by a young lad, and certainly not by one who is not of this outer world.

"What would you have of us?" a priest asks.

"I seek naught of you, but come to give a gift to you. As my words have been given to you, so do I give to you from my heart and spirit. There are many paths ahead, many choices, and those who will come to you and say, *Cast away that one who speaks truth and speaks it with authority.* My gift to you, then, is this: If all seek the God within and, finding His love and compassion in the center of their being, thereafter bring it forth in word and deed to others, might we not, in truth, all become one? And the world in which we live blessed many-fold over by the gifts of the many, rather than the few?"

"Where have you been?" Joseph asks Jesus and the Sisters who follow Him only a step or two behind.

"I am come from my Father's work," Jesus answers lovingly and respectfully, seeing in Joseph a love which is eternal, a spark of light that is as a child of God, yet the conditioning of one who has been given the ward of the Promise of God.

Mary speaks not a word, but goes to Him, brushing back His hair, touching His cheek. "You are aglow, My Son. Truly the Word of God has passed through you this day."

"It is so, my sweet Mother, and a great door opened. I could feel it. Many of the truths that you ..." He turns to look at the Sisters behind him, and then at Joseph and Mary, "Much of the truth you have handed me, lovingly, patiently, stirs into its rightful position."

"Judging from the reaction of those who followed Him

out of the temple," Hannah laughs discreetly, "it would be an understatement to say that what took place therein was of some impact upon them."

"Yes," Zephorah adds. "I saw one in tears. Another walked off to the side shaking his head, as though someone had struck him upon it with a rock. Two of them stood," she points, as though seeing the temple steps, "arguing about what this young lad had spoken."

Rebekah adds laughs lightly. "It was something, Joseph!"

"Well, come, all of you. We must return to our peoples. It will not be well for us to tarry here now. You are now known, my Son, and we must have a care."

Two of the guardians lead the small entourage from the School, making their way up the hillside to the encampment of Essenes. After they are cleansed and nourished, and the prayers have been offered, they join the gathering of the elders, the prophets, and seers around the evening campfire. Elob is speaking.

"Well, Joseph, He has come forth, it would appear."

"No question of that. And with clarity and authority!" He looks down and laughs. "Would that I had been there to hear and see those rigid, stodgy … Well, no offense meant." He looks about the group, for some here are Rabboni.

"None taken." Zechariah laughs, too. "I would have to agree with your description. But, can you imagine! Why I was not in the temple that day will be a question I shall ask myself many times."

Elob states, "Soon it will be time to take Him and many with Him to our School. We will share with Him those things that are of our teachings. Thereafter, shall He depart from there, or be returned here?"

Several of the elders and seers converse quietly among themselves. Then one speaks.

"His journey shall commence from your temples."

"Thank you, Benjamin. We shall make ready then. During those several years we are to be blessed by His presence and by offering Him that which we know, we shall interact with you, keeping you apprised of all that is transpiring. We would ask the same of you."

"Indeed so. Indeed so," Joseph replies softly.

Jacob nods, and they begin to form into smaller groups and speak among themselves.

Stretched out upon the earth, which is cooling very rapidly now, several gather about themselves the blankets that they cherish and hold sacred.

"I ponder why some do not blink and others blink or twinkle constantly. Some of these over there in the patterns ... Well, they do not seem to have much life. They are just there. Is the fire of life like that, do you suppose? Do you think the nature of our being, our life, is seen by God as we are seeing these stars?"

"I believe so, Timothy," Jesus replies. "I think we are, each of us, at differing times like any one of these stars."

"I can not completely agree with that," John counters. "I know some who are like that rock over there ... immobile."

They all laugh lightly.

"I know what you mean, but I think that within them is the potential to be as any of these ... brighter, more vibrant, more colorful, more alive. Do you agree with that?"

"I would have to agree with that as a potential, Jesus. But for some, it seems hopelessly lost within." John starts laughing, as he knows the nature of the comments that this will elicit from his brother Jesus.

After the laughter subsides and the gentleness of the night resumes, Jesus continues. "Do you remember Rebochien's teachings about the alignments? How these always point us in the direction that is the cardinal point?"

"I do," John answers. "I love those teachings. No matter

where I am in the night, I can look up and see, *Ah-h. Here are the positions. Here are the alignments.* Then I know that my destination must be in this direction."

"Well, I think that an answer to some of your feelings about those who are like great rocks in life has to do with patterns such as these, which they have created."

"Zelotese calls that karma," interjects James.

"Yes," replies Jesus, "and that is the pathway of life that is forged by one in the past. But it is not mandated. Using the word *forged* makes it sound of iron, but it is not so for the soul. The soul chooses its steps freely. Even though the burden may be heavy of habit, there is always the right to choose."

"How about one who is in bondage right this moment?" queries Thomas. "Perhaps with chains about them. They are not free literally, so what you are saying has to do with their inner freedom, their spirit. How do you equate these two things, my Brother?"

"I do not equate them. I only know that they are. I know the body can be imprisoned, but the spirit, heart, and mind are always free. It is only that individual whose willingness imprisons these aspects of themselves, along with the imprisonment of the body, who is truly in bondage."

"I have a powerful sense of that," John adds pensively, "and I know it will serve me and many of us well in the years ahead."

"Do you think that the prophecies will be as specific, as literal, as we have heard to this point?" Phillip asks.

"I think the essence of them is just as they have given," Jesus replies, "and I feel within that more will be known as time passes. But this I know in the Light of God in my spirit: We are the greater. We are the masters of that which comes before us. Those who would have us believe otherwise dwell in the finiteness of their own habit and illusion, and believe not unto that which shall follow this life and hereafter. But we have been guided, taught. We have, together and individually, gone into the future and seen the Light of God. We have been shown the paths that have brought us to this point, and we have been shown the paths that are offered to us that take us into the future.

"If we choose one of these according to that which we hold as the highest and best within, and we go forth upon that choice of paths with joy and expectancy, claiming the light within, then we shall emerge from these experiences in the full glory of God to embrace one another thereafter with love and laughter. We shall sing and dance and celebrate this journey, and place it righteously in its position of the heritage that we offer to those who will follow."

"The pains and challenges, the humiliation, the sorrow … all of that, as well, Jesus?" Thomas asks softly.

"Especially those. Those are the step-stones upon which we can reach the greater light, within and without. For if we have naught with which to call forth the best within, how could we give it to others? If we are left idle, to find merely joy and wonder and celebration over what we hold within, what is the inspiration to give of it to others? It is the knowledge that, as we bear these, these are the seeds that we, ourselves and all of us, will harvest in a time to come."

Whatsoever you seek, dear friends, know that as you seek it in an attitude of openness and truth, it shall be given.

In those instances when you know it not according to that which you have asked, stay a time upon it, openly, lightly. Hold it outward in your hands, turn it about, and, if need be, set it down aside from self.

But if in the examination you find the op-
portunity, the potential ... yes, even the gift,
then as you take of it, you are enriched and
blessed. Then comes the greater power, for
your sight and spirit are opened, and the Way
within you is made all the more passable.

Chapter Nineteen

The Dawning of His Light

A small cloud moves across the nearly full moon, yet a shaft of bright light illuminates the little group gathered upon this summit, centered around a small campfire whose flames are minimal compared to the brilliance of the moon's reflective light.

"It matters not how much I fast, how much I pray, there is this feeling of heaviness, sorrow. My mind and my training come forth to try to counter it with the reassurances that we have been given by the elders, the teachers, the seers, the prophets, our sisters. It brings to mind that day ... Remember, Mary? When we were about to ascend the temple steps and you were chosen? It seems lifetimes ago in one way, and yesterday in another. Give to me, my Sister, of your peace, that I may be as you. That I may release and love and rejoice in the work that lies ahead, casting off this mantel of grief at the thought that He shall leave us."

Mary smiles gently and leans Her head forward as though to reflect upon something, an image perhaps that She sees in the flame of the small fire.

There is a feeling of distance as the other Sisters look upon Her face, illuminated from beneath by the light of the fire and from above by the light of the moon, as though the finger of God is touching Her once again.

Her eyes are awide and glisten with the reflected light.

As She begins to speak She does not look up, as though discerning the words from the flame. "There is no dishonor in feeling what you feel, Zephorah. Indeed, you must know that I have these same callings, this same force beckoning me ... at times to such an extent," She lifts Her face to make eye contact with Zephorah, "and of such power and intensity that I want to rush to Him and plead, *Do not go forth! Let us do our Lord God's work from here, or along another pathway.*"

She sighs deeply, as do all the Sisters, as they are each one contemplating this.

"But then, a wonderful thing happens. First I see His bright beautiful eyes, filled with reassurance and hopefulness. Then I see His smile. You all know it. He has generously given it to any who would look upon Him. And I know that I must not tempt, nor imply any diversion from the path that is prophesied ... the prophecy that is, in fact, the Word of God."

She speaks no more, but smiles the sweet smile of Her eternal grace and looks back down at the flame, and then up here and there to connect with the eyes of Her other Sisters.

For a while longer, they speak quietly to one another or in small groups of three or four. They are awaiting the arrival of the men, who have been upon their own time of prayer and fasting.

Here on the eve of that day when the Master and those with Him will depart into the wilderness to the sacred School, and beyond, they know as they anticipate the arrival of their brothers there must be a work completed: The final stone laid in place carefully, lovingly, that the foundation of the work can be strong and endure. They know from the teachings and the prophecies that they are the wellspring of the Light and Spirit of God, to which this, their Brother (and those with Him, to be sure), will turn. They know it will be the energy of their faith that the Master will seek often, to enhance and to fortify that which will be challenged by the illusion, challenged by that which believes not.

"God's blessings be upon you all," Jacob offers quietly, but with his great smile that seems to grant each perceiver a wondrous, heartfelt hug. As he moves about the group of Holy Maidens, some stand to receive an embrace from him. Others, he bends to touch upon the shoulder or head, caressing them, offering them special blessings and greeting of brotherly love.

As all are now assembled and positioned, Jacob begins to speak. "Certainly you, our Sisters, have felt some of the things that we, your brothers, have also felt in our own time of fasting and prayer. So, here we are gathered together at the threshold of that which we have always known would one day be upon us, and it is here.

"We know that there is that part of the heart, that part of the spirit that calls out, *Leave me not, but stay. Tend to the garden of God's harvest here, together with us. Let us send forth our prayer, our intentions, and whatsoever else might be of need. But go not. Suffer not unto them that which we so love in You.* We also know, dear Sisters, that just as we, you have passed through this and found the Light of the Promise. That while we might hold this special Light within our group and cherish it, protect it, we also know that that Light is meant for the world ... the world as it is and as it shall be.

"We have been told by those we love so dearly, who hear the Word of God and who see the future, that we ourselves might return again and again, and that by giving of this now, so shall we receive it in those journeys ahead. Whether they are one or many, His light will be there. We will know it, and He will know of us, and our journeys will be filled with the joys we have known in this life, in this work.

"Surely you have arrived at that state of God's Grace." He turns to glance with absolute adoration at Mary and smiles. She, nodding, returns it. "In dwelling in that state of God's Grace, as you have looked for it and claimed it, we know that you have found, as have we, a great sense of anticipation and joy, the wonder of knowing that we have contributed to God's Gift to the world ... the Christ."

Smiling serenely, Jacob connects with each pair of eyes now steadily looking upon him. He raises his hand to his heart, to his lips, to his forehead, and up to God, leaning his head back as he does. "In my heart, Lord God, do I ever find Thee. In my words, Lord God, do I ever speak Thy goodness. In my mind, do I think those thoughts to create that which is Your Promise. I lift all these up to Thee and mine own spirit. Open me, Lord God, and all my brothers and sisters through spirit, mind, word, and heart, that Thy work shall be the joy of our existence."

A period of silence follows. Then Elob speaks: "It is well that each of us remembers that one who departs from our midst separates only the physical from the physical. All the moreso are our love and dedication in prayer, in meditation, and in all those things that we know to do of such wondrous power. From this eve forth, ever shall there be two or more of us, each hour, in joyful prayer and meditation, that as we might discern a call from our brothers or sisters who are in the outer world, we can be with them. The call will be heard and the power will be summoned.

"Look you all into your hearts and minds carefully. It is a time to release and rejoice. Between now and the dawn's light, we ask of you," gesturing to his brothers and sisters from the School of the Prophets and the Essene elders, "seek out that which would limit. If ye find it within, transform it, that when the day's light begins, we all begin anew, holding the Promise in a vessel which is pure ... our own spirits, our hearts ... that naught within us can be used to limit. That within us are only the magnitude of God's Promise and the joy and gratitude of having dwelled with Jesus and His brothers and sisters who shall be about our Lord God's works. Tomorrow we shall open our hearts, spirits, and minds to receive our brothers and sisters. Those of your group who have been in different locations will rejoin us, and we will celebrate together. Let us receive them, as we know they are preparing to receive us. Though their paths have taken them along differing routes, these paths come together tomorrow. Let us take from this the strength of our peoples, your tribes, the heritage from each, the highest and best that each has to offer, setting aside any illusion of separateness."

So they begin their meditation and prayer. Some gather together in small groups, others are seated by themselves, throughout the remainder of the night.

The first sounds that are heard invoke celebration and gladness. Songs, hand-clapping, and various musical tones come forth here and there from the rudimentary instruments that some from the various tribes of the Expectant Ones have brought.

Delighted chatter among the thirty-six maidens fills in the gaps of time since their separation and renews bonds that stem from very early childhood. Over here, a group of the men are similarly engaged. Occasionally they come together, and rivulets of laughter can be heard as old stories are recounted and humorous memories are relived.

Feasting breaks the fast, and song invokes the power of joyful expectancy, bringing it forth into this gathering of those who hold the Promise to come.

The inner circle is comprised of the Holy Maidens. In its center is Mary. Having offered a beautiful prayer, She raises Her head and holds Her hands out to Her sides, as She turns ever so slowly to pass a blessing to all those of the gathered tribes of Expectant Ones.

Beyond the inner circle is yet another, greater in number than the first. It is comprised of the other sisters from the two locations to the north and west, who are swaying this way and that as though offering a silent song.

Mary steps over to Her sisters, and Zephorah and Hannah part hands to accept her. Their group expands as Mary becomes one of them once again. First their heads go this way and that, then their bodies. Then we hear their song. First one then another, the voices all join. The sheer beauty of their song inspires the best within each who hears it.

The second group of maidens begins to offer their own song, joining in with the first. These, the thirty-six, are smiling, their heads upturned as they glance this way and that. Their celebration is joyous, their focus upon its being a true capstone, the accomplishment of an intent set very long ago. Now the dawning of His Light begins.

Beyond this group are the others ... another circle, and yet another ... a great swirling energy of circle upon circle of the Expectant Ones literally creating something tangible.

On it goes, the celebration and ceremony continue.

Now night has fallen and the great ceremonial fires have been lit. We find the great teachers leading the long file of Expectant Ones as they pass among the sacred fires, weaving this way and that between the individual ones, as though they are rising up in consciousness. They seem to cast something into the flames as they pass by, and we know that they have transformed a limitation, a fear, an emotion found deep within them during the previous night's prayer and meditation. That they have, figuratively and literally, tossed it into the appropriate flame which symbolizes one of the seven steps, the seven great Waves of Light, that have brought the Expectant Ones to this point.

As each of the sisters and brothers, young and old, teachers, prophets, seers, weavers, storytellers ... As each casts into the flame anything that would limit, we can see on their faces that they have been freed. A power is in their eyes, pure, easy, simple, a sense of timeless light, a quality of faith unshakable.

Now they form into a great circle, embracing not only the sacred flames, but all of those who shall, in the morning's light, depart, including the Master. Within this circle of hopeful anticipation are those who will come to walk with Him when His work begins, those whom He shall call and send forth bearing His blessing and His Name, and those who shall walk with Him and preserve His Light, even giving their lives in their appointed time, that the Light can endure and that the Promise will be eternally offered to those who will follow.

Gathered in this circle, ringed by the Essenes, one steps to the center. It is Zelotese. He turns and extends a hand this way and that, and calls to his side Anna, Judy, and each of the other great teachers, seers, and prophets.

He then gestures to Judy, who offers a beautiful prayer, asking that the Spirit of God be as a river of light between them all, that wherever and whenever one, anyone, shall encounter darkness, illusion, or limitation, that this living river of light shall cleanse them, strengthen them, and give them the power of a child of God.

Many take turns speaking, giving of themselves to the entire group, offering an inspired prayer.

Lastly, Zelotese leads Mary to stand beside him, flanked by Judy, Anna, and all the other teachers.

She steps into the inner group and extends a hand.

The group parts. From their midst, the Master comes forward and grasps Her outstretched hand.

Pausing for a time, they gaze at one another. He embraces Her.

He then turns to the circle of the Expectant Ones and walks about to touch and bless each one. His movement is fluid and swift, but His gaze and words will be felt, known, remembered throughout eternity by each soul so graced. Only as He has completed His blessing of the very last one does He return to stand beside Mary once again.

Mary gestures to Her Sisters, and the inner group and the outer group make way that the Sisters can encircle the Master and Mary.

Then, silence. An unbroken silence that reaches beyond time and space, a silence in which each one hears God speak to them. A golden silence in which the Promise comes to life.

As the Sisters stand heads bowed, eyes closed, the silence embraces them. Then, one by one they lift their heads and see Mary and the Master kneeling. Before they can even react, there is a hushed gasp as He rises, bathed in light.

He walks straight to the first of the Sisters. His outstretched hands receive hers, and we hear His gentle voice. "My sweet Andra, my mother Andra, tell me of your Gift that I might bear it on the journey ahead, and as I give it, I pledge to you, you shall stand with me and we shall give it together. And I shall hold your name within, just as I hold and treasure the gift you have given me."

Then, unto each of the Sisters, He does the same, and each leans forward to place her forehead against the Master's.

They speak softly.

"I gift You with the gift of Faith."

"I gift You with the gift of Compassion."

"I gift You with the gift of Truth."

"I gift You with the gift of Joyful Expectancy."

"I gift You with the Law of God."

On and on, each gives a blessing and is blessed.

Then He turns and walks back to the center.

Mary, who has been kneeling, head bowed, looks up to receive His hand.

As She rises, He kneels before Her and, from His kneeling position, looks up into Her eyes, sweet, gentle, filled with the grace of the certainty of God.

We hear Him speak again. "These are as Thee, my sweet Mother. Each has held and nurtured my life to this day, as Thou hast. Each has given unto me that to fill my need now and in future, as hast Thou. Our Father is God. Our Mother is God. But Thou art unto me that through which the Spirit of God has flowed, that this which is the temple of flesh could have life, that God might speak through this life and give light and return the Promise unto those who would have it.

"I am ringed by a circle that is filled with the Light of God. But as I hold Thy hands, it is the Grace of God, the very Compassion of God, that I receive as Thy true gift to me." He leans to place His forehead upon the backs of Mary's hands.

After a time, She removes one of Her hands from His, and strokes His hair. We hear Her ever so softly, ever so sweetly, "The Peace of God be upon You, my Son."

You are in the Earth in that time of preparation for the Light to enter the Earth once again.

✩

He shall return to awaken that which is the Christ spirit within you, each of you, when you have made the Way passable for Him.

And, then, as the sons and daughters of man shall illuminate the Earth, just so as we here have illuminated the heavens for Him, know that He may again walk from here to thee collectively. That time of Light thereafter shall come to be and sustain itself for many Earth years to follow.

-- Lama Sing

ABOUT LAMA SING

More than thirty years ago, for our convenience, the one through whom this information flows accepted the name Lama Sing, though it was stated they, themselves, have no need for names or titles.

"We identify ourselves only as servants of God, dedicated to you, our brothers and sisters in the Earth."

–Lama Sing

ଔ

ABOUT THIS CHANNEL

"Channel is that term given generally to those who enable themselves to be, as much as possible, open and passable in terms of information that can pass through them from the Universal Consciousness or other such which are not associated in the direct sense with their finite consciousness of the current incarnation."

–Lama Sing

Books by Al Miner & Lama Sing

The Chosen: *Backstory to the Essene Legacy*
The Promise: *Book I of The Essene Legacy*
The Awakening: *Book II of The Essene Legacy*
The Path: *Book III of The Essene Legacy*

In Realms Beyond: *Book I of The Peter Chronicles*
In Realms Beyond: *Study Guide*
Awakening Hope: *Book II of The Peter Chronicles*
Return to Earth: *Book III of The Peter Chronicles*

How to Prepare for The Journey:
     Vol I. Death, Dying, and Beyond
     Vol II. *The Sea of Faces*

Jesus: *Book I*
Jesus: *Book II*

The Course in Mastery

When Comes the Call

Seed Thoughts
Seed Thoughts to Consciousness

Stepstones: Compilation 1

The "Little Book" Series:
     The Children's Story

About Al Miner

A chance hypnosis session in 1973 began Al's ten-
ure as the channel for Lama Sing. Since then, nearly
10,000 readings have been given in a trance state answering technical and personal questions on such topics as
science, health and disease, history, geophysical, spiritual, philosophical, metaphysical, past and future times,
and much more. The validity of the information has been
substantiated and documented by research institutions
and individuals, and those receiving personal readings
continue to refer others to Al's work based on the accu-
racy and integrity of the information in their readings. In
1984, St. Johns University awarded Al an honorary doc-
toral degree in parapsychology.

Al \is no longer accepting requests for personal readings, but, rather, is devoting his remaining time to works
intended to be good for all. Much of his current research
is dedicated to the concept that the best of all guidance is
that which comes from within. Al lives with his wife in
Florida.

You can read more about Al's life and works at the
Lama Sing website: *www.lamasing.net*.